THE

DICTIONARY

OF

FEMINIST

THEORY

THE

DICTIONARY

OF

FEMINIST

THEORY

Maggie Humm

Ohio State University Press
Columbus

Published in the U.S.A. by Ohio State University Press.

Published in Great Britain by Harvester Wheatsheaf.

Library of Congress Cataloging-in-Publication Data

Humm, Maggie.
    The dictionary of feminist theory/Maggie Humm.
       p.   cm.
     ISBN 0–8142–0506–2.—ISBN 0–8142–0507–0 (pbk.)
     1. Feminism—Philosophy—Dictionaries.   I. Title.
  HQ1115.H86 1990   89–16237
    305.42′01—dc20   CIP

Printed in Great Britain

9 8 7 6 5 4 3 2 1

The master's tools can never dismantle the master's house
Audre Lorde

Feminism reconceptualizes the connection between being and thinking
Catharine MacKinnon

A theory in the flesh means one where the physical realities of our lives – our skin, color, the land or concrete we grew up on, our sexual longings – all fuse to create a politic born out of necessity
Cherríe Moraga and Gloria Anzaldúa

CONTENTS

PREFACE

I would like to begin by making clear the dictionary's and my own place. The book is a broad, cross-cultural and international account of contemporary feminist thought. But since writing across too many cultural boundaries very often produces a hybrid text, ill at ease with itself and the world, I focus primarily on Anglo–American and French theory which is already a complex and exciting area.

The book aims to broaden knowledge of, and to stimulate research about, women and feminism. I hope that the dictionary will be a source book for the feminist activist, for the student who wishes to know more about feminist theory and for the general reader who wants an introduction to feminism. I hope too that the dictionary contributes to the future of feminist theory by helping to prevent the eclipsing of feminist ideas. What I have tried to do is to take some of the commonest terms and issues in current English-speaking feminism and make them accessible.

Aims

The goal of the dictionary is to show how feminist theory both challenges, and is shaped by, the academy and society; to present feminist theory as a body of research in its own right and to explore the nature of feminist theory for the future of feminism.

The work I explore is relatively new, having its source in the political changes of the 1960s and the 1970s and in the fundamental transformation of social theory. The 'master' narratives of history or politics have undergone a crisis in legitimation. Categories such as 'class' or 'period' are inapplicable to the historical experience of women. An explosion of recent theory in the writings of Kate Millett, Susan Griffin, Adrienne Rich, Barbara Smith, Juliet Mitchell, Julia Kristeva and many others describe the different historical, psychological, sexual and racial experiences of women and how feminism can be a source of power and knowledge.

Definitions

Feminist theory is an area of writing which represents a crucial and original contribution to contemporary thinking. Unique to feminist theory is its insistence on the inextricable link between theory and practice and between public and private. Theory and experience have a very special relationship within feminism encapsulated in its slogan 'the personal is political'.

Certain terms in contemporary theory are used to sum up what appear to be the key experiences of women. Among these are 'work', 'family', 'patriarchy', 'sexuality'. These concepts reflect feminism's effort to reveal core social processes and to find what constantly reappears in various guises in the course of women's history.

A fundamental goal of feminist theory is to understand women's oppression in terms of race, gender, class and sexual preference and how to change it. Feminist theory reveals the importance of women's individual and shared experiences and our struggles. It analyses how sexual difference is constructed within any intellectual and social world and builds accounts of experiences from these differences.

The dictionary describes the conceptual tools we need to understand economic, political and sexual discrimination and the modes of analysis which are useful for feminist politics. For example, with increasing acts of physical aggression towards women there is an even greater need for feminist psychoanalytic theory which investigates sexual identity.

Issues

Some voice misgivings about feminist theory. But I feel that to deny the potential to feminist theory is to deny the basis of feminist practice. Feminism will always need a framework within which it can explore diversity. Feminist theory represents that potential for a broader politics. Its vision and forms of practice constitute a major break with traditional definitions. The issues of feminist theory – ecological feminism, pacifism, anti-pornography, Third World affairs, sexuality debates – all focus on women's specificity grounded in the sexual division of labour and reproduction.

Most misgivings are really doubts about traditional theory not about feminism. As Edward Said and others argue, the *cult* of theory reduces existence to elements in a self-confirming, intellectual operation. Feminist theory, on the other hand, enables women to recognise our interests and status as historical agents. Feminism actively refutes the arrogant mystification involved in traditional theory which is often obscure or abstract and has a proclivity for losing contact with the world. Traditional theories have been applied in ways that make it difficult to understand women's participation in social life. Feminist theory is immediate, and urgently about the world of women.

The notion that reason is alien to women has held a prominent place in many men's reading of the social world. Mary Wollstonecraft was the first to point out the awful prospect if women do not 'cultivate their understandings' (Wollstonecraft 1789, p. 33). In modern Western culture 'nature' is conflated in our understanding of the female. Women stand for, and symbolise, the body and all that is not reason. To refuse to think theoretically is to imply that feminism is not complex enough to need theorising. Without practice, feminist theory could never develop, yet theory is essential to feminist practice. In feminism theory is a vehicle for consciousness-raising not for hierarchy. The power of knowledge is the greatest argument to be made in theory's favour. The other argument is that feminism already has an indigenously produced theoretical tradition of some sophistication.

Criteria

In general the criteria for feminist theory include the principle of contextualisation, the principle of active agency and accountability; the causes and effects of ideas and the principle of diversity. Feminist theory is fundamentally about women's experience. Its subject is women's past and contemporary history and through utilising, and often rejecting, the explanations of economics, religion, or politics it brings into consciousness undiscovered aspects of women's lives.

I have not examined the role of feminist women as public figures in any major way in this dictionary, for example the pathbreaking careers of critical activists such as Betty Friedan or Gloria Steinem. Such an analysis is more properly the concern of feminist social research and in any case would need a hugely expanded text to begin to answer the question: What are the meanings of women's contributions to public life?

The structure of this selection is almost wholly shaped by French and Anglo-American theory. I have for the most part selected writing which is shaped by three concerns: first the redefining of the *content* of knowledge; second the development of an alternative epistemology; and, finally, the mapping of possible new configurations of knowledge.

I include writing which gives a general account of women's situation and history from the early work of Mary Wollstonecraft to current feminists Kate Millett, Gerda Lerner, Sheila Rowbotham, Dorothy Smith *et al.* Women's situation is also part of complex material relations and I include theory which describes economic and ideological structures, for example the writings of Michèle Barrett, Heidi Hartmann and Catharine MacKinnon. There is now an insistence that 'feminism' has been for too long a metaphor for white, first world, middle class or heterosexual experience. The theoretical reflections of Barbara Smith, Audre Lorde, Adrienne Rich, Cherríe Moraga and Gloria Anzaldúa are included to demonstrate the specificities of feminism(s).

Writing is included which appropriates, or derives from, specific disciplines, for example the analysis of gender identity, by way of psychoanalysis, by Dorothy Dinnerstein, Nancy Chodorow and Juliet Mitchell. Feminist theory is included which analyses the relation of identity to sexuality, and to sexual preference, in the writings of Gayle Rubin, Adrienne Rich and Linda Gordon. Theories of the subject based on the representation of identity in the symbolic order are included: those that intimately involve language in the work of French feminists Hélène Cixous and Luce Irigaray, and those that explore the figural, for example Laura Mulvey and Linda Nochlin.

Finally, these enquiries necessarily raise questions about the role of theory and knowledge itself in the work of Julia Kristeva, Evelyn Fox Keller, Sandra Harding; and they incur the naming of a feminist ontology in women's studies by Gloria Bowles, Renate Duelli Klein and other educators.

The second criterion of selection was to choose writing which has not only transformed the disciplinary and androcentric structure of knowledge but also its epistemology. For example, Tillie Olsen in *Silences* and Rachel Blau DuPlessis in 'For the Etruscans' have developed a 'body' of writing which speaks openly of its origins — the daily experience of women.

A final criterion was to include theory about our futures. The visionary goals of feminist theory give intelligible form to both the ontology and the epistemology of feminism in the other worlds of Virginia Woolf, Mary Daly and Dolores Hayden.

To specify the terms of this selection I need to place it for an abbreviated moment in my own personal history. One of feminism's most provocative challenges to existing theory is its insistence that we contemplate our agencies. The personal and intellectual circumstances that shape my particular viewpoint on feminism have luckily changed from undergraduate porridge to the crunchier flakes of libertarian feminism. As an undergraduate studying English in the late 1960s at one of Britain's first New Universities, I was required to take and pass a first year course in empirical philosophy. The discussion about whether tables, or indeed cows, continued to exist if you stopped looking at them had an unsituated stance (*sic.*).

I found this fantastical labour of epistemology difficult because it was not an interpretative order in which I had a part. I made tentative insertions in the first seminars and a 'kindly' (1989, 'paternal/patriarchal') male student explained that cognition from the 'senses' (1989, 'personal feelings/intuition') should be no part of an academic enquiry. There was no effort then (1966) to give me, a working class girl who could drop her Geordie accent but not her gender, a self-reflexive place at the high table of British academicism. It was hard to imagine, until I read *Sexual Politics* much later, that theory and ideas about 'human' nature (or tables and cows) could be anything other than a patriarchal Pictionary – a merely technical and unreflective pluralistic enquiry into language.

So I *do* want to privilege isomorphism, even sisterhood. I *do* want to maintain a significant sense of the agreements within feminism despite our important differences. Only with a sense of collective identity can students proceed as feminists. Second, there is a crucial need for *all* readers, feminists *and* misogynists, to have access to general overviews which prevent the transformative passion of feminism from being devalued or ignored.

Theories are tools and change constantly and we need woman-centred theory to give us strategies for change. Feminist theory is an uncompromising pledge of resistance against relativism as an intellectual stance.

Design

A work of this size cannot do justice to individual feminists who make that pledge. The entries devoted to them are necessarily brief, but offer an outline of their work and their contribution to feminism. Biographical information is more properly the work of an encyclopaedia (see Tuttle 1986) and details of their publications are in my *Annotated Bibliography* (Humm 1987). The dictionary is more a helpful short cut to their ideas than to their lives, particularly since many readers find some ideas difficult to understand and frequently seek information about them, for example French psychoanalysis.

Again, in the book as a whole, 'gender' or 'sexuality' occupy far more space than names. This is because the former subjects are the central ones and because the dictionary is a celebration of feminism's self definitions. Of course the feminist reader will be able to find a term used in ways I have not mentioned. It can only be misleading to offer precise definitions of feminism because the process of defining is to enlarge, not to close down, linguistic alternatives; it is to evoke difference and to call up experience.

As is usual in the making of anything, one of the main problems is to decide what to put in and what to omit. There is one conspicuous absence from the dictionary. I do not want the term 'theory' to mean largely critical theory and therefore have not included entries such as deconstruction or postmodernism. I think the condition of deconstruction and postmodernism is receiving the attention it deserves elsewhere and therefore its ideas are more sparingly represented here. For me the political theories of feminism are more attuned to the historic crisis. It has not been easy to write this account of feminist theory because most feminists refuse to categorise feminism. Like all dictionaries, this is a compendium of terms arranged in alphabetical order, together with definitions, citations and commentary. In each case I have tried to plot the evolving use of terms and the contributions made by the different politics of feminism, for example liberalism or radicalism. I have also made connections between feminist thought and Western social theory generally to set feminism in its historical context, for example by including entries on Freud, Lacan and Marcuse.

Yet in some respects the book is different from what many people might expect a dictionary to be. One main difference is that I refuse to offer single definitions. Instead, each entry tries to address the politics of dictionary-making by offering different definitions set in the historical *process* of feminist meaning making. The dictionary is therefore a summary of the meanings of concepts that have a special significance for feminism. By refusing homogenised entries I have tried to refuse ethnocentricity and heterosexism and to celebrate the exciting diversity of feminist theory which can only be described as revolutionary.

Dictionaries have a particular role as authorities and women and minorities are often made invisible or stereotyped in them. Feminism has always had a self-conscious attention to the meaning of words as the titles of key feminist books reveal – *Dream of a Common Language, Silences, Man Made Language*. This is not a dictionary of new vocabulary since there are now many challenges to traditional lexicons (see Daly 1978, 1987) but a conceptual grid of the agenda of contemporary feminism. While agreeing that language is the site where female subjectivity is inscribed, I feel that a dictionary of feminist theory should do more than invent new terms. It needs to describe the political functions and possibilities of feminism in order to help others oppose patriarchy.

Feminism presents especial difficulties for creating the style and format usually necessary for a dictionary. Feminism cannot be subdivided. It is, and must be, a collage of continuously changing ideas. For example some French feminists argue that 'woman' does not exist while 'womanism' is a key concept in Afro-American feminism. This is the excitement, the subversiveness of feminism.

But I am aware, for instance, that particular theorists have informed my work. Adrienne Rich seems to me a model of authorship in the way she struggles against ethnocentrism, for example by being one of the first White feminists to index in her work separate entries for white as well as for Black women (Rich 1986). In other words, I do not agree with all the definitions included and instead prefer to describe the controversies and be stimulated by their arguments. But terms and references are precise. For example, I cite the original user of particular ideas. Another problem was whether to include all the terms used by feminists working in each discipline but I decided that this was the role of a disciplinary encyclopaedia. I would like to have provided examples of how each feminist idea has been put into practice but again this was not feasible. What I have endeavoured to do, then, is to provide an accessible and comprehensive digest of feminist terms which I hope will therefore become of more general interest.

In preparing final entries, I have adopted a number of conventions as follows:

1. An entry followed by a reference indicates a summary of that writer's ideas. Verbatim quotations are in quotation marks followed by their reference.
2. Each entry is arranged in chronological order of the development of a term within feminism. For example I describe the changing definitions of motherhood from 'oppression' to distinctions between the institution and experience of motherhood and between biological and cultural mothering.
3. Entries try to describe the differing contributions of lesbian, heterosexual, Black, White, radical or liberal women where appropriate.
4. Entries are under both the names of particular writers and the ideas they have produced, for example 'sexual politics' and Kate Millett.
5. I include entries under the names of writers who, though not feminist themselves, have provided a foundation for feminist

theory, for example Freud, Lacan and Althusser. I assess how feminist writers, for example Irigaray have derived ideas from such figures or reacted to them.

I have used a wide range of sources, some of them unusual to dictionary-making, for example small journals and poetry. All are listed in full at the end of the book but represent a tiny summary of the rich material I found while working in the Women's Research Library, London, Stanford University and University of California libraries, the Fawcett Library and in correspondence with Centre de Recherches Interdisciplinaires, Institut voor Theorentishe, National Women's Studies Association, Mary Capek and many others.

The dictionary is a personal book but I hope that it is not just my personal pleasure, although in the course of making it I have written about ideas which stimulate me.

I must thank Sue Roe, formerly of Harvester Wheatsheaf, for first suggesting that I write a dictionary of feminist theory and for the continuing encouragement of Harvester Wheatsheaf and my family and friends. Thanks particularly to students in my seminars on feminist theory at the Polytechnic of East London for allowing me to test out my ideas on them. Thanks most of all to Joyce Lock for her immaculate word processing skill and her willingness to undertake such a huge task as the typing of this dictionary.

Finally, feminist theory, for me, will always be a topography of voices, anchored in the lives and experiences of individual women in my classroom, my family and my history.

Abolitionist feminism

One of the main theories of nineteenth-century feminism. It took the view that woman's oppression and emancipation paralleled the struggle for Black liberation from slavery. The nineteenth-century movement to abolish slavery in the USA preceded, and provided strategies for, the development of feminism. For example Sarah Grimké based her feminist ideas on Abolitionist politics. She argued that the democratic goals and values of the American revolution must apply to women as well as to men. See Grimké (1838).

Sara Evans argues that in its trajectory from civil rights to women's liberation, second wave feminism (dating from *Sexual Politics*) recapitulated the history of first wave feminism. 'Twice in the history of the United States the struggle for racial equality has been midwife to a feminist movement . . . in the abolition movement of the 1830s and again in the civil rights movement of the 1960s' (Evans 1979, p.24).

Abortion

The termination of pregnancy. Although there are many feminist theories of abortion, it is a fundamental demand of the women's movement that a woman has a basic and inalienable right to limit her reproduction.

The issue of abortion is central to feminist theory and politics for several reasons. First, it is the most visible manifestation of a healthcare system that is 'anti-woman' in the way the system limits women's access to, and legal rights to, abortion. Second, abortion controls are part of the ideology of sexuality in capitalist patriarchy on which depend the meanings of family, state and motherhood. Third, the abortion issue is part of a political battle over women's liberation because the curtailment of abortion rights is the main aim of both the American and British new right anti-feminist campaigns. Fourth, feminists understand that anti-feminist and some feminist arguments about abortion are very Eurocentric. For example in Brahmin scriptures abortion is possible until the fifth month, when 'quickening' is confirmed.

Adrienne Rich says that the legal and extra legal coercions regulating abortion are part of the institutionalising of motherhood (Rich 1976). Kathryn Parsons argues that the concept of abortion covertly sustains a hierarchy of patriarchal power since it derives from a reasoning based on rights, as opposed to a reasoning expressed as needs by feminists and women's clinics (Parsons 1977).

While acknowledging the moral dilemmas of Christian women, feminists agree that women's control over the termination of pregnancy is central to the future of women.

Action research

Research in which theories and techniques from social science are combined with practical politics in order to create social change. Where the traditional researcher provides an objective analysis of social events, the action researcher has a conscious interaction with research subjects.

Maria Mies describes feminist strategies which translate life experiences into role playing, and involve subjects collectively in the history and politics of research projects (Mies 1983).

Action research is a methodology which allows women to study women in an interactive way without the artificial object/subject split between researcher and researched.

Activism

The theory that militant action is a more effective agent of social change than electoral politics. It encourages political or symbolic activities which can directly challenge women's oppression. Generally, feminist activism precedes the creation of feminist theory but is subsequently strengthened and renewed by theory.

Contemporary feminist activism draws on several traditions: civil rights and anti-war movements, trade union history, libertarian theory and theatre and performance art.

In the USA, second wave feminism became visible with the activism of feminists demonstrating at the 1968 Miss America contest. In France, contemporary feminist theory developed from the pro-abortion demonstrations supported by Simone de Beauvoir, in particular the 1970 demonstration when a wreath to 'the unknown wife of the soldier' was placed on the tomb of the unknown soldier. Currently, peace theories depend on the activism of women in peace camps at Greenham Common and elsewhere.

Addams, Jane

American social reformer.

In 'Why women should vote' (1909), 'The larger aspects of the women's movement' (1914), 'Women, war and suffrage' (1915), and 'Women and internationalism' (1915) Addams argued that women must participate in public affairs, because she believed that women had a special contribution to make to society, particularly as pacifists. See Addams (1965).

Adultery

Sexual intercourse by a married person with someone other than their spouse. In many countries adultery by women is punished more than adultery by men. This is because most societies are shaped by a system of moral restraints which discriminate more against women than men. Feminist historians draw attention to matrilineal societies where women could freely leave husbands and confer 'matrimony' upon another. See Walker (1983).

Advertising

The process and the industry which attach images and ideology to consumer products in order to sell them to the public. Feminist theories of advertising agree that Western advertising is sexist, homophobic, ageist and racist. Betty Friedan collected evidence of the *manipulative* effect of advertising in stabilising an image of post-war women as consumers of American life rather than as active workers. See Friedan (1963). Socialist and Marxist feminists extended this critique to argue that advertising obscures the social relations of class and gender with identifications made by consumption not production; and it obscures history with a false sense of the present. See Barrett (1979).

Radical feminists draw attention to the conservative signifiers of mother/child relations and families in advertisements which reinforce patriarchal ideas of the nuclear family. See Daly (1978).

Feminists, drawing on psychoanalysis, show how advertising represents women as fragmented objects and trades on women's desire for coherence by offering women an artificial unity through product consumption. See Williamson (1978).

For most women advertising is the most visible and most constant evidence of social and sexist mythologies. For feminist theory it is the clearest evidence of patriarchal ideology.

Aesthetics

Literally, the school of philosophy which analyses the forms, values and experience of art. Since this activity concerns the relationship between a work's moral, psychological and social content and the work's production, form, function and effect, aesthetic questions are particularly relevant to feminism. Feminist aesthetics begins with the premiss that all art is gendered. A feminist investigation relates the sex of the artist to the gender values of art institutions and art audiences.

Feminist aesthetics encourage alternative feminist art. Notable examples are Judy Chicago's *Dinner Party* and *Birth Project* which symbolically represent women's experience and history.

Within the framework of feminist aesthetics, the relationship between the formality of art and a subjective, collective appropriation of it for women has to change. See Ecker (1985).

Mary Kelly calls feminist practice a 'radical' intervention against individualist practice. See Parker (1987).

Affirmative action

Affirmative action dates from the programme introduced by President Lyndon Johnson in 1964 prohibiting employment discrimination. The programme requires contractors to establish measurable integration goals and timetables in order to achieve equal opportunity regardless of race, colour, religion, sex or national origin.

Feminist researchers are developing new theories of organisations to promote equity objectives in trade unions, labour markets and technology.

Feminists claim that the principle of affirmative action recognises that market mechanisms cannot, by themselves, bring about conditions of equality. Feminist theory focuses not on equality in *treatment* but on equality of results and provides evidence to rectify past and future discrimination. In Britain the Equal Pay Act (1970) did little to change the material circumstances of women's lives due to women's segregation in industry and services. The 1984 amended act allowing women to claim equal pay for work of equal value has more potential.

Theories of affirmative action have implications for education and culture. Meaningful change in access to, and participation in, work necessarily involves changes in education. And, since the beliefs that women hold about their opportunities (like the importance of work relationships) may differ from those of management, theories which explain the cultural environment of women's work and lives are essential to enable change to take place. See Kendrigan (1984) and Wilkinson (1985).

Mary Daly dismisses affirmative action as reform tokenism, which she says is used by patriarchy to deter women. See Daly (1978).

African women

Women whose experience has been shaped by the ethnic history of Africa. Many Afro-American women identify their roots in Africa.

Feminist theory by, and about, African women has fuelled reinterpretations of Black women's history, and of the relationship between women's productive and reproductive labour in the Third World. See Robertson and Berger (1986).

Areas that need more research in the African context are ideology and psychology in relation to gender, since findings cannot be applied cross-culturally or across classes. See Shostak (1981).

The history of African women contributes to the development of Western feminist theory. Adrienne Rich argues that the economic and social sororities of African women are examples of resistance to male power. See Rich (1976).

Ageism

A process of systematic stereotyping of and discrimination against people because they are old (Butler 1975). Research on ageism in the media reveals a male bias in representations of the elderly: older women are less visible than older men and comedy stereotypes discriminate more against older women than against older men. See Adams and Laurikietis (1980).

Images of ageism reinforce internalised attitudes of subordination and maintain practices of inequality which are mainly experienced by older women. See Itzin (1986).

Aggression

Assertive behaviour which attacks by physical, verbal or psychological means. In biological research by men, the term is synonymous with male dominance and aggression is used to define sex difference. See Tiger (1969).

Because Freud claimed that aggression was a manifestation of Thanatos, a masculine death drive, feminist psychoanalysts argue that this manifestation must be socially constructed rather than a biological inevitability. See Mitchell (1974).

Feminist sociologists emphasise the importance of social modelling in the acquisition of aggression. See Oakley (1972). Anthropologists show that aggressive behaviour can be equally masculine or feminine depending on its cultural context. See Mead (1949).

Susan Brownmiller argues that male aggression *is* a genetic inevitability and cites the critical function that rage plays in its expression (Brownmiller 1975). Alternatively, Ruth Bleier proves that the concept of aggression has been fallaciously anthropomorphised. See Bleier (1984).

Alchemy

A chemistry which changes base metal into gold. Feminist

spiritualists document how alchemy began as women's great natural science, which led to its prohibition by the church and the opposition of later science.

Alchemy was founded by Mary the Jewess who invented the double boiler – the bain-marie – and alchemists seek for the divine female power in gnosticism. Alchemy is permeated by sexual symbols of reproduction, feminine colours and Goddess imagery. See Stone (1976).

Alienation

A state of estrangement from oneself, or society. In Western philosophy, Hegel first uses the term to describe the human condition of estrangement from nature. This is overcome by self-knowledge. Marx reinterpreted Hegel's concept to describe the condition of labour in capitalism which can be altered by social and economic changes.

The concept of alienation is central to feminist theory. Women's alienation has so many different elements, feminists argue, that a new theoretical framework can be used, but it must go beyond Marxism. It must link women's oppression in the home, in culture and in sexuality, with our experience in wage labour. Even within wage labour, the sexualisation of women's work and the sexual harassment of women create a gender-specific form of women's alienation.

Socialist and Marxist feminists agree that the first step is to eliminate the sexual division of labour in every area of life 'while alienation reduces the man to an instrument of labour within industry, it reduces the woman to an instrument for his sexual pleasure within the family' (Foreman 1977, p. 151). Sandra Bartky claims that alienation defines the relation between contemporary forms of female sexuality and other features of women's lives, since sexual fetishisation or reification is the extreme form of alienation. See Bartky (1979). Women are alienated from science and scholarship, which presents a male-biased model of human nature and social reality. These forms are interrelated. For example Sandra Bartky argues that the form taken by woman's sexual alienation results in an even more damaging alienation from her intellectual capacities. In addition, women's participation in male-dominated political activity might also be described as alienated.

Ann Foreman sums up these theories by declaring that femininity itself is alienation. To the extent that men and women conform to stereotypes of masculinity and femininity, they will be alienated from each other in incompatible ways.

Althusser, Louis

French Marxist philosopher who has influenced feminist theory with his idea that the family, school and other sites of ideology are *not* some natural sphere outside capitalism. See Althusser (1971).

Some Althusserian problematics are important to feminism. For example, Althusser argues that different paradigms (problematics) contain questions which in turn find or construct different facts about the world. The absences in these questions are as significant as what is present. Feminist theory has been influenced by this idea and by Althusser's polemical attack on the Marxist view that the economic base is the sole determinant of social and historical actions. To Althusser, ideology functions not only through economics but by addressing individuals who are 'interpellated' as subjects. Feminism agrees that it is by the concrete functioning of ideology in the material rituals of everyday life that a woman will recognise herself as a subject. See O'Brien (1982).

Feminism breaks with Althusser in the area of subjectivity both because he retains a concept of the individual, which is pre-Freudian, and because he argues that the economic function does determine the construction of subjectivity. Feminist theory prefers to privilege images, language or emotions.

Amazons

Women warriors from North Africa and the Black Sea region who worshipped the Goddess. Evidence collected by feminist researchers suggests that Amazon society was a matriarchy in which males were nomadic or slaves. Although traditional scholarship claims that Amazon culture was mythical, the terms and images of Amazons, for example the moon sickle, have been appropriated by contemporary feminists to symbolise the power of feminism.

Mary Daly makes Amazon into a metaphor to describe women who are fighting to affirm the true identity of our foremothers. This accepts that aggression can be used by women to develop an entirely separate and self-contained women's culture. See Daly (1978).

For example, Merlin Stone suggests that the term was used to describe Goddess worshippers who fought to protect their temples. See Stone (1976).

French theorists use Amazon as a metaphor for harmony. See Wittig and Zeig (1976).

Black feminism draws attention to the incipient racism of representations of Amazons as black female animals. See Hooks (1981).

Anarchist feminism

A theory that female subordination is determined as much by a system of sexual and familial relationships as by State controls, and that legal change cannot in itself provide equality without full psychological independence. Anarchist feminism would eliminate all social restraints and replace these with decentralised, organic communities of women. Early feminist anarchists, for example Emma Goldman and Voltairine de Cleyre, believed that social attitudes would grow organically into sexual and psychological freedom. See Kornegger (1979).

Anarchist feminists argue that the State and patriarchy are twin aberrations. To destroy the State is to destroy the major agent of institutionalised patriarchy; to abolish patriarchy is to abolish the State. This theory is more revolutionary than radical feminism because it believes that *any* State (matriarchal or otherwise) is always illegitimate. Perhaps for this reason many feminist science fiction writers are anarchist. See Le Guin (1969).

Anarchist feminists also believe that the means used to change society must be models of the future society in themselves. Therefore women's cooperatives and consciousness-raising groups can make a more significant social and ideological contribution than their numbers or economic status might imply. This is encapsulated in the slogan 'The personal is political' first coined by Carol Hanisch. See Hanisch (1971).

Anarchist feminists reject devices such as consent theory because these justify the limited use of State power and liberal feminism which will coopt rather than radicalise the Women's Movement. See Ehrlich (1979).

Androcentrism

Male centredness, which is the value set of our dominant culture based on male norms. Charlotte Perkins Gilman first used this term to draw attention to male bias (Gilman 1911). Any account which characterises aspects of women's lives as deviant is androcentric. Androcentrism affects theory, not only because universities and research institutions are largely male domains but more subtly in the choice of areas of research, research policies, theoretical concepts and research methods. For example, feminist anthropologists draw attention to the androcentric paradigm 'Man the hunter' which is used by neo-evolutionists to propagate the idea that all human development began with male hunting.

Renate Duelli Klein suggests that feminism will only defeat androcentricity when 'man-as-the-norm stops being the only recognized frame of reference for human beings' (Duelli Klein 1983, p. 89).

Autonomous women's studies can fundamentally alter the nature of knowledge by shifting the focus from androcentricity to a frame of reference in which women's different and differing ideas, experiences, moods and interests are valid in their own right. See Bowles (1983).

As Elizabeth Minnich puts it: 'What we [feminists] are doing, is comparable to Copernicus shattering our geocentricity, Darwin shattering our species-centricity. We are shattering andro-centricity and the change is fundamental' (Minnich 1982, p. 7).

Barbara Du Bois calls the attack on androcentricity by feminist theory 'passionate scholarship'. See Du Bois (1983).

Androgyny

Greek word from andro (male) and gyn (female) which means a psychological and psychic mixture of traditional masculine and feminine virtues. It is to be distinguished from hermaphroditism, which is primarily a physical condition. Androgyny has a long history. Many Indo-European religions combine male and female in a Primal Androgyne.

The first feminist theories of androgyny described a hybrid model. For example Elizabeth Cady Stanton in *The Woman's Bible* (1895-8) describes the Heavenly Being as androgynous. Virginia Woolf defined androgyny, in *A Room of One's Own* as a spectrum on which human beings could choose their places regardless of history or tradition. Second wave feminism suggests that androgyny could offer a new monogendered personality. Carolyn Heilbrun describes how, in Western literature and mythology, there is a long-standing tradition of androgyny which could be drawn on to replace contemporary dualisms. See Heilbrun (1973).

In feminist psychology, Sandra Bem devised a test, the Bem Sex Role Inventory, which showed that the brightest people were the most androgynous. See Bem (1974).

Many feminist philosophers claim that androgynous personalities are holistic and have a capacity to experience the full range of human emotions. See Trebilcot (1977). Andrea Dworkin uses the concept of androgyny to propose a physical transformation of human biology: 'We are, clearly, a multisexed species . . . where the elements called male and female are not discrete' (Dworkin, 1981, p. 183). This is a goal shared by the French writer Monique Wittig. Julia Kristeva argues against the destructive power of any metaphysical belief in fixed gender identities. See Moi (1985).

Other feminists argue that androgyny is a static concept because it ignores issues of power which can promote individual psychological transformation through material change. See J. B. Miller (1976).

Radical feminists, like Mary Daly and Adrienne Rich, argue that even if androgyny *were* an adequate moral ideal, it would be totally inappropriate as a *political* objective because it fails to name differences. The idea of androgyny obscures the need to struggle for separatism. See Raymond (1975).

Anima

The female soul, derived from *an* 'heavenly', and *ma* 'mother'. Anima is the basic principle of alchemy because alchemists believed that all spirits were female. Anima is also an important concept to feminist Jungians because, in Jungian terms, anima represents the intuitive part of the mind and one's first experience of the anima is with the mother. See Hall (1980).

Anorexia nervosa
Self-starvation.

The first mention of anorexia nervosa is usually credited to Richard Morton's *Phthisologia* (1689).

Traditional psychoanalysis defines anorexia nervosa as a psychomatic illness and includes it in the group of so-called personality disorders where symptoms focus on weight loss.

Because anorexia involves a breaking of social rules and norms of conduct, feminist theory redefines the behaviour characteristics of anorexia as social and mythical rather than as disturbed or organic. See Orbach (1978).

Current writing traces the history of anorexia nervosa to women's religious and secular fasting in the past, and also to contemporary family identity crises. See MacLeod (1981).

Because anorexia nervosa appeals to those who desire to escape from traditional images of femininity and women's roles (for example adolescent girls) it has been described as a feminist gesture. See Chernin (1981).

Anthony, Susan B.
American, Susan Anthony was both a theorist and a brilliant political organiser. She elaborated a fundamental natural rights doctrine in her statements and abolition writings. Anthony edited a radical women's newspaper, *The Revolution*, from 1868–70 and contributed to the *History of Woman Suffrage* with Elizabeth Cady Stanton and Matilda Joselyn Gage. See Anthony (1902).

Anthropology
The study of cultures. Feminists argue that traditional anthropology has ethnocentric biases, for example its use of the concepts of

dominance and subordination, hierarchy, power and authority and its views concerning production and reproduction, nature and culture, the domestic and political spheres. Anthropology is a dynamic and influential area of feminist scholarship because it centralises kinship and gender and can take a holistic perspective looking at gender as a principle of social organisation. Anthropology offers an unparalleled possibility to enlarge the scope of feminist theory and scrutinise Western assumptions because it provides the cross-cultural perspective needed by Western feminists.

Building on the work of Margaret Mead and others, contemporary theorists show how gender behaviour is a social artifact. Michelle Rosaldo suggests that all societies assign women to the domestic sphere and give male activities greater significance. She argues that there is a direct relationship between the degree of women's subordination and the degree to which the realms of public and domestic are separated. Feminist theory has to understand the structure of the whole sexual order. See Rosaldo and Lamphere (1974).

Michelle Rosaldo later qualified her original argument to suggest that gender characteristics are not universal but 'the complex product of a variety of social forces' (Rosaldo 1980, p. 401).

Sherry Ortner makes a parallel argument that the devaluation of women is universal because all societies distinguish nature from culture and associate women with nature which is inferior. See Ortner (1974).

Feminist theorists favour an examination of the cultural and symbolic significance of reproduction and the domestic sphere, rather than the economic division of labour lending the authority of anthropological theory to Shulamith Firestone's hypothesis that women's need to reproduce is the root cause of our oppression. See Firestone (1970). Karen Sacks, refining Engels' *Origin of the Family*, claims that men's production for exchange eclipsed women's production for use and formed an important basis for male power. See Sacks (1974).

Feminist theories of anthropology challenge existing ideas of 'natural' human behaviour by pointing to cultural patterns which disguise women's inferior social position.

Architecture
The art of constructing buildings for human use.

Feminist architects describe examples of communes, non-sexist settlements and fantasy environments which can maximise personal choices about child rearing and sociality and become women's architecture. See Hayden (1976 and 1980).

There are three dominant aims in current theory about women and architecture: to attack the conventional division between public and private spaces; to create architecture that fits the environment and behaviour paradigms of home and neighbourhood; and to provide equal access to public goods and social services. See Wekerle (1981).

Writers on feminist aesthetics argue that an ideal architecture would be one where buildings for women are designed by women. They could be symbolic expressions in circular form 'in freely flowing creativity to formal principles completely freed from patriarchal tradition' (Erlemann 1985, p. 128).

Art
Creative expression.

Feminist criticism questions the principles of art history, adjusts its historical perspective and creates new definitions of craft and technique. See Linda Nochlin's pathbreaking essay 'Why have there been no great women artists?' (1971). It argues that art, through its imagery, associations and cultural status has functioned as an instrument of sex role socialisation using exaggerated emblems of female virtue and vice. Feminist theory attacks the basic premises of the discipline, for example the idea that only individual artistic innovation is progressive or that the institution of the avant-garde depends on free (male) artists. See Parker and Pollock (1981).

'To re-experience art from a feminist perspective is to divorce it from an ivory tower context of universal value and to see it not as a passive reflector of social history, but as a tool that can be used and has been used in every historical period as a powerful social force' (Broude and Garrard 1982, p. 14).

Feminism creates a context for women artists to make a new art which affirms the personal and collective experience of women and uses the materials of women's lives. See Chicago (1979). Women's contemporary art is characterised by anti-classical techniques. For example, Lucy Lippard includes performance, action art, and ready-mades as recurring elements in women's art: 'a uniform density . . . often sensuously tactile and repetitive or detailed to the point of obsession: the preponderance of circular forms, central focus, inner space . . . parabolic form that turns in on itself, layers or strata, or veils; an indefinable looseness or flexibility of handling; windows; autobiographical content; animals; flowers; a certain kind of fragmentation; a new fondness for the pinks and pastels' (Lippard 1976, p. 49).

Black feminists draw attention to the Eurocentrism of early feminist theory and they describe a wider framework of women's art, for example by including gardening and practical skills. See Walker (1983).

Associational thinking

A way of representing theory as thoughts in a process based on the idea that no theory is final.

In literary criticism feminist theorists use associational thinking to create a mixed mode of autobiography and criticism. See DuPlessis (1985).

Dale Spender uses associational thought to suggest that female experience is continuous. For example many women writers work things out on the page in order to show the correlation of thinking with various permutations of language. See Spender (1983).

Astell, Mary

English writer.

In *Serious Proposal to the Ladies* (1694) Mary Astell made an early critique of male learning. She argued that learning is flawed by a male interest in maintaining male supremacy. She advocated reorganising knowledge from a feminist standpoint, for example in women's colleges.

Astrology

The study of the heavens.

Like alchemy (q.v.), astrology is an example of how women's early scientific skill was later devalued both by the church and by the scientific establishment.

In both astrology and astronomy women were responsible for determining calendars, seasons and future events by charting the movements of planets and stars. Both sciences inform much of contemporary feminist anthropology, for example by suggesting symbolic, interpretive frameworks that can escape traditional anthropological paradigms. See Hall (1980).

Atkinson Ti-Grace

American activist.

In 'The institution of sexual intercourse' (1970) Atkinson argued that this institution is a political construct used to keep women in their place (prone). It was in *Amazon Odyssey* that Atkinson created the radical feminist theory that women are the first exploited class. Atkinson claims that women must develop a new identity apart from their political class identity, and that love is a pathology rooted in the incomplete identities of men and women.

A crucial part of contemporary feminist theory is its development of a lesbian perspective. Atkinson argues that lesbians are the radicals of the feminist movement because, as lesbians, women can reject stereotyping and can think radically and profoundly about social change. See Atkinson (1974).

Authentic relations

From Carl Rogers. The idea that people who behave in accordance with their values are behaving genuinely. This encourages others to behave genuinely. If genuineness is experienced by both parties, the relationship is called authentic. Shulamit Reinharz argues that feminist researchers should be interested only in information derived from authentic relations. Research processes based on authentic relations will be those which formulate questions of concern and interest to the 'subjects' who will want to collaborate – particularly if the research process provides an opportunity for catharsis or self-discovery. See Reinharz (1983).

Authority

Institutionalised power whose use usually goes unquestioned because authority is regarded as routine. Feminist theory draws attention to the ways authority depends upon language, for example by using stereotypes. See Spender (1980). Feminist writers provide alternative etymologies of women's words which can represent women's power. See Daly (1978). These theoretical critiques are supported by the political activity of feminists who, in consciousness-raising groups, identify alternative sources of authority drawn from personal experience. This is called the authority of experience.

Autonomy

Women who retain a sense of self-direction and self-determination that grows with the help of affiliation and connection with others, rather than in competition against them, are autonomous. See J.B. Miller (1976) and Eisenstein and Sacks (1975).

A respect for autonomy is basic to the liberal concepts of freedom and equality and this aspect provides one of liberalism's main arguments for limiting the power of the State. Feminist theory argues that this liberal position is problematic unless it takes account of the ways in which human beliefs, desires and interests are socially constituted.

Feminism places autonomy as a struggle concept in the context of sexual politics. For example feminism rejects any tendency to subsume the woman's question into general movements. Women's autonomous organisations are expressions of the desire to preserve both the qualitatively different character and identity of the feminist movement, as well as its independent power base. See Mies (1983).

Others link sexual autonomy with economic autonomy. See Ehrenreich and English (1979). In feminist theories of science, Nancy Chodorow argues that male gender identity stems from separation and autonomy and E.F. Keller suggests that autonomy, separation and distance connote masculinity. See Keller (1978).

Autonomy of colour for women involves articulating an independent Black experience and the historical and cultural differences that give feminism a distinctive meaning in Black lives. See AAWORD (1980) and B. Smith (1982).

Barrett, Michèle

A British feminist who has widened the definition of women's politics. In *Women's Oppression Today* Barrett developed a comprehensive account of Marxist theory to argue that it is the monogamous family, not simply the sexual division of labour, which enables men to dominate women. This is because the family controls access to resources and defines women's sexuality as reproducers and pleasers of men, thereby restricting women's access to paid labour. See Barrett (1980).

Barthes, Roland

A French theorist of semiology – the sociology of signs, symbols and cultural representations. Barthes' accounts of the semiotics of fashion, advertising and culture in *Mythologies, S/Z* and *Camera Lucida* opened up definitions of culture and art which helped feminists writing about cultural production. See McRobbie (1984).

Barthes attacked the centrality of the author as a fixed point of meaning in criticism, in what he called 'the birth of the reader'. While supporting Barthes' rejection of the humanist notion of the artist, feminists argue that semiology needs to address gendered subjects. See Wolff (1981).

Battered women

Physically abused women.

There is no single feminist theory of battering but most feminists locate violence against women within the broader context of women's subordinate position relative to men. Feminist theory defines battering as the historical expression of male domination which is manifested in the family and currently reinforced by the institutions, economic arrangements and sexist division of labour within capitalist society. See Schechter (1982).

Battering was first raised as a feminist issue by Frances Power Cobbe in *Wife Torture*, and is regarded as the extreme end of a continuum of oppressions suffered by all women. See Dobash and Dobash (1980).

Beard, Mary Ritter

American historian.

Beard was a political activist who went on to initiate and develop a new scholarship of women's history. Gerda Lerner cites Beard's *Woman as a Force in History* (1946) as the first critique of history from a feminist perspective.

Beauty

Attractive appearance. Feminist theories about beauty describe women's need to be beautiful as creating false object-selves. See Bartky (1982). De Beauvoir argued that this objectification functions to perpetuate male supremacy and Susan Griffin argues that women's objectification is pornographic. See Griffin (1981). Black feminists point out that in any case most concepts of women's beauty are based on white male values. They argue that definitions of Black beauty must respond to Black history and Black culture. See Joseph and Lewis (1981).

Beauvoir, Simone de

French philosopher. Author of *The Second Sex (Le Deuxième Sexe*, 1949). Simone de Beauvoir was a major contemporary feminist writer. Her main contribution to feminist theory is her argument that, in a patriarchal culture, the masculine is set up as the positive or norm and the female or feminine is set up as the negative, or what de Beauvoir called 'the Other'. De Beauvoir believed that Otherness is a fundamental category of human thought. She speculated that women's identity as Other and her fundamental alienation derive in part from her body – especially her reproductive capacity – and in part from the historical division of labour dictated by childbearing and rearing.

De Beauvoir argues that women need to strengthen their rationality and critical power in order to achieve transcendence. See de Beauvoir (1953).

Bebel, August

In *Women and Socialism* (1879) Bebel provided an early Marxist theory about women's position and analyses the sources of women's oppression and the strategies by which oppression could be changed. His ideas of sexual independence and the decline of marriage were influenced by early socialist feminism and Alexandra Kollontai referred to the text as 'the woman's bible' (1977).

Benston, Margaret

The first contemporary feminist to argue that *all* women are exploited as domestic workers. Benston argues that women's domestic condition is analogous to that of wage labourers. See Benston (1969).

Bernard, Jessie
American critic.

Bernard applies perspectives from the sociology of knowledge to sex differences research, and argues that sex difference is an institution whose objectives, method and ideology mirror a male-controlled and male-defined environment. See Bernard (1968).

Biology
The study of human and physical life. Questions of biology are central to feminism because women's oppression is deeply determined by our ability to give birth. Feminist theory has always explicitly recognised the importance, for women, of freedom from reproductive control although de Beauvoir, Juliet Mitchell, Firestone, Griffin, Rich and others describe different paths to freedom.

Feminist research is investigating how women's bodies function within the context of our lives and argues that our biology develops in reciprocal and dialectical relationship with the ways in which we live. See Lowe and Hubbard (1983).

Some feminist theorists argue that reconstructions of women's 'intrinsic' biological nature are scientifically meaningless and are usually politically or ideologically motivated. Sociobiology in particular is attacked by feminist theorists because it renders the biological as more important than the social origins of women's roles. See Bleier (1984). All feminists agree that feminist theory must dispel naturalistic explanations which provide biological justifications for women's economic and social limitations.

Biological determinism
The concept that physiological differences between men and women determine social roles. This concept is the basis of discriminatory legislation which prohibits women from full expression of our potential. Some feminists, in particular radical feminists like Shulamith Firestone, believe that biology does determine women's nature but that we can be freed by technology. See Firestone (1970).

Other feminists use notions of biological determination to suggest that women *do* have certain biologically determined attributes, for example our pacifism. See Griffin (1978).

Birth control
Control over the conception of children. Birth control is used in

eugenics and campaigns in the Third World as a form of social control and racism. In areas where women do have total responsibility for their own birth control, for example Hunza women, such controls are not used in sexist or racist ways. Birth control is an issue involving more than just technological politics, and feminist theory argues that the right to reproductive freedom must be a cornerstone of women's liberation. The theory and practice of birth control stems from a female condition that is more basic than class. See Gordon (1976).

Bisexuality
The condition of enjoying both heterosexual and homosexual sexuality. The term is an important one in contemporary French feminist theory. Where bisexuality is linked with hysteria in traditional psychoanalytic theory, Catherine Clément and Hélène Cixous use the word 'bisexual' in their texts like *La Jeune née* to name some sort of positive goal. Both Clement and Cixous are talking about 'other bisexuality': one that accepts the imaginary and the symbolic; both theory and body. See Cixous and Clément (1975).

In other writings Cixous argues: 'In saying "bisexual, hence neuter," I am referring to the classic conception of bisexuality . . . self-effacing, merger-type bisexuality, to this I oppose the *Other bisexuality*, that is each one's location in self (*repérage en soi*) of the presence of both sexes; non exclusion either of the difference or of one sex, which is multiplication of the effects of the inscription of desire' (Cixous 1976, p. 881).

Black feminism
The theory of Black-defined women's struggles. Black feminism has built on a tradition of leftist activism, adapting models of socialist feminism. Initially Black feminism argued that meaningful change in a social order which represses both men and women could be accomplished by building coalitions between women of colour and progressive movements. Black feminists like Barbara Smith, Audre Lorde, Gloria I. Joseph, Gloria Hull or Alice Walker are creating theories which meet the needs of Black women by helping Black women to mobilise around issues that they perceive to have a direct impact on the overall quality of life. Black feminist theory examines the boundaries of sisterhood with white feminists in order to deal fully with the contradictions inherent in gender, race and class within the context of a racist society. See Amos and Parmar (1984).

Black feminists argue that all feminist theory must understand imperialism and challenge it. 'To look at the crucial question of how we organize in order to address ourselves to the *totality* of our oppression. We cannot prioritize one aspect of our oppression to the exclusion of others. Only a synthesis of class, race, gender and sexuality can lead us forward' (Amos and Parmar 1984, p. 18).

Black women and other women of colour point to the insensitivity of white feminists in assuming that white experience could speak for that of all women. For example by using the experience of Blacks as a metaphor for white women, without noticing the unconscious racism of their language and assumptions. See Hooks (1981). Audre Lorde took Mary Daly to task for talking about the experience of women of colour only in the context of victimisation without describing their full experience. See Lorde (1984).

Only Black women can understand the role gender has played in Black male thinking. See Combahee River Collective (1981).

As Barbara Smith argues: 'Acknowledging the sexism of Black men does not mean we become "man-haters" or necessarily eliminate them from our lives. What it does mean is that we must struggle for a different basis of interaction with men' (B. Smith, 1979). Currently, Black literary critics are deconstructing the signifying processes around words like 'mulatto' to articulate a theory of difference for Afro-American women. See M. Davis *et al.* (1987).

Black woman

'I capitalise "Black" because I regard it not simply as a colour but as a cultural, personal and political identity' (Joseph, 1983, p. 134). Being Black and female is a double burden but Black women are developing a new conceptual framework to encompass the autonomous values, behaviour, attitudes and beliefs of Black women. There are conflicting theories about Black women. For example, Black women more than white women have an ambiguous relation to traditional roles. In her review of research on the 'black matriarchy', V. O'Leary concludes that is a myth that cannot be defended on any empirical grounds. See O'Leary (1977).

Yet in literature, Mary Helen Washington argues, there is a persistent image of the strong Black mother. She claims that the relationships of Black mothers and daughters can only be discovered as one comes to terms with history. See Washington (1975).

Body

Theories about the sexuality of the body, power and the political control of women's bodies by patriarchy, are central to feminism.

In contemporary society a woman is usually represented *only* as her body. Accurate information about the body is withheld from women and our bodies are regarded in functional terms. Kristeva argues that, if women came to power the representation of power as opposition *to* the body would cease. She claims that a woman's body is 'unrepresentable' power. See Kristeva (1974).

Jane Gallop suggests that the conflict is always 'between body – as the inadequate name of some uncommanded diversity of drives and contradiction – and power, between body and law, between body and phallus, even between body and Body' (Gallop 1982, p. 121).

A feminist theory of the body is based on concepts of sexual self-determination. Cherríe Moraga argues that 'a return to the body' implies an acceptance of lesbian desire. See Moraga (1981).

Robin Morgan extends this definition to celebrate the erotic and essential life instincts of women's bodies. See Morgan (1977).

Dorothy Dinnerstein proves that women's subordination stems from women's ignorance of the erotic and a general cultural revulsion for female flesh. See Dinnerstein (1976).

Body politics
The term refers both to physical power relations and to the struggle against all forms of indirect violence against women. Nancy M. Henley argues that the body language of contemporary society is inherently sexist. See Henley (1977).

Other feminists use the concept of body politics to describe violence against women embedded in other exploitative and oppressive relations like class and imperialism, as well as in the patriarchal institutions of family, medicine or education. See Brownmiller (1984).

Feminists writing about body politics share one main theme. This theme is the insistence on the human essence of women, on our dignity, integrity and inviolability as human beings and a rejection of women's objectification.

Browne, Stella
A British feminist who wrote and campaigned about abortion and birth control during the 1920s and 1930s. Sheila Rowbotham argues that Browne's critique of women's reproductive rights influenced contemporary socialist feminism. See Rowbotham (1977).

Brownmiller, Susan
In *Against our Will: Men, Women and Rape* (1975) Brownmiller makes a comprehensive study of rape. She believes that sexual violence against women is not only culturally condoned and pervasive but that rape is a primary means by which some men establish their 'manhood'. Rape is the secret of patriarchy. Both the

possibility and the actuality of rape, Brownmiller argues, serve as the main agent of the 'perpetuation of male domination over women by force'. Brownmiller suggests that rape culture and the ideology of rape are socially produced.

Bunch, Charlotte

A founder of *Quest*, the leading journal of lesbian theory, Bunch drew on socialist feminist theory to argue that the organisation of labour depended on heterosexual assumptions. Bunch's writings helped to establish lesbian theory as a major element in contemporary feminism. Lesbian feminist politics is a political critique of the institution and ideology of heterosexuality as a cornerstone of male supremacy. It is an extension of the analysis of sexual politics to an analysis of sexuality itself as an institution. (Bunch 1981).

Bunch, along with Adrienne Rich, provides a comprehensive plan for the dissection of compulsory heterosexuality as an oppressive social institution.

Canon

A term for the list of literary *master*pieces in traditional literary studies. The canon is an informal institution of literature whose specific inclusions and exclusions, deletions and exceptions are nowhere codified. Elaine Showalter points to the intrinsic sexism of a canon where whole literary forms and periods do not represent a single female author. See Showalter (1971). Feminist criticism argues that the canon must be patriarchal because it has chosen so few women writers as major figures and it has relegated so many women to obscurity. See Humm (1986).

Feminist critics looked first at the historical process of literary evaluation and argued that the canon should be studied like any other historical phenomenon. See Ellmann (1968).

Others questioned definitions of 'classic' literature and modified the range of texts regarded as great works. See Moers (1977).

Feminist theorists attack the institutionalisation of literature (Rich 1979). They reveal the class, race and homophobic elitism of traditional literary syllabuses. See B. Smith (1980) and Zimmerman (1981). Marxist feminists deconstruct the canon by showing how it is historically constituted by relations of production and consumption. See Barrett (1980).

Capitalism

The economic system in which the means of production are in private ownership. Marx described the exploitative forms of capitalism in his theory of the capitalist mode of production.

Radical feminists, liberals and socialist feminists agree that there can be no understanding of the nature of contemporary capitalist society without placing the oppression of women at the centre of such an analysis. Nor can any adequate feminist theory simply *add* women as a 'missing ingredient' to an overall Marxist theory.

Zillah Eisenstein argues that the systems of capitalism and patriarchy are mutually supportive. These systems have *relative* autonomy from each other and are dialectically related. Woman is a site of the contradictions in capitalism because advanced *capitalism* has required the married woman to enter the labour force against the interests of *patriarchy* as encapsulated in the arguments of the contemporary New Right. Eisenstein argues that the wage earning wife's double day of work (outside and inside the home) is the result of this contradiction. See Eisenstein (1982).

Other feminists argue that analysis must link the two main forms of capitalist oppression – the sexual division of labour in the home and in production *and* the historically specific organisation of procreation and sexuality. See McDonough and Harrison (1978).

Socialist feminists look at the impact of the needs of a late monopoly capitalist economy on the position of women domestically and internationally. This strand of feminist analysis places feminist issues such as reproductive self-determination in the context of an overall political struggle for democratic socialism. See Sargent (1981). They look, too, at the interaction of psychology and materialism which need to be linked in discussion of sexual issues such as pornography. Feminist theory describes the uses of sexuality by capitalism, its packaging as a commodity, and forms of cooption (for example the 'marketing' of homosexuality).

Capitalist patriarchy
A historically specific form of patriarchy in which patriarchy operates through class and productive relations. The subordination of women is shaped by specific modes of production. One instance of the collaboration between capitalism and patriarchy, which has been a focus of discussion among feminist scholars, is the combination of protective legislation and women's exclusion from male dominated trade unions. See Hartmann (1976).

Career
A pattern of mobility in a profession. The term applies more to white male middle-class occupations. Feminist critics point to the gender differences in careers. Adult white women lack mobility due to unstable life patterns, and adult Black women suffer the double discrimination of career instability combined with a lack of vertical achievement. Ann Oakley attacks the notion of 'career-woman' as representing illegitimately wielded authority. See Oakley (1982).

Caste
From *casta* meaning race and *castus* meaning pure. Usually used to describe the Hindu system of social organisation which relies on the practice of endogamous marriage and precise rules of social contact, occupations and ritual.

Feminists draw attention to the important differences that occur between lower-caste women and middle-class women and challenge ruling class ideologies about Indian womanhood. They argue that these oppressive ideologies which govern women's role in society are founded in a specific relationship to men. They are products of unequal structures and practices arising from within Indian society itself, and are lent weight by colonialism rather than only by religion. See Jayawardena (1982).

Censorship
The control of offensive material.

This is a hotly debated issue in radical feminism in relation to its campaign against pornography. Radical feminists are sometimes fallaciously linked to the contemporary New Right because both favour a return to censorship. Susan Griffin and Andrea Dworkin argue, on the contrary, that pornography itself is a form of censorship because it silences the authentic voice of women. See Lederer (1980), Griffin (1981) and Dworkin (1981).

Census
An itemised list of a country's population obtained by means of a compulsory demographic, social and economic questionnaire.

In census classifications the unit of analysis is not the individual but the household or family. Feminist historians attack the sexist assumptions implicit in census codes. Officials, when assigning a household to a single social class or socio-economic group, typically attend only to the occupation of the head of the household and take this to be the husband or father whenever present or the principal earner, who usually happens to be male. See Beddoe (1983).

Chesler, Phyllis
American psychologist. In *Women and Madness* (1972) Chesler argued that psychiatry oppresses women and described how women are made mentally ill by the social processes of sex role conditioning. Chesler's main contribution to feminist theory is her argument that women's sex role stereotyping is a prescription for failure, for victimisation, and in extreme cases, for severe mental illness.

Chicana theory
The culture of women of Mexican ancestry. Writers Cherrie Moraga in the USA and Rosario Castellanos in Mexico redefine the image of Mexican woman and the framework of Western culture.

Despite their diverse backgrounds these Chicana writers focus on similar aspects of Chicana oppression and steps that might eradicate it.

Chicana women are triply oppressed: as members of minority culture, from their gender roles and from the machismo culture of Chicano men. Mexican/Chicano patriarchy translates women into archetypes of motherhood, virgin or deviant.

The most valuable part of feminist theory thus far has been its re-evaluation of Chicana history from a woman's perspective and its re-evaluation of Mexican/Chicana female figures that were early examples of subversive femininity, for example the figure of La Malincha.

In addition Chicana theory describes the strong and essential bonds between mothers and daughters in Chicana culture. See Castellanos (1975) and Moraga (1986).

Childbirth

Women's unique psychological, psychic and physiological experience of parturition. Until the eighteenth century childbirth was the province of women but, with the development of an elitist male medical profession, women were alienated from the experience of their labour by the demands of male obstetrics. See Ehrenreich and English (1979).

The feminist self-help health movement encourages women to see reproductive functions as natural and normal and thereby to question alienating and unnecessary medical procedures. See Arms (1975). Feminist theory, by describing the power of prepatriarchal women, has helped to locate women's unique biological capacities in a new culture of childbirth. See Boston Women's Health Collective (1971).

Childcare

Childcare services in Britain after World War II emphasised the importance of children staying at home with their mothers. This anti-institutional approach was influenced by John Bowlby's work on maternal deprivation in *Child Care and the Growth of Love* (1953). Feminist theorists attack State ideology because it reinforces the idea that mothers should be sole child carers. American government administrations share a similar view that childcare is primarily a family responsibility. The women's liberation movement has consistently shown that child care responsibility is a cause of women's second class status. See Riley and Leonard (1986).

There are many diverse feminist accounts of childcare but all agree that the first step is to break down society's idea that women should be solely responsible for the caring of children. Marxist feminists like Michèle Barrett argue that women will never be truly equal until childcare becomes society's responsibility. For example women's dependence on part-time work is the direct consequence of their responsibility for childcare. See Barrett (1980).

Shulamith Firestone suggests that the physical hardship of childcare can be overcome through abolishing women's physical and psychological responsibility for reproduction and the socialisation of childcare. See Firestone (1970).

Juliet Mitchell in *Woman's Estate* (1971) emphasises how important it is to demystify ideologies about the socialisation of children and the social cult of maternity. She suggests that woman's activity of bearing and raising children came to be seen as replacement for paid work.

Sherry Ortner points out that it is the universal association of women with childrearing and domesticity which contributed to women's association with the natural and therefore led to her devaluation. See Ortner (1974).

Sandra Bem argues that the issue of women's sole capacity to childbear will become a non issue once people become psychologically androgynous because then the relationship of women to childcare would be a matter of free choice. See Bem (1976).

Dorothy Dinnerstein argues that women's monopoly of childcare is a central cause of human malaise. Women's control over men as infants leads men to dominate women in later life. Only when men take an equal share in the task of nurturing can women enter history. See Dinnerstein (1976).

Nancy Chodorow suggests that men and women's personality structures are determined by the responses each makes to the mother as main childcarer. Boys learn autonomy through learning not to mother – not to nurture. Chodorow calls for a conscious break in the cycle of 'mothering' and the reallocation of childcare. See Chodorow (1978).

Whatever the various positions within feminist theory and the differences within women's own experiences of childcare, the issue is a crucial point of contact between feminist theory and feminist politics.

Childhood

According to Philipe Ariès in *Centuries of Childhood* (1962), the institution of childhood developed in the eighteenth century among the bourgeoisie based on a notion of demographic segregation and moral instruction. Infants become children through socialisation in the family.

Feminist research has shown how boys and girls are treated

differently and socialised in childhood into sex specific gender roles. Juliet Mitchell, in *Psychoanalysis and Feminism* (1974) argues that social identity is a gendered identity. Other feminists argue that girl children are defined, in childhood, by their relationship with their mothers. See Chodorow (1978).

Chodorow, Nancy

American sociologist whose text, *The Reproduction of Mothering* (1978) is an influential feminist reinterpretation of Freudian theory. Chodorow's central thesis is that gender personality is shaped within the psychodynamics of the family and in particular within the 'object relations' the child forms with the mother.

Basing her thesis on her observations of gender differences in the 'preoedipal period', Chodorow drew on the theoretical perspectives of Talcott Parsons and those of the Frankfurt School to create a new theory of object relations. This theory takes the self to be constructed out of social relationships. The term 'object relation' signifies the idea that aspects of these relationships become internalised − become 'internal objects' for the self. By placing the question of gender differentiation at the centre of her work Chodorow could ask how object relations theory might be used to explain psychological differences between men and women. Chodorow argues that since each child's initial relationship is to the mother, boys achieve male identity only in contradistinction from the mother. The girl, because of her continuing tie to the mother cannot, and does not need to, repress her infantile experience or relational capacities. Girls are more likely to define themselves in relation to others.

Christian feminism

Feminist theories of Christianity fall into three categories: those that challenge the theological view of women and the androcentricity of traditional theology; those that challenge the theological laws that bar women from ordination; those that evaluate the church as an institution and aim to upgrade the professional status of women in the church.

Feminist theologians dispute the continual use of masculine terms to refer to God or the Holy Ghost. In research about the imagery of women in the church and in Christian history, theologians reveal that there are only two images of women − the transgressor (Eve) or the virgin (Mary), which includes motherhood and obedience. See Daly (1968).

Sara Maitland contests the nature of dualistic theology. She argues that this dualism, by creating a sense of the other, is inherently racist, sexist and could lead to the destruction of the planet. See Maitland (1983). Feminist Christians are not *anti* Christian but argue instead that Christianity has excluded transcendental biblical themes in favour of anti-women images.

City

A term for a major town which carries the feminine gender in several languages. The shape of cities both enhances and constricts women's lives. Since the 1960s, women's groups have organised to change the repressive effects of cities, for example in campaigns for public transport, housing and urban cooperatives. See Ettore (1978).

Feminists who are critical of urban structures claim that current forms are inefficient and reinforce women's roles as household members. For example the separation cities make between work and home corresponds to the division of labour between men and women in household and wage labour. Feminists challenge the patriarchal structuring of urban space, which operates in tandem with work constrictions. See Stimpson (1981).

Civil rights movement

A social movement organised to fight segregation in the USA in the 1960s. Second wave feminism grew out of the ideas of women movement members who were activists and grew too, from the oppression women experienced from male members of the movement. See Morgan (1977).

The beliefs of feminism and civil rights intersect. Both re-evaluate the power structures of the family, education and racism. Both grew from the theories of R.D. Laing and Franz Fanon among others. But feminists broke with the civil rights movement in order to develop a radical perspective which could focus on the theory and politics of gender, rather than simply on left-wing activism. See Eisenstein (1984).

Cixous, Hélène

A French writer.

Cixous's theories about feminine sexuality combine psychoanalysis with literature and anthropology. For example, Cixous took her idea of generosity/expenditure from the exchange theory of Lévi-Strauss. Cixous believes that the feminine can be discovered and released when women interrogate our sexual pleasure. She describes this female libidinal economy in *Le Sexe ou la Tête*, and argues that bisexuality nourishes and compounds differences.

Cixous believes that writing is a forceful, cultural expression of women's alterity. She argues that the feminine text has no end and that it will inscribe a feminine libidinal economy into culture. See Cixous (1976).

Class

People of the same social and economic level.

Existing concepts of class, whether they are formations in history or categories of occupation and social groupings, are inappropriate for feminism. Socialist feminists argue that a full social analysis must accommodate both class and gender. They claim that the category of female interacts in a complex way with class but never overlaps it completely. See Rubin (1975).

Kate Millett in *Sexual Politics* (1970) claims that class is a social and economic hierarchy which sets one woman against another.

Marxist feminists argue that since a married woman inhabits her husband's class position, women's relationship to the class structure is mediated by the configuration of family, and domestic labour. Michèle Barrett argues that this duality is an important determinant of women's consciousness of class. See Barrett (1980).

Christine Delphy adds that women's class can best be understood in terms of the institution of marriage as a labour contract. See Delphy (1977).

Other feminists claim that a class analysis cannot incorporate family structure without a theory of sexual stratification. See Eichler (1980).

Zillah Eisenstein draws attention to the need for a class analysis which can adequately accommodate women who work only in the home. Radical feminists, on the other hand, argue that women form a class (or caste) unto themselves. Shulamith Firestone attacks Marxist feminism for paying inadequate attention to women as a 'sex class'. She developed a materialist view of history based on sex/gender and claimed that this axis is a basic division of society.

Feminist theories of class are now accommodating women's differences in race and sexual preference. See Snitow (1980).

Clitoridectomy

The severing of the suspensory ligament of the clitoris. This can involve the cutting of the tip of the clitoris ('suma') or infibulation where the two sides of the vulva are sewn together after excision.

The issue of clitoridectomy is a contentious one in feminist theory because the ritual is both an example of male power over women within the ideology of monogamous marriage and, in some countries, is conducted solely by women on other women. Anne Koedt claimed that clitoridectomy needs the perpetuation of a male supremacist ideology, but Mary Daly provides a more comprehensive response to the problem of duality. Daly argues that clitoridectomy is an example of sadomasochism because it embodies a symbolic murder of the Goddess in a reality of women -hating. The 'active' collusion of other women in the ritual, Daly can excuse as a 'passive, instrumental' role since only mentally castrated women can participate in the destruction of their own kind. See Daly (1978).

Black feminist discussions of the clitoridectomy now suggest that the issue must be seen in the context of modernisation in Africa and they argue for research into women's differences. See Abdalla (1982).

Collaborative research

Where the subject's role expands to all phases of research, rather than the traditional subject role which is one on whom research operations are performed.

Collaborative research begins with shared topic formulation. The participants act as partners or consultants shaping the research focus, selecting research procedures and their implementations; collaborating on data analysis and publication in a relation of 'equality, sharing and trust' (Vaughter 1976).

Phrases which describe the results of this research are 'shared feedback loops', 'joint interpretation of meaning', 'unpredictable discovery based on intersubjectivity' (Westkott 1979).

Barrie Thorne suggests that collaborative talk is feminine because women are more able then men to collectively share knowledge and emotional experience. See Thorne and Henley (1975).

Collective

A group in which each member's work is collaboratively shared and of a similar kind. Collective work is often suggested as an answer to the isolation, competitiveness and monotony of routine capitalist work plants.

Feminist historians study female collectives to call attention to emergent feminist consciousness. Kaplan argues that it is possible to examine a range of motivation in the everyday lives of women that might lead them to act collectively in pursuit of goals they could not attain as individuals. See Kaplan (1982).

The collectivisation of women's experiences helps women overcome the structural isolation of families and helps women understand that individual sufferings have social causes. Feminist researchers believe that if a woman is committed to the cause of women's liberation she cannot choose her area of research purely from a career point of view but must try to use her relative power to take up issues that are central to the movement. Maria Mies suggests that women cannot appropriate their own history until they collectivise their own experiences. See Mies (1983).

Colonialisation
A system of domination over subject countries. Feminist theorists argue that this process is analogous to women's experience of oppression in patriarchy.

In the absence of external colonies women become 'a last colony' (Werlhof *et al.* 1983).

The colonial process 'naturalised' colonised women as the counterpart of the 'civilising' of European women. The two processes are causally linked because the creation of 'savage' and 'civilised' women and the polarisation between the two is an organising structural principle of patriarchal capitalism. The colonisers used a diametrically opposed value system *vis-à-vis* the women of the subjugated peoples as that used to their 'own' women. See Reddock (1984).

In *Sexual Politics* (1970) Kate Millett was the first to point to the colonialisation of women in contemporary patriarchy. This colonial-isation, Millett claims, functions by a mechanism of the 'interior colonialisation' in women of male values. Robin Morgan adds the dimension of sexuality to Millett's argument, by describing women's bodies as the 'land' of male colonisers. See Morgan (1977).

Dalla Costa claims that the family and household are a colony. Adrienne Rich draws on Fanon's theory that colonialisation is a metaphor never an explanation, to argue that women's oppression as mothers is a form of colonialisation because men define and appropriate motherhood. See Rich (1976).

Combahee River Collective
A Black feminist group founded in 1974. The name comes from Harriet Tubman's guerrilla action which freed more than 750 slaves and is the only military campaign in American history planned and led by a woman.

In 1972 the collective published an important manifesto which described the issues in Black feminist politics and theory. The manifesto points to differences between Black and white feminism particularly in relation to Black men. 'We struggle with Black men against racism, while we struggle with Black men about sexism' (Combahee River Collective 1981, p. 213).

Coming out
The formation of a homosexual identity.

In the late 1960s 'coming out' was thought to be a single event, the first time that a homosexually orientated individual identified herself as such to another person. As a result of lesbian theory 'coming out' is now described as a *process* rather than as a discrete point in time. See Freedman (1985).

Communal research

A feminist alternative to mainstream methods of social research. Communal research involves the techniques of uncontracted co-operation, nonlinear patterning and a fusion of subject and object and ego boundary diffusion.

A communal epistemology which would link to communal ontology is 'naturalistic observation' of behaviour where the investigator combines autobiography with research. See Sharff (1981) and Fox Keller (1978).

Community

A group with common interests. In sociology community has several meanings, for example it can stand for a group culture or for local kinship.

Feminist theory defines community as a type of relationship – a sense of shared and warm identity between individual women.

Community can also mean a separatist women's group. For example Adrienne Rich speaks of the importance of community in feminist work and scholarship. She suggests that if we split ourselves off from the common life of women and deny our female heritage and identity in our work, we lose touch with our real powers and with the essential condition for all truly realised work: community. See Rich (1977). Cherríe Moraga argues that this separatist meaning of community is vital to the survival of women in the Third World. See Moraga (1981).

Other feminists define community as 'model' – a feminist guide for the whole of society. Nancy Hartsock suggests that generalising the activity of women to the social system as a whole would raise, for the first time in human history, the possibility of a fully human community. See Hartsock (1981).

Compensatory

The idea that equality, particularly in education, can offset disadvantage if additional resources are channelled to minority groups. The notion builds upon work on social justice by J. Rawls in *A Theory of Justice* (1971).

An original goal of women's studies aimed to compensate for women's invisibility by adding women to existing academic fields from which they were absent, for example in the 'canon' of literature.

Historians, like Gerda Lerner, argue that women's lives and accomplishments must be *added* to the professional chronology before we can rethink the whole concept of periodisation.

Women scholars in many fields produced what we now, following Catharine Stimpson, call 'compensatory' scholarship. This scholarship was a necessary first stage of feminist research which had to precede the current radical challenge to disciplines and institutions. See Bowles and Duelli Klein (1983).

Compulsory heterosexuality

A term in radical and lesbian theory for the enforcement of heterosexuality. It includes the ideological and political control of women's sexuality.

In her keynote essay Adrienne Rich describes compulsory heterosexuality as the main mechanism underlying and perpetuating male dominance. She argues that the assumption of heterosexuality both reflects and reinforces ignorance about lesbians and lesbian perspectives. See Rich (1980). If heterosexuality were not presented as, or perceived to be, *the* 'natural' form of sexual relations then the erotic choices of both women and men and our gender identities would be very different. Critiques from Marxist feminists claim that Rich's theory is too ahistorical. See Kaplan (1986).

The assumption that heterosexuality is innate has been a theoretical and political problem for many women as well as for men. Marilyn Frye contends that even in women's studies the supposition of heterosexuality is complete and ubiquitous. See Frye (1980).

Conflict

Literally a struggle between opposing interests.

Women are socialised to manage and internalise conflict as part of the acquisition of femininity. Men are allowed acceptable social outlets for their aggression, while women's experience of conflict (for example in domesticity) is often pathologised.

Education theorists describe the way girls in schools are taught to displace conflict. See Steedman (1985).

Feminist researchers argue that because knowledge is socially constructed and thus dependent on given social, cultural and historical contexts, the explanation of women's knowledge (which is grounded in these different contexts) will itself involve perspectives in conflict. See Beechey (1985). Women-centred research must be multi-dimensional (in conflict).

Feminist psychoanalysts suggest that when women become fully aware of the forms of conflict in our lives, these forms could be a source of creativity and growth. See J.B. Miller (1976).

Conscientisation
The term *conscientizacao* was first defined and applied by Paulo Freire in his teaching programmes in the Third World. The term describes the way that a teacher in illiteracy programmes can encourage collective pupil participation by beginning with key words from the pupils' own experiences and needs (Freire 1970).

Feminist theory applies Freire's theory of conscientisation in different ways. First, one becomes conscious of one's individual suffering as a woman (see consciousness-raising), which is a subjective precondition for liberating action. Then women make a collective conscientisation be sharing the formulating of problems and also by studying women's individual and social history. See Mies (1983).

Consciousness
Feminist consciousness depends on understanding socio-economic conditions, and knowing how they can change.

Feminism argues that 'facts' are really 'contradictions' requiring resolution. Feminist consciousness is primarily a consciousness of women's victimisation. See Bartky (1978).

Temma Kaplan suggests that female solidarity expresses consciousness when it reorients political theory. 'By placing human need above other social and political requirements and human life above property, profit and even individual rights, female consciousness creates the vision of a society that has not yet appeared' (Kaplan 1982, p. 56).

Feminist philosophers describe consciousness as a series of 'negotiations' between ideology, social reality and desire. These negotiations depend on a conscious, if unarticulated, understanding of the morality of a situation, of praxis. See Eisenstein (1983).

The goal of radical feminist theory is a 'change in consciousness', often described as a paradigm shift, for example Susan Griffin describes feminist consciousness as an entirely new way of perceiving reality.

Consciousness-raising (CR)
A form of verbal self-examination taking place with the support and collaboration of other women in small groups.

The American group the Redstockings, based their theory of CR on the Chinese 'speak bitterness' technique described by William

Hinton in *Fanshen*. CR relies on the idea that theory must grow out of feelings and experience and that women speaking together can generate collective political change. Jo Freeman suggests that from a sociological perspective, the recovery of experience begun in CR or 'rap groups' is the most valuable contribution the women's liberation movement has made to the tools for social change. See Freeman, (1973).

CR proves that individual experiences fit into a pattern which reflects a structure of oppression. CR de-emphasises women's differences by focusing on experiences women have in common. However, generalisations about the condition of women necessarily reflect class and race limitations. See Allen (1970). But CR can be described as a form of political practice because it reveals that gender relations are a collective fact neither simply personal nor dependent on class relations.

CR is analogous to a psychoanalytic model in which unconsciousness is 'below' the conscious mind and where unbearable knowledge is kept unconscious by repression. To raise one's consciousness is to become aware of one's own repression (known as subordination). The therapeutic processes that occur in CR are akin to personal growth groups and achievement-orientated training. See Mitchell (1971).

Feminist theory took several axioms from CR:

1. The validity of women's personal experience as a source of authority.
2. The source of new knowledge, for example about abortion or rape, comes from understanding that women's symptons are part of our general victimisation by men.
3. That public and private realms are interconnected and that the facts of individual oppression are the substance of the politics of the women's movement.
4. There is a commonality underlying the diversity of women's experience, which in its concrete form is the concept of women as a sex class.
5. That the CR group represents a social experiment in microcosm.

The early days of CR are now recalled in the intensity of debates about pornography, because these debates question personal and public sexuality as a feminist issue.

CR also influenced the techniques of feminist research. Alix Shulman suggests that CR is a process of *data collection* and therefore can be a crucial source of feminist theory.

The articulation of lesbian consciousness carries the CR process one stage further by pointing the way to a woman-centred perspective. For example, Mary Daly's *Gyn/Ecology* (1978) is a linguistic version of CR practice.

Women's studies uses CR as a teaching device in the classroom when staff and students collectively reconstitute the meanings of social experience as they have lived through it as women.

'What it is to raise consciousness is to confront male power in this duality . . . in consciousness-raising, women learn they have *learned* that men are everything, women their negation, but that the sexes are equal' (MacKinnon 1982, p. 28).

Conscious partiality
In social science this means a partial identification with the research subject. According to Maria Mies it is the basis of feminist research. Conscious partiality is opposed to spectator knowledge, which takes an indifferent, disinterested or alienated attitude towards the research objects. Conscious partiality implies that researchers and researched join together in their work which is part of a bigger social whole.

Contraception
Methods of birth control.

In *Woman's Estate* (1971) Juliet Mitchell suggests that contraception is an innovation of world historic importance and she calls for feminists to create a history of reproduction. Reproductive rights has always been a feminist issue because it represents women's right to win self-determination. See Gordon (1976). In science, feminist theorists claim that contraception has not been given the scientific attention its human importance warrants and that what attention it has been given has been focused primarily on contraceptive techniques to be used by women. This is because men predominate in science, which leads to a bias in the choice and definition of problems with which scientists concern themselves. See Keller (1982).

Catharine MacKinnon argues that contraception should not be isolated from any other aspect of sexuality. The defining theme of the whole is the male pursuit of control over women's sexuality. See MacKinnon (1982). Other radical feminists locate the issue of contraception politically. Linda Gordon argues that the laws regulating contraception and abortion are one of the connecting fibres of the institution of motherhood – the coercion of women by legal and extralegal means. See Gordon (1976).

Contradiction
Susan Griffin defines contradiction as 'at one and the same time I agree with a political description of reality and with a psychological description of reality. At one and the same time, I see that social and

economic forces shape human behaviour and that human behaviour is shaped by the life of the child' (Griffin, 1982b, p. 240).

This definition of contradiction is close to a feminist dialectic. Griffin argues that contradiction bears directly on our condition as women because the word 'woman' signifies a duality of false concepts. Women's struggles necessarily involve mutually exclusive categories of being, and feminist thinking must become that which can cultivate paradox and welcome contradiction.

Conversation
Verbal interaction.

Feminist linguistics describes the forms and contexts of different conversation patterns. It finds that conversation strategies, for example the withholding of personal information, contribute to one's maintenance of power and that in mixed-sex groups this control is the prerogative of men. Lee Jenkins suggests that this has to do with the supposed male difficulty in dealing with the personal. See Jenkins and Kramer (1978).

Jo Freeman points to socio-cultural problems women experience when holding conversations in public because there are few public spaces for women's conversations. See Freeman (1975).

CR groups helped to create alternative spaces for women's conversations because single-sex conversations give women the advantage of using cooperative verbal strategies. See Aries (1976). Dale Spender describes these very complex processes of conversation in *Man Made Language* (1980). Feminist researchers are especially interested in women's gossip as a unique form of conversation. Women's gossip functions as an important source of social power for women in small communities. See Yerkovich (1977).

Cott, Nancy
American historian whose studies of nineteenth-century America helped to reconstruct our idea of capitalist culture. Cott argues that the male/female dialectic of Victorian culture is an important characteristic of nineteenth-century sexual repression and domesticity. Cott's work helps scholars gain a new understanding of social processes by concentrating on the victims of progress – frequently women. See Cott (1977, 1987).

Counter institutions
Radical and socialist feminists argue that counter institutions, for example women's peace camps, both represent feminist models of future social structures and act to raise women's consciousness in present society. See Rowbotham (1979).

Creation

The making of life.

Creation myths can begin with a splitting from an essential Mother, which is signalled by the coming of light.

In an extensive cross-cultural study Peggy Sanday found that in societies in which women and men are more equal to one another, origin myths describe a primary female, while in other societies the original creator is male or an impersonal force. See Sanday (1981). Gnostic creation myths are telling versions of a pre-eminent female principle which is why gnosticism was made uncanonical.

A writer's self-creation is the focus of Sandra Gilbert and Susan Gubar's *Madwoman in the Attic*. Gilbert and Gubar argue that women writers give 'birth' to themselves by confronting the assumptions that render women writers a kind of fiction. Writers create their creativity as part of their lives and as an enabling relationship with language. See Gilbert and Gubar (1979).

Susan Griffin links a fear of creativity to a fear of nature since society uses culture as a way to deny the power of the natural. See Griffin (1982a).

Dale Spender suggests that the artificial alignment by man of creativity with 'innovative' and 'original' is used to exclude woman from entry into the 'worthwhile' records of society. See Spender (1982).

Adrienne Rich argues that women's greatest creativity lies in our experience of motherhood. See Rich (1976).

Crime

Crime is generally defined as unlawful social activity. Feminist theory shows that this meaning is implicitly sexist because it defines crime in terms of public welfare not private concerns.

Feminist criminologists argue that women in prison are a subculture ignored by the larger society. Women prisoners are an oppressed group whose problems are an exaggeration of the problems of all women. See Smart (1977).

Susan Brownmiller suggests that women are often victims of violent acts but that these acts are not considered criminal either because they occur in the private sphere (for example wife battering and rape) or because they occur to women branded as deviants (for example prostitutes). See Brownmiller (1975).

Radical theory deconstructs myths about crime, for example, the myth that some kinds of women collude in their own rape. It argues that violence against women is very extensive, for example, wife-battering occurs in 30 per cent of marriages.

Criminal justice is a racist system and Black feminists draw attention to the unconscious racism of white feminism, which is insensitive to the relation of violent crime and racism in American society. See Davis (1981). Susan Griffin defines rape as 'the all-American crime'. Griffin connects crime with American imperialism and shows that crime is an issue for social theory rather than just criminology. See Griffin (1979).

Criticism

Feminist criticism reads writing and examines its ideology and culture with a woman-centred perspective. Criticism is feminist if it critiques existing disciplines, traditional paradigms about women, nature or social roles, or documents such work by others, from the point of view of women. See Humm (1986).

Contemporary feminist criticism starts with Kate Millett's *Sexual Politics* (1970). Millett's special contribution lay in placing literature in the political context of patriarchy. Millett, and the critics Judith Fetterley and Mary Ellmann, examined ideologies in male writing and revealed the misogyny of the literary establishment. See Fetterley (1978) and Ellmann (1968).

A second form of feminist criticism reclaims women's writing and constitutes women's literature as a specific field. See Moers (1977), Showalter (1977) and Gilbert and Gubar (1979).

Subsequently, many branches of feminist criticism, including Marxist, Black, lesbian, myth, psychoanalytic and linguistics, developed sophisticated analyses of feminist aesthetics. See Spivak (1987), Christian (1985) and Rich (1979a). While all feminist criticism depends heavily on theory, Anglo-American criticism reconstructs the history of women's writing and reading. 'It is not nature we are looking at in the sexual politics of literature, but history' (Jehlen 1982, p. 199). French feminist criticism defines literature as a symbolic system. See Hélène Cixous (1976).

Whatever the 'moments' and 'modes' of feminist criticism, all critics call for a re-evaluation of the concepts, history and politics of literary studies in terms of gender in order to create a new literary landscape.

Cross cultural studies

The study of correlations and variables within cultures. Margaret Mead made the first major feminist studies of different cultures. Mead found significant evidence that gender is a social artifact. See Mead (1949).

Feminist theory shows that the universal subordination of women cannot be explained biologically without reference to cultural diversity. For example feminist anthropologists point to the wide variations between societies in the sexual division of labour. In two influential accounts Sally Slocum and Elizabeth Fee argued that past anthropology by male anthropologists was dubious because it ignored women, or did not have access to women's experience. See Slocum (1975) and Fee (1973).

Michelle Rosaldo claims that all cultures distinguish male from female by assigning appropriate behaviours and tasks to each. See Rosaldo and Lamphere (1974). Sherry Ortner adds that this assignation led to the association of women with nature and hence to women's devaluation. See Ortner (1974).

In psychoanalysis, Nancy Chodorow proves that 'historically and cross-culturally we cannot separate the sexual division of labour from sexual inequality' (Chodorow 1978, p. 24).

Cultural anthropology

Literally the study of daily interaction in the non-industrial world. Feminist anthropologists argue that by studying the way women pattern perceptions, we can understand the significance of the categories and codes societies make. They focus on women's activities of cultivation, fuel collection, water carrying and childbirth, because in many societies women's ability to participate in other spheres of activity is limited by taboo and myth. Such studies of family life, kinship and female cooperation provide an alternative to structural anthropology's sole concern with the institution of the family. See Ardener (1981).

Cultural anthropology is used by feminist sociologists to analyse aspects of Western culture, for example in the study of adolescent culture. See McRobbie and Nava (1984).

Feminist literary critics use cultural anthropology to explore popular culture, for example in reader reception accounts of romance. See Radway (1984).

Cultural feminism

Feminist theory which is dedicated to creating a separate and radical women's culture. Charlotte Perkins Gilman in *Herland* (1915) gives fictional expression to cultural feminism in her account of a society of strong women guided by female concerns of pacifism and cooperation. Cultural feminists describe how a powerful female culture of music, art, poetry, science and medicine would be anti-authoritarian and anti-structure. See Bunch (1981).

Some radical feminists think that patriarchy is a transhistorical and all-embracing culture and therefore believe that women will only be free in an alternative woman's culture. The hegemony of patriarchy encourages some feminists to withdraw from traditional political action and turn instead to creating a separate woman's world. Mary Daly in particular describes many cultural feminist strategies for social change. In *Gyn/Ecology*, she calls such resistance a process of 'Sparking the fire of female friendship'. By 'Spinning cosmic tapestries' women will create a new culture with its own feminist rituals, symbols and a new language. See Daly (1978). Critics argue that cultural feminism ignores the extent to which femaleness functions as the complement to maleness. See Echols (1984).

Culture

The symbolic realm of the arts. Feminist theory extends the definition to include all symbolic products of society. This frees women from being defined by the expression 'sub-culture'.

Feminist historians use the term culture to refer to the broad-based commonality of values, institutions and relationships focusing on the domesticity and morality of late eighteenth-century and nineteenth-century women. Carroll Smith-Rosenberg suggests that the concept is one of the most creative developments in contemporary historiography because it enables feminists to discover and make sense of an enormous amount of information about women's lives. For example the discovery of women's rich and meaningful networks contradicts the notion that women were totally identified with the concerns of nuclear families. See Smith-Rosenberg (1975).

Gerda Lerner argues that to speak of women's activities and goals from a woman-centred point of view is women's culture. Lerner uses the term to mean the redefinition of women's lives in our own terms. See Lerner (1978).

Radical feminism describes women's culture as a society informed by values of wholeness, trust and nurturance. According to radical feminists, the bifurcation between male and female experience means that every society has, in effect, two cultures – the visible, or male and the invisible, or female. For example Susan Griffin suggests that society's artificial dualism between culture and nature, intellect and emotions comes from a fear of the body and leads to a pervasive division of labour. See Griffin (1982a). Audre Lorde argues that society's definitions of culture and its concomitant fear of poetry's connection with the unknown regions of the mind are allied to a patriarchal fear of the female, of darkness and of black values which signify an older secret knowledge. See Lorde (1984a).

Shulamith Firestone suggests that woman culture is essential. 'We are proud of the female culture of emotion, intuition, love, personal relationships, etc. as the most essential human characteristics. It is our male colonisers – it is the male culture – who have defined essential humanity out of their identity and who are 'culturally deprived' (Firestone 1970, p. 178).

Temma Kaplan defines culture as consciousness. She argues that most studies of women's culture focus on the middle class because the middle class leaves written evidence, but that working-class women have cultural traditions with their own networks and institutions. Working-class culture has a solidarity built around networks and communal rituals passed on through an oral tradition, and 'consciousness appears as the expression of communal traditions' (Kaplan 1982, p. 60).

Feminist anthropologists argue that women's oppression occurs because all societies distinguish between nature and culture and relegate women to nature. See Ortner (1974). This has led to what Dorothy Dinnerstein calls the essential illness of modern culture – the 'megamachine' myth or the attempt to use rationality to extend human control. See Dinnerstein (1976).

Feminist scientists examine cultural definitions of masculinity and femininity as these affect the practice of science. Science celebrates the cultural features of autonomy and separatism because science is a masculine arena. See Keller (1978). There are several feminist accounts of alternative cultures. Mary Daly describes a women's culture created by witches, crones and hags, and literary historians describe fictional counterparts of Carroll Smith-Rosenberg's communities and sustaining networks of lesbian relations. See Faderman (1981) and Auerbach (1978).

To use the term 'culture' in feminist theory is to assert women's sisterhood and communality.

Curriculum theory

The study of the way learning is organised in formal educational institutions such as colleges and schools.

The curriculum is usually understood to be a group of subjects based on disciplines operating a syllabus of material and a particular pedagogy.

Feminist educators research both this overt curriculum and the 'hidden' curriculum which represents the conscious or unconscious ideology of any institution. They argue that all curricula reinforce sex-role stereotyping by encouraging girls to study 'female' subjects like the arts or biology, which reinforces existing gender stereotypes and reduces girls' future employment opportunities. See Byrne (1978) and Deem (1978).

Radical feminists argue that any curriculum is essentially patriarchal because all devalue girls by operating on a principle of 'male as norm'. See Spender (1982a).

Dalla Costa, Mariarosa

A feminist activist who in 'Women and the subversion of the community' (1972) argues that woman's isolation in the home and her dependency on men are the main factors of woman's oppression. Dalla Costa claims that factory work is potentially less alienating than housework because it is collective. Together with Selma James, Dalla Costa founded the Wages for Housework campaign.

Daly, Mary

Radical American philosopher.

In her first books *The Church and the Second Sex* (1968) and *Beyond God the Father* (1973) Daly examines misogyny in Christianity and the church. Using existentialist theology, Daly rejected the idea of God as a fixed image of a supreme male being and argued that the power of patriarchy over women depends on Christianity.

Daly claims that the women's movement is 'spiritual revolution'. She argues that if women reject their status of Otherness and refuse sexual stereotypes women will find new modes of seeing and being beyond the destructive and narrow modalities of technical reason.

In *Gyn/Ecology* (1978) Daly creates a philosophy for radical feminism. She argues that since reality is constructed through language it is only through a radical destruction or 'deconstruction' of language that women can gain a new reality. This involves women in a voyage of new words which constitute a 'gynomorphic' language, which is a process of consciousness-raising and new women-identified consciousness.

Gyn/Ecology contains a number of premisses with important implications for feminism:

1. Women embody life forces.
2. Spiritual change is *the* mode of political change.
3. Women's energies can develop only in a separate and self-contained women's culture.

Arguing that the women's movement produces only token reforms, Daly defines 'radical' to mean a metaphysical, even elemental women's sexuality – as the title of her subsequent book revealed – *Pure Lust: Elemental Feminist Philosophy* (1984). In *Webster's first New Intergalactic Wickedary of the English Language* (1987) Daly created a feminist dictionary.

Daughterhood
The relation of females to parents.

Feminist psychoanalysts agree that the construction of women's gender identity is interdependent with our psychic and cultural experience as daughters. Nancy Chodorow argues that by being daughters women, unlike men, learn to affiliate with others triggered by our initial affiliation with our mothers. See Chodorow (1978).

Radical feminists define the political expression of this experience as 'daughter-right'. Janice Raymond uses the term to describe women's need to bond with mothers and Mary Daly argues that women's recognition, and memory, of daughterhood puts them in touch with women's history. See Daly (1978).

The tradition of daughter/mother relations in literature and myth has been described and anlysed by literary theorists. See Davidson (1980).

French theorists provide conflicting definitions of daughterhood. According to Julia Kristeva, daughters need language – the paternal, symbolic order – to protect themselves from the mother. See Kristeva (1974a). The exclusion of the woman from production, according to Luce Irigaray, is because she is daughter to the father. Irigaray argues that a feminist revolution must undo the vicious circle by which the daughter's desire for the father's desire (for his penis) causes her to submit to the father's law. See Irigaray (1974a).

Davis, Angela
A Black American writer and political activist who in *Women, Race and Class* (1981) and other writings describes her experience of, and the issues in, Black feminism. Davis describes historical examples of Black resistance to oppression and attacks misnomers of Black women (for example the matriarch archetype). See Davis (1971). Davis, in describing the insensitivity of white feminism to Black women, argues for a larger historical reconstruction of Black experience. (Davis 1981).

Davis, Elizabeth Gould
American cultural feminist whose book *The First Sex* (1971) influenced the development of feminist theories of myth and culture. Davis collected a compendium of information about

women's matriarchal past based on a theory of women's superiority over men and the nature of female power.

Declaration of Sentiments, 1848

A crucial document of nineteenth-century feminism. The declaration was drafted primarily by Elizabeth Cady Stanton, signed by 100 women and men and approved at the first women's rights convention in Seneca Falls. The declaration was rooted in natural rights theory. It represents a feminist counterpart to the Declaration of Independence, and contains the radical themes of women's right to suffrage, the right of women to serve in government and the right of women to proper training to enable such service.

Definition

The explicit meaning of a word.

Feminist theorists argue that existing definitions are prescriptive ways of ordering language. Mary Daly in *Gyn/Ecology* rejects what she calls a masculine control of language and chooses to define words 'gynomorphically'. This involves not simply rejecting terms and definitions but replacing them with a playful celebration of 'cerebral spinning' and new definitions. Daly reveals the manipulable ambiguity of language, for example the way women are trained to accept definitions or designations which force us to self-split. See Daly (1978).

Other feminists attack the way definitions themselves restrict us, and call for a re-vision of the process of language in terms, not of 'correct' definitions, but of purpose and audience. See Morahan (1981).

Cheris Kramarae and Paula Treichler wrote *A Feminist Dictionary* (1985) which illustrates women's linguistic contribution and substitutes quotations for definitions in order to encourage reflection and theorising about women, language and society.

Other writers refuse definitions completely. For example Luce Irigaray argues that definitions only work to fix plurality into unified representations. Women should replace definitions with a process of questioning and contextual associations. See Irigaray (1977b).

Delphy, Christine

French Marxist feminist who was a founding member of the journal *Questions Féministes* in 1977. Delphy argues that women are a sex-class. She dislikes the Derridean punning of other French theorists and, in her analysis of materialist feminism called for research into the construction of femininity rather than research about biological difference. See Delphy (1977, 1980, 1984).

Democracy

One distinctive difference between socialist feminism and other forms of feminist theory is the value socialist feminism attaches to democracy. Socialist feminists argue that it is essential to institute, not only democratic control of the economy as traditionally construed, but also democratic control of procreation. Socialist feminism provides an incisive critique of the ways in which centralised forms of political organisation replicate sexual and other divisions in the larger society.

One alternative to centralised forms of organisation is 'participatory democracy' in which decisions are made by those present at meetings. However, Sheila Rowbotham points to weaknesses in this form of organisation because it relies on white, middle-class techniques. 'Participatory democracy only works if everyone accepts a certain give and take, a respect for one another's experience' (Rowbotham 1979, p. 41).

Dependence

A state of subordination.

Feminism rejects women's dependence on men. In *The Second Sex* (1953) de Beauvoir argues that woman's problem is her need for men to complete her 'being', whereas men are socially independent. Indeed dependence, Mary Daly says, contaminates and pollutes words like 'sister', 'friend' or 'lover'.

Dependency theory is the term used by feminists working in a Marxist tradition — the major school of modernisation theory — to explain the experience of women in industrialisation. In the Third World when women's sources of income (for example agricultural work and handicrafts) are undermined women become more dependent on men who, in turn, become more dependent on international corporations for survival. See Nash and Fernandez (1983).

The psychologist Jean Baker Miller argues that some of what are sometimes seen as women's weaknesses can be strengths. She criticises feminists who think that *any* form of dependence on others is a threat to autonomy. See J.B. Miller (1976).

Derrida, Jacques

French philosopher, whose ideas about 'différence' and language in *Grammatologie* (1967) and other writings have influenced feminist theory.

Derrida coined the term 'logocentrism' to characterise Western philosophy's preoccupation with first principles. He claims that Freud's treatment of sexual difference appears essentialist, because it reproduces the old hierarchy: male-originary-superior/female-tributary-inferior. Derrida defines this way of thinking as 'phallogocentric', represented in the paradigm that posits the male and his sexuality as the norm and the female and her sexuality as a variation. These terms and ideas encouraged feminists like Gayatri Spivak (Derrida's American translator) to find new ways of thinking and writing which could change a masculine domination of criticism.

Desire

An essential need whose social construction is sexuality.

Historically, female desire has been restricted to the areas of marriage and the family. Feminist theory aims to understand and redefine woman's sexual desire and its public expression. Since 1980, feminist attention has turned to historical and psychoanalytic explanations. Psychoanalytic theory explores how desire is structured and feminists examine the historical context of desire to investigate the relationship between patterns of desire and the social institutions of sexual relations. See Coward (1984).

In psychological discourse desire is that position of pre-articulated need which finds itself left out of demand – the demand being the register of ethical discourse. Juliet Mitchell distinguishes between desire and need. 'Need changes to demand (articulation), and if unsatisfied or unreciprocated, to desire . . . Desire is therefore always a question of significant interrelationship, desire is always the desire of the other' (Mitchell 1974, p. 396).

French feminist definitions of desire grew out of the work of Jacques Lacan. Lacan defines desire as a metonymy. He has it that the phallic order short circuits fluid desire by fixing it onto an object. Desire is always mediated by signification. See Lucan (1966).

Luce Irigaray suggests that 'love' is sublimated, idealised desire, which moves away from bodily specifics towards dreams of complementarity, and the union of opposites where difference is resolved into the one. See Irigaray, (1977b).

Kristeva suggests that 'the desire of a subject that ties him to the signifier obtains through this signifier an objective, extra individual value' (Kristeva 1980, p. 117). Kristeva argues that this occurs in literature, and in psychoanalysis.

Development

Feminist theories of development assess development in terms of improved human well-being rather than in terms of economic growth targets. This frees the concept from traditional definitions based on industrial patterns of development.

Ester Boserup found that women's status had deteriorated in most Third and First World countries in all spheres: politics, economics, education, health and law. See Boserup (1970). Modernisation, she argues, has brought a gender-linked division of labour, or 'dualism' which leaves women to subsistence tasks and processing.

A feminist theory of development is multi-dimensional and encompasses the political, cultural and social, as well as the economic. See Boulding (1976).

Deviance

Resistance to patriarchy has always been labelled as deviant. For example women who resist 'wifely duties' are labelled neurotics or frigid and women who resist heterosexual alliances are labelled spinsters.

Feminist theories of lesbian identity offer alternatives to these definitions of deviance. Ann Ferguson suggests that a definition that appropriately describes resistance to male domination cannot be expressed in terms of a deviance concept. See Ferguson (1982).

Lesbian theory challenges distinctions between 'natural' and 'unnatural', and between 'deviant' sexuality and sexual identity. Researchers examine the motivations that lead women to accept a deviant label and adopt a lesbian identity, and find that a growing resentment of male domination in the family and the economy may lead some women to turn from sexual relations with men to sexual relations with women.

Deviance concepts are used by those in power to 'naturalise' their way of doing things as normal and to label other ways of action as deviant. Lesbian theorists prefer to use 'counter culture' as a term rather than 'deviant'.

Dialectic

The term derives from Hegel who claimed that reality develops by means of contradictions and the reconciliation of contradictions. Marx and Engels use the term 'dialectical materialism' to define how all production and reproduction is governed by these dialectical laws.

Feminist theory argues that the structure of necessity is a bipolar and dialectical relation between production and reproduction. Mary O'Brien suggests that women's emancipation can come only from an understanding of this dialectic. An autonomous feminist praxis depends on historical change within the social relations of reproduction. See O'Brien (1982). In *The Dialectic of Sex* (1970) Shulamith Firestone argues that this dialectic of production and reproduction is the material base of patriarchy which requires women to reproduce the species.

Dialogue

Feminist researchers use a method called 'dialogic retrospection', which is defined as an open and active exchange between the researcher and participant in a partnership of co-research.

Susan Griffin has called dialogue 'the form of all thought'. See Griffin (1982b).

Diary

A private account of daily life.

In feminist research diaries are used as records of the researcher's feelings and ideas. Diaries draw attention to the researcher as a human being and offer clues to the social environment being studied. In this way diaries can be as significant a part of data as empirical evidence. See Reinharz (1979).

Private diaries have been used by women to record religious inspiration, to examine themselves and educate themselves in a safe context. A diary allows women to be their own theorists in the way women use a diary form to examine social and psychological problems. Feminist historians regard diaries as a crucial, sometimes only means of access to the voices of our predecessors. See Kolodny (1975).

Dichotomy

A difference between the 'subjects' and 'objects' of research. In traditional research, a researcher is in opposition to, and above the particular and lived experience of his 'objects'. Liz Stanley and Sue Wise argue that rejecting the scientist/person dichotomy will dismantle the power relationship which exists between researchers and researched. See Stanley and Wise (1983). The alternative to dichotomy is a dialectic woman-centred theory.

Barbara Du Bois argues that dichotomy is not, in any case, a property of nature but of a learned mode of thought, a way of seeing and knowing that turns reality into rigid, oppositional and hierarchical categories. She says that the challenge for feminist science will be to see and describe without recreating these dichotomies, without falling into the old pattern of objectifying experience. See Du Bois (1983).

Difference

A necessary polarity between women and men and between women.

Feminists define difference politically, not simply in terms of sexual categories.

Defining difference has been the single greatest contribution of second wave feminism to theory. Difference has two senses in feminism. A primary meaning is that women have a different voice, a different psychology and a different experience of love, work and the family from men. Difference also means a negative category which includes the exclusion and subordination of women.

Kate Millett and Shulamith Firestone express the view that women's differences from men are the chief mechanism of women's oppression. 'Difference' is an artifact of patriarchy and male and female are really two different cultures.

Much of the theoretical writing of the 1970s focused on gender difference and therefore on psychological rather than on political, economic or social issues. For example Nancy Chodorow argued that gender difference stemmed from childhood psychosocial affiliations. Audre Lorde and more contemporary theorists attack the false universalism in feminist analysis as a form of neo-colonialism or neo-imperialism. They point to crucial differences between Black and white women, for example to the enormous differential of power. 'Difference is that raw and powerful connection from which our personal power is forged' (Lorde, 1984b, pp. 111–12).

French theorists locate the meaning of difference in power relations. Monique Wittig argues that the ideology of sexual difference functions as a form of censorship because it masks as 'natural' the social opposition between men and women. Masculine/feminine, male/female are categories which serve to conceal the fact that social differences always belong to an economic, political, and ideological world. See Wittig (1982). Colette Guillaumin adds that difference is quite simply the statement of the *effects* of a power relationship. Difference is a fact of dependence and a fact of domination. See Guillaumin (1982). Jacques Derrida uses *la différance* meaning both to differ (in space) and defer (postpone) as an antidote to totalitarianism. See Derrida (1967).

Radical feminism defines difference as a great positive. Mary Daly claims that to simplify differences would be to settle for a less than dreadful judgement of the multiple horrors of gynocide. Adrienne Rich suggests that an epistemological revolution can stem from the different physiology of women. A new revolution of consciousness comes from women's unique capacity to nurture.

Diner, Helen
American myth theorist.

In *Mothers and Amazons: The First Feminine History of Culture*

(1932), based on the work of J.J. Bachofen and Robert Briffault, Diner described empowering images of semi-mythical women warriors and argued the case for a prehistory of matriarchy.

The book encouraged later feminists to look for historical evidence of women's symbols and myths.

Dinnerstein, Dorothy

American, feminist psychologist, whose book *The Mermaid and the Minotaur: Sexual Arrangements and Human Malaise* (1976) influenced a great many feminists writing about gender difference.

Dinnerstein argued that the division of the world into male and female and the assignment of life and growth to women's care doomed culture. The fateful symbiosis of minotaur and mermaid must end and all human beings, male and female, must embody aspects of each other. The text provided ammunition for those feminists interested in androgyny.

Discipline

A field of study. Feminist research examines the sets of assumptions around which the disciplines ask questions and form conclusions and the way each discipline has its own language and way of ordering the world.

Florence Howe argues for a return to the original meaning of 'discipline' – the exercise of one's mental faculties. According to Howe, disciplines fragment education and are antithetical to women's holistic view. See Howe (1978).

A new feminist scholarship would entail historical perspectives, criticism and empirical practice centred on women. This would generate new learning in what Adrienne Rich calls 'the woman-centred university'. See Rich (1979b).

Gloria Bowles suggests that the concepts of women's studies derive from questions which are quite unlike those of traditional academic disciplines (Bowles and Duelli Klein 1983).

Feminist scholars argue that the development of women's studies theory must go beyond disciplines because such theory is beyond the limits of received perspectives. Some feminists argue that women's studies is a discipline; a study in its own right. See Coyner (1983).

Discourse

The relation between language and social reality.

Sheila Rowbotham argues that discourse is *the* instrument of patriarchal domination and that struggle for power within discourses is an issue of political importance for the women's movement. See Rowbotham (1973b). Ros Coward argues that in order to understand the construction of gender difference we need to look at the contexts, transformations and definitions of sexuality in several discourses and how these are produced. See Coward (1978). Jean Elshtain suggests that the nature and meaning of feminist discourse itself must be a subject for critical enquiry. She defines feminist discourse as a political discourse directed towards the construction of new meanings. See Elshtain (1981).

Sara Ruddick has called 'maternal thinking' a feminist discourse which is imbedded with maternal values and ways of seeing. See Ruddick (1984).

Discrimination
The unfavourable treatment of women based on the patriarchal belief that women possess undesired attributes. Statistical discrimination means that a woman may be denied a job not only because she is a woman but because she is thought 'statistically' more likely than a man to have to care for families. Policies which provide more favourable treatment for women are known as positive discrimination. This is a form of theoretical discrimination against the major part of an institution in favour of women.

Heidi Hartmann states that discrimination is the result of a long process of interaction between patriarchy and capitalism. She argues that discrimination cannot end without the eradication of the sexual division of labour. See Hartmann (1976).

Division of labour
An exploitative relation in society and in economic production.

Marxist feminism argues that the unequal relation of the sexes derives from the sexual division of labour. This division structures women's work, confining women to 'female' jobs and to working for men irrespective of technical or education differentials, since the attribution of skill is a patriarchal not an empirical matter. See Kuhn and Wolpe (1978).

Firestone argues that the division of labour is one of the major and fundamental differences in power between women and men. Anthropologists show that whatever form the sexual division of labour takes, tasks and roles assigned to men are given greater significance and importance.

Feminist psychoanalysts, for example Nancy Chodorow, argue that women's mothering is a primary cause of the sexual division of labour and of the continued domination of women by men because both are linked to, and generate, male dominance. Susan Griffin suggests that in total the division of labour in Western culture has artificially assigned language control to men and nature to women.

Domestic feminism

An important theory in feminist historiography. P. Branca defines domestic feminism as the middle-class British and American woman's search for greater personal autonomy within the home, including the desire to control her fertility. Feminists use the concept to create a woman-centred history which can focus on women as actors rather than on women as victims. See Branca (1975).

Domestic labour

The way in which women regenerate labour power for capitalism by servicing the home and socialising their families.

The analysis of domestic labour is a central focus of feminist anthropology, history and economics. The most fruitful debate so far in feminist theory has been the domestic labour debate, in which feminist ideas challenge the political concepts and theoretical positions of the traditional left.

The domestic labour debate was initiated in 1969 by Margaret Benston in 'The political economy of women'. She drew attention to the fact that housework must be taken seriously in any analysis of the workings of the economy, and not relegated to a marginal or non-existent status (as it was by Marx and Engels). Housework could be recognised both as productive labour and, simultaneously, as an area of exploitation and a source for capital accumulation. At the centre of the debate is the question of whether Marx's theory of value could be applied to domestic labour or not. Heidi Hartmann argued that it is only within capitalism that men are able to exclude and marginalise domestic labour. See Hartmann (1976). But Third World studies show the coexistence of different modes of production.

Other Marxists focus less on capitalism and more on domestic labour in relation to men — the domestic mode of production. For example Christine Delphy suggests that marriage is a labour contract by which men appropriate women's labour power in exchange for upkeep. See Delphy (1984).

Ann Ferguson identifies another kind of domestic labour overlooked by social theorists which she calls 'sex/affective production' or women's work in providing sexual relations and child nurturance. See Ferguson (1979).

A more positive view of domestic labour is provided by Lisa Vogel who suggests that because housework produces use values it is relatively unalienated and domestic labour may be a glimpse of a future society organised around unalienated labour. See Vogel (1984).

Domesticity
A nineteenth-century ideology which assigns the sphere of the household to women as their proper and ordinary place. Feminist historians describe how the ideal domestic woman was to be pious, pure and submissive and devote her energies to the harmonious functioning of the home. Increasingly, as the nineteenth century progressed, these ideas became less a description of what women actually did and more a way of structuring a masculine ideology of women's lives. See Cott (1977).

Domination
The power of one group or individual over another group or individual.

A distinctive part of contemporary feminist theory is its analysis of the basis of male dominance and all feminist theory is designed to show how a male domination of women can be ended. Liberal feminism believes that male dominance is rooted in irrational prejudice and can be overcome by rational argument. Marxist feminism defines male dominance as an ideology by which capital divides and rules and which will be overcome by a 'cultural revolution' based on a socialist transformation of the economy. Radical feminists believe that male domination is grounded on men's universal control over women's bodies and our sexual and procreative activities, which will only end when women achieve sexual and procreative self-determination. Socialist feminism argues that male domination is part of the economic foundation of society and its abolition requires a transformation of the economic foundation of society as a whole.

Feminist psychoanalysis describes the forms of expression of dominance and its relation to objectification. Evelyn Fox Keller claims that the emphasis on domination which is so prevalent in the rhetoric of Western science is a projection of a specifically male consciousness because it conjoins the domination of nature with the insistent image of nature as female. She argues that the impulse towards domination can be understood as a natural concomitant of defensive separateness. See Keller (1982). Jessica Benjamin defines dominance as a way of repudiating sameness, dependency and closeness with another person. See Benjamin (1980).

Double consciousness
The way women inhabit the world – we are in and of our society but in important ways not 'of' it. Women see and think in terms of culture yet have always another consciousness, another potential language. See Du Bois (1983).

Double standard

A term which describes how even when two features are the same, they are measured by different standards for women and for men. Eichler describes how the sexual double standard is ingrained in all aspects of social life: law, economics, education, the media and the family. Attitudes to prostitution and rape are at the very core of the patriarchal double standard.

Feminist theory aims to abolish the double standard, but Eichler argues that identified sex differences should only be of concern if they involve the double standard. See Margrit Eichler (1980).

Douglas, Mary

A feminist anthropologist who made an extensive examination of ritual and taboo in terms of women's themes, for example domesticity and social boundaries. As well as influencing the sociology of education (e.g. the work of Basil Bernstein) Douglas provided very influential theoretical constructs, particularly in *Purity and Danger* (1966), for feminist writers in disciplines other than anthropology.

Julia Lesage uses Douglas's ideas in film theory and Douglas's ideas were very useful to Marina Warner in her analysis of female heroism in *Joan of Arc*. See Lesage (1981) and Warner (1981).

Dualism

A concept which describes the social and economic structure of underdeveloped countries.

Feminist theorists attack those dualisms which are institutionalised in patriarchy, for example: culture and nature, public and private, death and birth. Alison Jaggar argues that underlying the philosophy of all political liberalism is a kind of dualism, because liberalism believes that mind and body represent two different kinds of being. See Jaggar (1983).

Nancy Hartsock suggests that dualism, along with the dominance of one side of the dichotomy over the other, marks phallocentric society and social theory. These dualisms appear in a variety of forms – in philosophy, sexuality, technology, political theory and in the organisation of society itself. See Hartsock (1981).

Adrienne Rich in *Of Woman Born* (1976) describes a feminist world which could reject dualisms, and other feminists argue that women's different lived experience of reproduction and motherhood offers a material basis for a more integrated relationship to the world and others. See O'Brien (1983).

Dual systems

A theory in feminist scholarship which argues that women's

oppression arises from two distinct and relatively autonomous systems in work and the home. The system of male domination, or patriarchy, produces the specific gender oppression of women. According to feminists who subscribe to a dual systems approach, male domination and concomitant female subordination is a relatively autonomous system of domination – autonomous, that is, with respect to any particular form in which it occurs. See Young (1980).

Dual systems theory, Young argues, leaves unchallenged the assumption that women's oppression is separable, and thus a peripheral element in social life, which obscures the integration of the two spheres.

Dworkin, Andrea

A radical American feminist who has made significant contributions to feminist theory in her analysis of the exploitative and discriminatory nature of patriarchy. In *Woman Hating* (1974) and *Pornography* (1981) she argues that the chief engine of male history is male sexual violence, possibly rooted in biology. In *Right-Wing Women* (1983) and *Intercourse* (1987) Dworkin makes a radical critique of the sexual politics of women's oppression. She extends the critique of masculinity begun by Chodorow to argue that pornography is at the heart of male supremacy. Women can be free only when pornography ceases to exist. Dworkin, together with Catharine MacKinnon, drafted a model antipornography law.

Eastman, Crystal

A major theorist of pacifist social reform. Influenced by the writings of Charlotte Perkins Gilman, Eastman argued that the primary task of politically enfranchised women must be to end war.

Eastman was one of the few women committed to socialism and an active advocate of the Equal Rights Amendment who could see that the women's battle was distinct in its objects and different in its methods from the workers' battle for industrial freedom. In 'Equal rights' (1924) and other writings Eastman describes the sexual hierarchy in production work and male domination in the socialist movement. See Eastman (1978).

Ecology

The study of interconnections between human life and environments. Ellen Swallow (1842–1911) was the founder of environmental science.

Feminist theories of the environment and behaviour provide solid evidence of the costs to women of living in environments, particularly in cities, which do not readily accommodate women's participation in the labour force or changing family patterns. A major paradigm guiding feminist research and environmental equity is the concept of equal access to housing, transportation and public services for women.

Eco feminism is normally regarded as part of cultural feminism. Susan Griffin argues that ecological or scientific environmentalism stresses the importance of sustaining a viable physical or biological environment; and that humanistic environmentalism stresses the incompatibility of modern scientific and technological developments with humanistic principles. See Griffin (1978).

A convergence between the political values of radical and of socialist feminism is their shared concern for ecology. Respect for nonhuman nature has always been important to radical feminism. In *The Dialectic of Sex* (1970) Firestone links feminism and ecology.

Other radical feminists link ecology with women's spiritual communion with nonhuman nature.

This concept of a dialectical unity between human and nonhuman nature constitutes the theoretical basis for socialist feminism's ecology, a basis which is not incompatible with a radical feminist view of the spiritual unity between human and nonhuman nature.

Economics

Theories which account for the making and consumption of wealth. Alexandra Kollontai provided an early feminist critique of economics in *Communism and the Family* (1920). She believed that the destruction of old social forms was an economic inevitability and believed in the emancipating force of collectivised domestic labour. See Kollontai (1977).

Marxist feminists examine the effects of class and the impact of a late monopoly capitalist economy on the position of women both domestically *and* internationally. See Kuhn and Wolpe (1978).

Theorists show how the economic vulnerabilities of women are not eradicated with legal equality and that women's increasing economic participation does not give us political power. See Jordanova (1981).

Most women's economic experience is one of destitution or hardship in the face of bad harvests, epidemics and desertion. By describing the international reach of the sexual division of labour, feminists have made visible much of women's hitherto invisible economic activity and demonstrated how this activity is organised for men's benefit. This new way of conceptualising the economic realm informs pioneering feminist theories of economics. See Parker and Leghorn (1981).

Other feminists argue that economics itself, while still a male-orientated discipline, has developed tools more open to women's concerns. For example there is now an extensive literature about discrimination and segregation. See Ferber and Teiman (1981).

Feminist economists feel that a radical solution to women's disadvantage would be a truly equal sharing between men and women of their domestic responsibilities. Otherwise liberal and Marxist economists will continue to prioritise socialised services rather than rethinking the ideology of economics.

Écriture féminine

The term for women's writing in French feminist theory. It describes how women's writing is a specific discourse closer to the body, to emotions and to the unnameable, all of which are repressed by the social contract. Writing and literature are crucial areas because literature reveals the repressed, the secret and unsaid and, in a 'potency' of the imagination, can be a space of fantasy and pleasure. See Marks and de Courtivron (1981).

The term's roots are in criticism, written by Barthes and Derrida in the 1960s, which denounced logocentric ideology.

Écriture féminine is one of the best developed areas in French theory. It includes Annie le Clerc's deification of woman's body, Monique Wittig's deconstruction and reconstruction of the lesbian body, the post-Lacanian analysis of Luce Irigaray, and the utopian revisions of Hélène Cixous.

Most French feminists are actively creating a new women's language while simultaneously critiquing the old one. Cixous claims that women write 'through' their bodies and Kristeva adds that this language can seem to come from a foreign land — from an 'asymbolic, spastic' body. Texts by the writer and film-maker Marguerite Duras are seen by many as the epitome of *écriture féminine*.

There are problems that can occur from tying women's writing to the physical pleasures of infancy and placing women outside of the established system of discourse, which posits a unified subject and discursive coherence. French feminism has seemed in danger of neo-essentialism and of isolating sexuality from social experience. However, its writings do foreground a highly accentuated erotics of language. 'Feminine' linguistics are characterised by simultaneity, plurality and mobility. By stressing the *metaphors* of sexual desire, *écriture féminine* is not a question of physical biology, but is instead a fundamental epistemological *and* historical form.

Education

This means both the process of social rearing and what occurs in institutions. Education is one of the most powerful ways in which the state reproduces the gender and social relations of production. The combined influence of gender and class construction in schools on both boys and girls is a central concern of feminist theory which aims to show how schools reproduce female subordination. See Howe (1975).

Feminist theory argues that the very transmission of culture and social hierarchies in schools reproduces gender differences. In the main, nineteenth-century feminists campaigned for equal access *into* education for women and against the separate acquisition of feminine skills. Contemporary feminists argue that the education system itself disadvantages girls through sex-role stereotyping and the use of a hidden curriculum which privileges boys' interests. See Deem, ed. (1978). Dale Spender has suggested that it is a mark of our sexist education system that we could believe that sexism in education is something new. See Spender (1982a).

Feminists challenging the basic structure and practice of education link the sex inequalities of education directly to the general subordination of women by men.

There are many feminist alternatives to education's patriarchal agenda. Virginia Woolf in *Three Guineas* (1938) wanted women to be Outsiders. See Woolf (1938). Contemporary feminists describe female models which encourage female experience as an alternative to the organised practices of education. See Rich (1979b).

The impact of feminism on education, for example in Women's Studies, lies in the challenge it makes both to male versions of education theory and practice *and* to male supremacy within education.

Eisenstein, Zillah R.

An American political theorist who in *Capitalist Patriarchy and the Case for Socialist Feminism* (1979) uses the metaphor of marriage to describe the relation of patriarchy to capitalism.

In *The Radical Future of Liberal Feminism* (1981) Eisenstein shows how feminism grew out of liberal theory but now seeks to transcend liberalism by advocating radical practice and theory, not simply legal reforms.

Elshtain, Jean Bethke

An American philosopher who in *Public Man, Private Woman* (1981) and *The Family in Political Thought* (1982) has thoroughly documented the misogyny of masculine philosophy. Elshtain claims that the dichotomy of public and private is an abstraction which ignores the complexities of human life.

Emancipation

Theories of emancipation depend on a belief that the position of women can change within the existing framework of society, where theories of women's liberation involve transforming the social framework itself. The concept of emancipation was central to early and first wave feminists in their campaigns for equal rights. See Smith-Rosenberg (1985).

Emotions

These are privileged, in theories of feminist consciousness-raising, as powerful sources of knowledge, as forms of cognition, appraisal, judgement or choice, and as tools for grasping the world and changing it. See Frye (1983) and Fisher (1981).

Engels, Friedrich

A German philosopher whose *Origin of the Family, Private Property and the State* (1884) represents the most sustained account of women's roles produced in early Marxism. Engels' central thesis is that a prehistoric 'communistic' matriarchy was overturned, or superseded, at a particular moment by patriarchy. Unlike contemporary matriarchal feminists, Engels associates this transition with economic development, in particular with the establishment of private property and the emergence of commodities to be used for exchange and profit.

Engels' solution to the problem of women's oppression is to urge that women enter more fully into the work force, thus eliminating their confinement to private, domestic labour.

Feminist criticisms point to Engels' false concept of universality, his suppression of the possibility of woman as the locus of the transmission of property and his presupposition of a natural division of labour between the sexes. Feminist interest in Engels' theory lies in his analysis of the family but argues that a fully materialist analysis of women's position must involve a more complex mapping of these different interrelations. See Young and Harris (1976).

Epistemology

The theory of knowledge. Ros Coward describes epistemology as a distinct realm of concepts and objects but rejects traditional epistemological theories as either too empiricist or too rationalist to be of great use in feminism. See Coward and Ellis (1977).

According to Virginia Woolf in *Three Guineas* (1938) a feminist epistemology would be the 'cheap arts', the arts of human intercourse, an understanding of women's lives and minds, and making combinations as wholes in human life.

Hilary Rose suggests that a feminist epistemology derives from women's lived experience, centred on the domains of interconnectedness and affectual rationality. See Rose (1986).

Feminist epistemology emphasises holism and a harmonious relationship with nature. Theorists identify five basic features: the principle of the contextualisation of knowledge, the principle of necessary human agency, the principle of predominant causality, the principle of intersubjective process and interactive process and the principle of scientific diversity or multi-formed regularities. See Vickers (1983).

Equality

The term incorporates several meanings. In sum, equality is based on the idea that no individual should be less equal in opportunity or in human rights than any other. Liberal feminism campaigns for the granting of the full equality of formal rights to women as the solution to women's subjection. Equality, as equal rights, would also, to liberal feminists be part of a progressive rationalisation of human society. Harriet Taylor in *The Enfranchisement of Women* (1851) pointed out that female inequality became a custom and tradition solely through men's superior physical strength. See Mill and Mill (1970).

One problem with liberal feminism is that even with the granting of equality to women in public life, women's domestic labour will always be unequal to that of men. More subtly, the hidden patriarchal agendas of public institutions can subvert the apparent equality of legal rights (see Education).

Contemporary American theorists argue that the principle of equality cannot be initiated in a meritocracy. Sandra Harding suggests that where standards of merit are more or less universally shared and uncontroversial the equality of opportunity principle might function, but that it is a reactionary device at times when social relations, structured by institutions, need deep changes. See Harding (1978–9).

Erotic passion

Psychiatry, by conflating the difficulties of psychodynamic functioning with modes of erotic conduct, limits eroticism to sexual behaviour. In *The History of Sexuality* (1979) Michel Foucault shows how the domain of erotic life is renegotiated in every historical period and how 'sexuality' is always sharply contested and overtly politicised. Feminist theory similarly aims to separate eroticism from gender characteristics and return it to politics, for example by characterising the 'eroticism' of pornography as objectified sexuality.

A particular contribution of contemporary feminism is the argument that each erotic identity is unique but that erotic identities have strong racial and class components. Lesbian theorists argue that erotic identities polarised around gender appear arbitrary and that gender categories cannot constitute erotic identities. See Newton and Walton (1984).

All theorists agree to refuse the compartmentalisation of the erotic from ordinary life, urging that it be integrated with all activities as an energising force. Adrienne Rich in 'Compulsory heterosexuality' suggests that we begin to discover the erotic in female terms in 'lesbian continuum' which involves the assimilation of the erotic and aesthetics into daily life. See Rich (1980).

Audre Lorde develops and extends Rich's description into the psychoanalytic. In 'Uses of the erotic' she recalls Eros in classical and psychoanalytic meanings as a life instinct, the assertion of the 'life force' of women. The erotic is then, not merely sexual desire, but an entire sensuality, a nurturer of all our deepest knowledge. See Lorde (1984). French feminism, particularly in the writings of Luce Irigaray, even argues for a female autoeroticism.

Essentialism

The belief in a unique female nature.

Feminists challenge assumptions that women are esssentially weaker, whether biologically, emotionally or intellectually, than men since these assumptions underpin misogyny and discrimination against women. For example feminist historians show how discrimination against women in medicine and science is often based on a fallacious essentialism. See Ehrenreich and English (1979).

Alternatively, radical feminism believes that there *are* essential feminine modes of perception which can be communicated in female creativity and culture. See Daly (1978).

This sometimes leads radical feminism to idealisations which often underlie essentialist views of women. For example women are described as superior pacifist beings by some peace groups. But if it is impossible to distinguish between 'genuine' and 'imposed' feminine essentials, all feminists accept that theory should be thoroughly genderised and that women do have preoccupations which are 'essentially' female, for example motherhood and female bonding, even if all women do not wish to mother or to affiliate with other women.

Ethics

The sharing, in notions of 'justice' or 'equality', or individual moral beliefs. Conservatives generally use appeals to universals in order to stabilise the status quo, for example: 'all women ought to want children'. Feminist philosophers argue that if ethics is grounded in the concerns of dominated groups, ethical norms could be used to encourage political forces and to change society. For example feminists agree that consciousness raising groups are an important source of feminist ethics. These groups affirm ethnic and demographic interests and enable women to work together in a feminist ethical agenda. See Harding and Hintikka (1983).

Ethnicity

In anthropology ethnicity characterises the culture of a distinctive, sometimes racially distinct, group. Feminist anthropologists are concerned about the arbitrariness of race categories and that, whatever the system of classification, women often remain a 'muted' group. See Ardener, (1981).

Feminists point, too, to how sociology has pathologised and problematised ethnic communities in Britain and America. These analyses have had an impact on Euro-American contemporary feminist thought by linking feminist theory to colonial experiences. Black feminists propose we engage with the *contradictions*, not with the similarities which shape our roles as women, and not be trapped by false universalism. For example Bell Hooks describes how women's communities are not a new feminist experience for Black women but have a long-term history. See Hooks (1987).

Other feminists argue that we should see ethnicity not as a cultural *problem* but in the broader context of State harassment and the double oppression of Black women. See Amos and Parmar, (1984).

Ethnomethodology

Founded by the American sociologist Harold Garfinkel, the school or method refers to research concerned with everyday life and face-to-face relationships. Liz Stanley and Sue Wise propose that the method is suitably feminist since ethnomethodology takes the everyday as both the topic of its research and also as the resource with which it works. Feminist researchers, using ethnomethodology, would explore the basis of their everyday knowledge as women, as feminists and as social scientists. See Stanley and Wise (1983).

Eurocentric or ethnocentric

A way of thinking which is unable to see difference and which universalises all values and ideas from the subject's experience of her own white ethnic group. Eurocentricity creates models which leave no room for validating the actual struggles and experiences of Black Third World women. An example would be the image of an Asian woman as 'passively' subject to oppressive family practices or to think that the strength of Afro-Caribbean women is located only in motherhood. Audre Lorde argues that eurocentricity characterises much of white feminism, and that white feminism's failure to recognise difference as a crucial strength is a failure to reach beyond the first patriarchal lesson. See Lorde (1984).

Evolution

The theory drawn from Darwin's *On the Origin of Species* (1859) that species and societies progress by natural selection and inherited capacities. Evolutionary theory regards change as progressive.

Feminist anthropologists demonstrate that a major bias in

evolutionary theory is its reliance on a Man-the-Hunter model of evolution. Sally Slocum describes a feminist version of evolution which takes into account the participation of women as gatherers and mothers and the critical role women's activities may have played in the evolution of food-sharing, cooperation and the invention of containers and tools. She argues, in other words, that evolution relies on cooperative patterns and gathering activities not on aggression. See Slocum (1975).

Experience

Women's private awareness and knowledge drawn from participation in social life. The experience of women is often denied as 'real' or important and our difficulty in accepting the validity of our experience is part of our cultural heritage and perpetuated in schooling. Feminists draw attention to the gap between women's experience of the world and the theoretical schemes we have available in which to think about experience. See D. Smith (1974).

The challenge is to convert women's private concerns into shared public concerns. This occurs in consciousness-raising groups and also in the revaluation of women's experience as a part of social science methodology and theory. Feminism argues that personal, lived experience is intensely political and immensely important politically. See Stanley and Wise (1983).

One hallmark of contemporary feminist research in any field is the investigator's continual testing of the plausibility of the *work* against her own experience. See Parlee (1979). Reversing a longstanding tradition of relying on (or being expected to rely on) the advice of male experts gives women an 'authority of experience'. See Diamond and Edwards (1977). Socio-historians argue that to study the history of women, especially as it is recorded through the consciousness of women themselves, is to discover how one's life experiences are joined to those of other women. Marcia Westkott calls this 'experiences of consciousness-in-history'. See Westkott (1983). Indeed, women researchers have to begin with personal experience since traditional disciplines do not often utilise women students' personal or emotional experiences. For women an emotional reaction is, however, often the foundation of critical thought and more astute theory. See Rutenberg (1983).

It is precisely the rich and varied experiences of contemporary feminism which contribute to the variety of its theories. Anthropologists argue that feminist theory must look for variety both in the experiences of women in other societies and in the experiences of women of different classes, races and nationalities in contemporary industrial society. The claim to a diversity of experience is an important part of the Black radical critiques of Audre Lorde and Angela Davis. As Gerda Lerner pointed out: if women's experience is the norm, men will become the Other.

Experiential analysis

This research technique involves interacting components: a collaborative relation between the researcher and subjects, where the researcher is a student rather than an expert; the researcher's own experiential knowledge and the usual problem formulation and data gathering.

Feminist sociologists argue that the method can fashion a nonmasculine reflexive model which represents growth and understanding, both in the area of the problem investigated and in the person(s) doing the investigation. See Reinharz (1983).

A feminine cognitive style would be artistic, sensitive, integrated, deep, intersubjective, empathic, associative, affective, open, personalised, aesthetic and receptive.

Exploitation

To use the experience, wealth or skills of others without reward. Feminist theory argues that exploitation is a historical category which is the basis of male and female social relations as characterised by patriarchy. Rosa Luxemburg first suggested that the relationship between male and female workers mirrors a permanent hierarchisation and exploitation between producers and consumers. She argued that exploitative social relations exist when non-producers are unable to appropriate the products and services of producers and that this characterises male and female relationships over large periods of history. See Luxemburg (1970).

Contemporary feminism adds the psychological explanation that women have 'acquiesced' in their exploitation through internalised ideology. See Gregory (1980).

'Super exploitation' is a term for the appropriation not just of *surplus* labour but of labour and time necessary for people's own subsistence, for example housework. See Mies (1983).

Family

An individual, or group, with children.

Feminism is the one radical political movement that focuses on transforming family relationships. The major feature distinguishing the new feminism of the 1980s from previous periods is the way it identifies the family as a major site of women's oppression. Kate Millett describes the family as a patriarchal unit within a patriarchal whole — mediating between the individual and the social structure. See Millett (1970).

Feminists are concerned about the family because it is the primary beneficiary and focus of women's labour as well as the source of women's most fundamental identity, that of mother. One of the most valuable achievements of feminist theory has been its effort to deconstruct the family as a natural unit and to reconstruct it as a social unit — as ideology, as an institutional nexus of social and cultural meanings and relations. See Thorne and Yalom (1982). For example feminist theory has created a complex understanding of violence in the family.

The main approach of socialist and Marxist feminism sees the family as the site of gender struggle and the 'reproduction' of persons — as a miniature political economy with its own division of labour. See Ferguson (1983). The family household is an important organising principle of the relations of production of the social formation as a whole, the ideological ground on which gender difference and women's oppression are constructed. In Marxist feminism the family is essentially an econometric model, a unit defined by its role in 'the provision of domestic labor and the reproduction cycle of labor-power through which it relates to the functional prerequisites of capitalism' (Humphries 1982, p. 138).

Jean Elshtain argues that the depth and complexity of family relations are too complex for this abstract, reductionist discourse (Elshtain 1982). Feminist theory about Third World women agrees the need for complexity. The family needs new definitions because existing ones come from assumptions about the predominance of men, for example the dichotomy between public and private realms is part of a map of the social order constructed by men. See Mickelwait *et al.* (1976). In addition Black feminism has criticised white feminism for assuming that the family has universal characteristics. For example the family in Third World history and practice has a different function. It can be a haven of self-determination for women in an exploitative world. See Sanchez and Cruz (1978). Feminists have proposed many alternatives to the patriarchal nuclear unit, but in the main, 'family communities' are one way feminism has transferred into practice the insight that the personal is political. For example the feminist architect Dolores Hayden proposed HOMES, groups of cooperative housing for women. See Hayden (1980a).

Family planning

The control of procreation in a family.

Feminists have long agreed that the association between sexual activity and procreation, endorsed by an ideology of motherhood, has restricted women from activity in the public sphere. The freeing of women from the reproductive consequences of sexual intercourse combined with the acceptability of contraception might seem then to be a liberating feature of post-war society.

However, contemporary feminists point to implicit problems in this development. First, the euphemistic term 'birth control' shows how patriarchy always constructs reproductive relations as hetero-sexual sexuality within the family. See Roberts (1981). Second, women's apparent 'freedom' is circumscribed by the assumption that women are primarily responsible for procreation. See Smart (1977). Changes need to come at the level of ideology not just at the level of the technology of reproduction. See Beechey (1986).

In any case feminist theory shows that we need to distinguish gender identity and social roles apart from sexual practices.

Family wage

Men's income, paid on the assumption that men are the only or major economic support of families. According to Heidi Hartmann the family wage is 'the cornerstone' of the present sexual division of labour since the term is based on the idea that women are not expected to make an economic contribution to the household and that women's priority is to domestic responsibility. In reality, very few families resemble this myth.

Challenging the concept of the family wage has raised funda-mental questions about women's economic dependence on men, about male trade union strategies, about State responsibility for childcare and about the whole economy of the nuclear family. See Land (1981).

Fascism

The most extreme form of the patriarchal capitalist State, which emphasises a masculine heroism exemplified in war. Fascist ideology constrains women in particular through its obsessive familialism and the way fascism imposes sexual difference to an absurd degree.

From Virginia Woolf's original analysis of the origin of fascism in *Three Guineas* (1938) to contemporary European and American feminist historians, feminist theories offer a unique understanding of fascism by looking at fascist ideas of the patriarchal family, marriage and the treatment of women and children. Luisa Passerini uses oral history to critique positivist and historicist conceptions of history and to connote areas of symbolic activity and ambivalence towards fascism in terms of subjectivity. For example she describes how a fascist consensus is achieved in forms of acquiescence to order and authority. She argues that fascism satisfied a passive, historically conditioned structure of needs — interconnecting family, State and peer groups. See Passerini (1979).

Only with a gender perspective can fascism's uniqueness (in contrast to other types of exceptional states) be understood. The 'law' of patriarchy is involved in fascist ideology. The originality of fascism does not come in *new* ideology but in its conjunctural transformation and recombination of existing elements, for example fascism's fusion of contradictory pro-natalism and euthanasia arguments.

Feminists show how fascism specifically curtailed women as social agents since it connected the biology of race with the biology of gender in a passion for motherhood. See Brindenthal, ed. (1984). Any ideological analysis of fascism needs to take into account the component of sexuality in terms of women's consent. Fascism enlisted the support of women by addressing them in an ideological — sexual language with which they were familiar through 'discourses' of bourgeois Christian ideology. 'The body of fascist discourse . . . is the death of sexuality.' See Macciochi (1979).

Fashion

The economic, cultural and psychological functions of fashion have been a source of concern and of fascination to feminists. Fashion has both a positive and negative construction in feminist theory. For example feminists in suffragette campaigns wore fashionable clothing in order to create an aura of respectability for radical ideas, whereas in Charlotte Perkins Gilman's *Herland* (1915) women are allowed only the mundane clothing of dress reformers.

The main aim of feminists writing about fashion is to expose its double ideology which stereotypes women into feminine objects while caricaturing feminists as masculine and unfashionable. Several different ways of understanding fashion have emerged in contemporary feminism. First, feminists condemn a culture of fashion which reproduces sexist stereotypes of women − a view represented by Simone de Beauvoir's *The Second Sex* (1953) and the utilitarianism of Susan Brownmiller's *Femininity* (1984). Second, some feminists adopt a populist liberalism, for example Janet Radcliffe Richards in *The Sceptical Feminist* (1980) attacks a feminist contempt for fashion as being conservative. A third area in which feminists have been active since the 1980s is in campaigns against the exploitation of women in the fashion industry and Third World exploitation. See Chapkis and Enloe (1983).

Feminists also argue that fashion can be used positively by women. For example Lois Banner suggests that fashion is a key element in producing a communality in women's experience. See Banner (1983). And feminists have consistently proposed alternatives of a more liberated dress style, while recognising the constant danger of recuperation by mainstream fashion (as for instance the thrift shop style of the 1970s). See Wilson (1985). Wilson has developed a complex theory of fashion, interweaving changes in fashion with economic and social change throughout history.

Fear of Success

A term coined by the American psychologist Matina Horner to account for sex differences in achievement behaviour. Horner's thesis is that women are motivated to achieve but fear the negative consequences of their success. (Horner 1972).

Horner based her explanation on the perceived inconsistency for women between achievement and femininity. It was not that women wished, or needed, to fail but that they thought achievement and femininity mutually exclusive. Horner's construct stimulated a new way of understanding motivation in psychology, although the concept has since been refined. Direct tests of a relationship between ability and fear of success are not possible, although several studies may be cited as showing indirect support.

Female

This is a term reserved in feminist theory for the purely biological aspect of sexual difference with 'feminine' as the term for the social construction of women. This avoids the deliberate confusion of these terms by patriarchy which constructs female as the binary opposite of male.

There are several ways in which feminist theory works to define female and discredit binary polarisation. In psychoanalysis, Nancy Chodorow describes the female personality as a process – as fluid and less unitary than male identity. See Chodorow (1978).

Another way of moving outside binary logic is through feminist history which asks what female has come to mean historically. See Jones (1985).

In feminist literary criticism arguments focus on how the female body influences, creates or controls a woman's language and writing, and affects a female tradition in literature. See Showalter (1977).

French theory is also closely bound up with the idea of a specifically female language, for example in Hélène Cixous's notion of the female body as the site of women's expression (see *Écriture Féminine*).

Female consciousness
Women's recognition of how a particular class, culture and historical period creates definitions of female. Female consciousness is not necessarily feminist but is an unconscious feminism, particularly when it occurs in women's groups. Temma Kaplan argues that female consciousness, though often conservative as for example in consumer groups, promotes a social vision embodying radical political implications that feminist theory needs to address. See Kaplan (1982).

Female ethic
This has three main features. It includes a critique of abstraction and a belief that female thinking is more concrete. It stresses that the values of empathy, nurturance and caring are values of women. It stresses too that 'choices' are really demands of situations. See Grimshaw (1986).

The American novelist Ursula Le Guin suggests that a female ethic is, or at least historically has been, basically anarchic since it values order without constraint, and rules by custom not by force. (Le Guin 1976).

Female eunuch
A phrase coined by Germaine Greer in her book of the same name to describe the 'castration' of women by aspects of patriarchy such as 'romantic love' and by male aggression. Greer used de Beauvoir's concept of woman as Other to argue that women's fate is to become

deformed and debilitated by the destructive action of male oppression in contemporary society which deprives women of contact with external reality. Greer suggests that the effect is to make women inner-directed. See Greer (1970).

Feminine

French theorists argue that the term feminine is an arbitrary category given to women's appearance or behaviour by patriarchy. Much feminist writing in France, therefore, has dedicated itself to eliminating the unitary feminine by focusing on the *process* of fictional representation rather than on the creation of individual character. Michele Montrelay suggests that the term 'woman' can be the locus of a primary imaginary dedicated to feminine *jouissance* and available to both women *and* men. In this sense, 'feminine' as a concept and as an identity can be read as a point of departure from such beliefs as 'subject' and 'Man' since, Montrelay argues, in the late nineteenth century 'woman' and 'the feminine' were dislocated in Western thought from passive negative concepts to problematic ones. See Montrelay (1977).

Feminine mystique

A term invented by Betty Friedan in her book of the same name to describe the discrepancy she found between the reality of the women's lives she investigated and the images to which women were trying to conform. 'Mystique' was the notion that the highest value for a woman is the fulfilment of her own femininity. Friedan looked at the non-careers of 200 Smith College graduates through lenses she borrowed from de Beauvoir. She drew her solution to the problem from liberal humanism. Friedan advocated greater educational opportunities to save women from the 'feminine mystique' (rather than radical reform) (Friedan 1963).

Femininism

A term used by cultural and essentialist feminists to describe the ideology of female superiority. Feminism, to writers like Hélène Cixous and Monique Wittig, represents a narrow bourgeois demand for egalitarianism. Femininism, on the other hand, can celebrate feminine plurality.

Femininity

A term which describes the construction of 'femaleness' by society and which connotes sexual attractiveness to men.

Feminists are concerned about cultural definitions of femininity in the media which represent sex role stereotyping. The assumption here that appearance creates identity was an early target of feminist writers. Drawing on the language of social psychology, Kate Millett attacked femininity for implying that anatomy is 'destiny'. Phyllis Chesler agreed that 'femininity' is in effect a sex role stereotype and in *Women and Madness* (1972) proved that women's attempts to achieve it were a prescription for failure, victimisation and severe mental illness.

Both French and American writers suggest that 'femininity' is part of an ideology which positions 'women as Other' against 'masculinity' which is regarded by society as the norm of human behaviour. For example Susan Brownmiller suggests that femininity is a way of making masculinity appear more masterly and competent. See Brownmiller (1984). Julia Kristeva argues that characteristics of 'femininity' can therefore be found in the writing of 'marginal' men like the modernist author Mallarmé. See Kristeva (1980).

Marxist and socialist feminism identifies 'femininity' more as a particular tendency of capitalist development by pointing out that the meanings of femininity and masculinity have varied historically and cannot be treated as static or unified. See Foreman (1977).

Third World feminists interpret 'femininity' more positively. For example Buchi Emecheta describes how the self creation of femininity enables her women characters to become strong and independent. See Emecheta (1979).

Feminism

The definition incorporates both a doctrine of equal rights for women (the organised movement to attain women's rights) and an ideology of social transformation aiming to create a world for women beyond simple social equality. Gerda Lerner argues that feminism must distinguish for itself between women's rights and women's emancipation. See Lerner (1978).

In general, feminism is the ideology of women's liberation since intrinsic in all its approaches is the belief that women suffer injustice because of our sex. Under this broad umbrella various feminisms offer differing analyses of the causes, or agents, of female oppression.

Marxist feminists identify mainly the sexual division of labour as a cause of oppression and Marxist feminism is then an agenda of economic change. Catharine MacKinnon on the other hand identifies sexuality as the primary social sphere of male power. She argues that feminist political theory must centre on the construction and social determination of sexuality, since to feminism the personal is epistemologically the political, and its epistemology is its politics. See MacKinnon (1982).

Feminism also incorporates various methods of analysis and theory, if feminism is taken to be the theory of the woman's point of view. Consciousness raising is the quintessential method of feminism, and since feminism means a knowledge of existing things in a new light it needs a distinctive account of the relation of method to theory.

Feminism's method recapitulates as theory the reality it tries to describe. For example feminism challenges universalisms and uses the pursuit of consciousness itself as a form of political theory and practice. See Hartsock (1979).

Indeed some French theorists have abandoned the use of the word 'feminism' altogether on the grounds that it is one more ism. See Makward (1980).

Definitions of feminism by feminists tend to be shaped by their training, ideology or race. So, for example, Marxist and Socialist feminists stress the interaction within feminism of class with gender and focus on *social* distinctions between men and women. See Mitchell and Oakley (1976). Black feminists argue much more for an integrated analysis which can unlock the multiple systems of oppression. See B. Smith (1981). (The different political theories of feminism are entered as individual categories. See, for example, Anarchist feminism or Marxist feminism.)

Feminism is the theory; lesbianism is the practice

A slogan coined by Ti-Grace Atkinson in the 1970s to affirm that lesbianism was the radical political practice and experience of the feminist movement. Feminist theory, Atkinson argued, would not be *compromised* by lesbianism but could be completed only by the lesbian experience of marginality and difference. (Atkinson 1974).

Feminist

Like feminism, there is not, nor could be, a single definition of feminist since feminists have many differing affinities — of sexual preference, class and race. In short a feminist is a woman who recognises herself, and is recognised by others, as a feminist. That awareness depends on a woman having experienced consciousness raising; a knowledge of women's oppression, and a recognition of women's differences and communalities.

Some feminists argue for a definition that is future orientated — that a feminist must have a concept of social transformation. See Eisenstein (1984). Others argue for a definition that recognises the validity of women's contemporary experiences. See Duelli Klein (1983). 'I myself have never been able to find out precisely what feminism is. I only know that people call me a feminist whenever I express sentiments that differentiate me from a doormat or a prostitute' (West 1982, p. 219). But all feminists share a commitment to, and enjoyment of, a woman-centred perspective.

Féminitude

A French term used to characterise 'cultural feminism'. Similar in construction to *négritude*, *féminitude* cultivates female difference and argues that the experience of *féminitude* is more significant than an examination of the political production of difference. See Marks and de Courtivron (1981).

Feminisation of poverty

A term coined by the American sociologist Diana Pearce to describe the situation facing increasing numbers of women in the Third World, and now facing minority and disadvantaged women in the USA and Europe. See Pearce (1978).

Feminist scholars focusing on the Third World show that its increased incorporation into the world economy has also increased women's disadvantages. For example women in the Third World suffer an increased dependency on men through reductions in their earnings, access to land, and legal autonomy. There is discrimination against women in education and job opportunities and an increase in agricultural labour for women. See Robertson and Berger (1986). The blurring of a distinction between productive and reproductive labour in such research helps feminist theory to rethink the relationship of class to gender.

Fertility

Women's ability to produce children. Feminist theory argues that fertility is not simply a biological or private concern of individual women but occurs within relations of sexual power. Fertility is an area of conflict because gender divisions and the position of women in society have a direct influence on fertility control practices.

Feminist ideas about fertility in the nineteenth and early twentieth century embodied a contradiction between an emphasis on the joys of motherhood and a eugenic justification for fewer, or no, children. See Ehrenreich and English (1979).

Since 1970 feminist activists have deprivatised fertility and located the issue in a political context. Feminist theories of fertility now relate fertility both to the historical and to the contemporary, lived experiences of women and children. Woman's position in the family is the primary shaper of woman's needs and desires about fertility. Feminist historical demographers show that in societies where women's power is strong, for example in matrilineal kinship,

women control their own fertility; and in societies where childbearing is a major source of prestige for women, fertility control
methods are less accessible to women. See Petchesky (1986).

Socialist feminism argues that women must have equality of conditions for reproductive choice. However, feminist psychoanalysis
argues that women's own responses to fertility are an area of conflict
and moral ambiguity. See Gilligan (1982).

The visionary idea of women organising around the relations and
tasks of fertility in reproductive collectives is described by Mary
O'Brien (1983).

Film

Analysis of the representation of women in mainstream films and
descriptions of feminist alternatives are an important area of feminist
theory.

The first wave of feminist film criticism adopted a broadly
sociological approach and analysed imagery and sex roles in film.
Then, influenced by semiology, feminist theorists became concerned
with the role of the medium in the construction of meaning. This
enabled critics to deconstruct patriarchal myths in Hollywood films
and patriarchal ideas of the family and sexuality. See Kaplan (1983).

Psychoanalytic methodology was an essential step in the feminist
project to understand film since the method enabled feminists to ask
questions about the role of spectatorship and sexual differentiation.
Using Lacanian analysis, Laura Mulvey created a theory about the
domination of the male gaze in the classical Hollywood film and
showed how film makes women's position be silent, absent or
marginal in a phallocentric language of film. See Mulvey (1975).

Psychoanalysis proved a fertile method for feminist criticism both
because it enabled feminist theory to relate film theory to other
feminist issues such as pornography and gender differentiation, and
also because it encouraged attempts by female film-makers to make
films which could avoid the dominant 'male' spectator, for example
Chantal Akerman, Marguerite Duras and Margarethe von Trotta.
New theoretical approaches are addressing issues of racism, Black
women and representation, female friendship and feminist distribution. See Brunsdon (1986).

Film noir

A term for Hollywood thrillers of the 1940s and 1950s which
feminist film critics have written about extensively because the films
reveal key examples of contradictions in patriarchal capitalist
culture. Christine Gledhill suggests that although women characters
in *film noir* are finally subjected to the moral evaluation of a male

investigator, the films portray strong women who can resist and
disturb this male-ordered world. Sylvia Harvey argues that the films
reflect a period of profound social changes for women. For example
the absence of 'normal' family relations in *film noir* registers the
shifting position women occupied in American society. See Kaplan
(1978).

Firestone, Shulamith
American radical feminist.

In *Notes from the First Year* (1968) and *The Dialectic of Sex* (1970)
Firestone uses a transhistorical theory to account for the subordination of women. Offering a radical reinterpretation of 'materialism',
Firestone suggested that the material base for women's oppression
lies not in economics but in biology. The fact that females and not
males reproduce, Firestone argues, is the reason for the gender
division of labour on which patriarchy, and its ruling ideology
sexism, are constructed. It is biological characteristics which create a
'sexual class system'. Firestone argues that a feminist revolution will
come when women seize the means of *re*production.

First wave
Sometimes known as 'old wave', the term usually refers to the
mobilisation of the suffrage movement in America and England
between 1890 and 1920, although an organised 'feminist' movement for women's suffrage had existed for 40 years earlier.
Contemporary feminism dates from the early 1970s with the
strength of 'second wave' or 'new wave' feminism and its search for
the political bases on which contemporary feminism rests. But both
movements share similar characteristics, for example a use of
militant tactics. First wave feminism represents organised feminism
with an emphasis on reforms in family law and economic opportunities, and international associations symbolised, in America, by
the 1848 Geneva Falls Convention of Women. See Du Bois (1978).

The term 'first wave' of course is only relevant for feminist
movements in the Western world. See Sarah (1985).

Flax, Jane
American philosopher and psychoanalyst.

Flax made a fundamental attack on the whole discipline of
philosophy by arguing that the 'psychic qualities' of maleness are
imprinted in both the methods and problems with which philosophy deals. See Flax (1983).

Fluidity
A rhetorical feature of women's writing and an important concept in

French feminist theory. Luce Irigaray suggests that fluidity is what 'leaks out' of solid discursivity. Women speak fluid, hysterical speech as opposed to the phallocentric rigidity and metaphysical privileging of identity in physics or metaphysics. See Irigaray (1974b).

Foreman, Ann

British Marxist who argued that femininity was inherently alienating because it quickly became reified into an expected form, an Other. Foreman claims that it was the relegation of women to being custodians of the emotional life which constituted a gender construction (Foreman 1977).

Foucault, Michel

French historian who influenced feminist theory with his interpretations of the sociology of knowledge and the history of sexuality. In *L'Archéology du Savoir* (*The Archaeology of Knowledge*) (1969) and *The History of Sexuality* (1979) Foucault examines the nature of the solidarity between knowledge and power, the historical discourses of exclusion and repression, and the social construction of sexuality. Of particular importance for feminism are Foucault's ideas that 'woman' is a discourse created by and for others, and that definitions of sexuality are politically created.

Freedom

Feminism describes three areas of freedom: political, economic and sexual, but feminist theories differ in deciding which area is most significant. Ann Ferguson argues that sexual freedom is most important because women need to define themselves as sexual subjects, not to be sexual objects. See Ferguson and Folbre (1981). Other feminists argue that feminism needs an awareness of the *relation* between sexual expression and other areas. Individual freedom and the freedom of all women are linked when women reach the critical consciousness that 'we are united first of all in our unfreedom' (Westkott 1983, p. 213). In particular, Westkott argues that the main source of knowledge about freedom will come from life experience rather than from theory.

Free universities

Radical education groups established in many European, and subsequently American, cities after the May 1968 student strikes in Paris. The collective pedagogy and radical politics of free universities were an inspiration to feminist theory and women's studies. In Britain the first women's studies course was taught by Juliet Mitchell at the London Anti-University and Florence Howe suggests that the first 'political' women's studies course in the USA was taught at the Free University of Seattle in 1968. See Boxer (1982).

Freeman, Jo

American activist and writer who founded one of the early women's liberation groups in 1967 and later documented the social history of the contemporary women's liberation movement. Her contribution to feminist theory lies in her argument that we use the term 'liberation' over other feminist terminology, her argument that 'communality' is the key substance of women's politics, and her advocacy of independent feminist action. See Freeman (1970 and 1975).

Freire, Paulo

Libertarian education writer and teacher who developed the method of '*conscientizacao*' to teach adult illiterates. By *conscientizacao*, Freire means a method of teaching in which student and teachers collectively choose political vocabulary in order to expose the ideological contradictions in their lives. See Freire (1970). Freire's approach influenced those feminist sociologists interested in finding techniques of consciousness raising which would also be instrumentally educative. The notion of learning in groups as a subjective precondition for liberating action was particularly attractive to feminist activists. See Mies (1983).

Freud, Sigmund

The founder of psychoanalysis whose theories about hysteria, infantile sexuality and gender acquisition, and the unconscious and its symbols were criticised and rejected by early feminists like Kate Millett but modified and developed by Juliet Mitchell and others.

Freud wrote about women in *Three Essays — on the Theory of Sexuality* (1905) which described the development of femininity in terms of a girl's penis envy and masculinity in terms of the oedipal complex and as a refusal of the mother. Feminist theorists who draw heavily on the original theories of Freud are those in the tradition of object relations (like Nancy Chodorow), and Juliet Mitchell who situates Freudian theory into a cultural context by reading it as the analysis of a patriarchal society. Dorothy Dinnerstein drew on Freud to explain that men's fears of women stemmed from their childhood fears of their mothers.

Feminists Kate Millett and Shulamith Firestone rejected Freud's concepts as inimical to women, arguing that his statements about women could not refer to biological differences but only to the patriarchal order. Millett in particular attacked Freud's biological determinism. Freud maintained that civilisation was built on the repression of sexuality, which Susan Griffin feels is a fallacious division of 'culture' and 'nature'. In Jean Baker Miller's elaboration of Freud, male 'dominants' had repressed not only sexuality but women. (J.B. Miller 1976). Adrienne Rich adds, in *Of Woman Born* (1976), that Freud's fundamental dualism of 'inner' and 'outer' was an organisation fundamental to a male ego but that such a dualism could not apply to female experience.

A new vein of feminist enquiry accepts Freud's notion of the 'instability' of the female as a positive characteristic of woman's psycho sexuality and claims that Freud's explanations of 'penis envy' and 'hysteria' were designed to control female potentiality. See Kofman (1987).

Friendship

A form of women's emotional bonding. The historical phenomenon of long-lived intimate, loving friendships between two women is the focus of much feminist history and historiographical studies have helped revise androcentric versions of women's contribution to history. See Smith-Rosenberg (1975).

In *Gyn/Ecology* (1978) Mary Daly makes an etymological study of the derivation and meaning of friendship. Claiming that the word comes from the Old English root of 'to love', Daly argues that 'sisters' friendship is radically different from male comradeship because it is self-affirming.

Fuller, Margaret

American writer. In *Woman in the Nineteenth Century* (1845), an early example of feminist theory, Fuller initiated the cultural feminist tradition by fusing ideas from English romanticism and American transcendentalism to argue that true knowledge is emotional, and intuitive. Drawing on the theories of Emmanuel Swedenborg, Fuller envisaged a future cultural androgyny which would be a psychic synthesis of masculine and feminine attributes in a dialectic of complementary opposites. See Fuller (1971).

Functionalism

The theory that every social institution or practice has a function in maintaining the social process. Functionalism defines social activities in terms of social needs or functions.

The approach is criticised by feminist theorists for over-emphasising a causal relationship at the expense of a proper consideration of contradiction and conflict. See Coward and Ellis (1977).

Furies

A lesbian feminist group which was based in Washington DC in the early 1970s. Together with their best known representative, Charlotte Bunch, the Furies created a theoretical analysis of class, women's oppression and lesbian separatism which influenced much of radical thinking in contemporary feminism. See Bunch and Myron (1974).

Gage, Matilda Joslyn

Nineteenth-century American activist and writer whose ideas are close to those of contemporary feminism, for example, Mary Daly.

Gage based her theories on doctrines of natural rights and in *Woman, Church and State* (1873) argued that the oppression of women is rooted in Christian beliefs, particularly in the belief derived from Genesis of women's inferiority and wickedness. Gage claimed that women have special intellectual capacities which are unique – in particular an intuitive faculty. She postulated that the notion of a 'lost name' is really the lost memory of the divine attributes of motherhood once exemplified by matriarchy. See Gage (1973).

Gatekeeping theory

The term used by Dale Spender to describe men's codification of knowledge. She argues that it is men who largely control access to print; and that this, in turn, means that the paradigms and scholarship of various disciplines will be androcentric. See Spender (1981). Mainstream scholarship still refuses to admit that knowledge has a politics.

Gay liberation

A movement (which began in America in the late 1960s) for political, social and cultural rights for homosexual men and women. Jill Johnston and other writers argue that the women's movement shares with gay liberation a common goal: a society free from defining and categorising people by virtue of gender and/or sexual preference. See Johnston (1974).

As feminism developed in the 1970s, lesbian replaced gay in feminist theories of liberation. 'Woman-identified woman' became a term for women whose self concepts are independent of all relationships with men. Lesbian theorists radically redefined 'lesbian' and described new political strategies, which moved far away from the narrow civil libertarian position of gay liberation. See Darty and Potter (1984).

Gaze

The theory of the gaze was first described by Laura Mulvey in 'Visual pleasure and narrative cinema' in *Screen* magazine. Drawing on Lacanian psychoanalysis, Mulvey argued that the stereotyping and objectification of women on the screen comes about through the way cinema is structured around three explicitly male looks or gazes. There is the look of the camera in the situation being filmed which is voyeuristic since most films are made by males; there is the gaze of men within a film narrative which is structured so as to make women objects of their gaze; and finally there is the look or gaze of the male spectator. See Mulvey (1975). Revised in 1981, Mulvey's concept greatly influenced film theory, even if subsequent work draws attention to its limitations. See Humm (1988).

Gender

A culturally-shaped group of attributes and behaviours given to the female or to the male. Contemporary feminist theory is careful to distinguish between sex and gender. Building on the work of Margaret Mead in *Sex and Temperament in Three Primitive Societies* (1935), such theory takes the view that sex is biological and that gender behaviour is a social construction.

Kate Millett and Shulamith Firestone radicalised contemporary thinking about gender. In the *Dialectic of Sex* Firestone argues that gender distinctions structure every aspect of our lives by constituting the unquestioned framework in terms of which society views women and men. Gender difference, she claims, is an elaborate system of male domination. The theoretical task of feminism is to understand that system. The political task of feminism is to end it.

Polarity is essential to gender construction since each gender is constructed as the opposite of the other. Simone de Beauvoir was first to describe 'woman' as Other or 'not man'. This concept of Otherness underlies categories of contrasting characteristics labelled feminine and masculine, for example 'hysterical' or 'angry' which reflect gender related expectations.

Traditional sex difference studies are designed to prove that these characteristics are not socially constructed but derive from biological differences. Feminists criticise pro-gender biological evidence as being fallacious. See Maccoby and Jacklin (1974). Feminist sociologists are able to show that attributes that Western society considers 'natural' for women are usually created by social pressures or conditioning. The internalisation of these attributes is called gendering. See Oakley (1972).

Feminist anthropologists ask us to study the significance of gender for the organisation of social life so that we can conceptualise a future society without traditional categories. See Rosaldo (1980). Gayle Rubin argues that gender is a product of the social relations of sexuality because kinship systems rest upon marriage. Every gender system exhibits an ideology or cognitive system that relies on repression in order to present gender categories as being fixed. See Rubin (1975).

This focus on gender as a locus of power relations set the terms of debate for much theoretical writing of the 1970s. The great strength of contemporary feminism lies in its dissection of the mythology surrounding gender. Psychoanalysts argue that the gender division of labour in the modern nuclear family, which gives exclusive responsibilities for early childcare to the mother, produces gender-differentiated people with desires and capacities to continue the gender division of labour. Basing her theory on gender differences observable in the 'pre-oedipal' period of development, Nancy Chodorow claims that only a transformation of the social organis-ation of gender can lead to the disappearance of sexual inequality. See Chodorow (1978). Dorothy Dinnerstein felt that symbiotic gender arrangements were leading to a planetary crisis affecting human future. Less apocalyptically, Carol Gilligan relies on Chodorow's view of female gender identity to argue that this identity formation makes momen relational, unlike male gender identity which stems from separatism and autonomy. See Gilligan (1982).

The analysis which Millett and Firestone began and which was extended and deepened by Adrienne Rich and Nancy Chodorow shifted feminist theory from a focus on sex roles to a woman-centred perspective. As Catharine MacKinnon argues, sexuality is the linchpin of gender inequality because gender is based on an ideology that attributes its learned qualities to nature. See MacKinnon (1982).

More positively, women can now see that gender relations are a collective issue like class relations. Mary O'Brien optimistically proposes that developments in contraceptive technology are a world historical event because they give a hitherto non-existent material base for gender equality. See O'Brien (1982).

Gender gap
A general term for differences between men and women in employment and income. The theory of the gender gap was created

in the early 1980s to explain the fact that women had voted differently from men in recent American elections and that women were more critical of right-wing administrations. Zillah Eisenstein argues that the gender gap reflects two contradictory realities simultaneously. First, it reflects the gendered reality of women's lives; the tendency for women to think 'like' women because they are nurturers and hence more peace loving than men. Simultaneously, women believe in their right to equality of opportunity and therefore they attack patriarchy as a sex class. See Eisenstein (1982).

Genderlect
A term used by feminist theorists in linguistics to describe the distinctive linguistic identity of women. They argue that both sexes have their own structural systems or codes sometimes called a language.

Anthropologists making comparisons of women's languages across cultures find that syntactical forms and linguistic competences are gendered. See Thorne and Henley (1975). The view that there are sex-linked differences in language use presupposes the effect on women's language of single-sex experiences. Linguist Robin Lakoff prefers a frequency model of genderlect rather than one based on essential gender differences. (Lakoff 1975). Sex-differentiated languages or genderlects are expressive of the social construction of gender identity.

Gender stratification
An extension of social theories of stratification made by feminist theorists to explain the gender inequality between males and females in class, status and occupation. Such critics argue that a social stratification by class or occupation is too inexact to categorise women because it fails to take account of women's work in the family or house. See Oakley (1982).

Genres
A term for a literary type or class. Ellen Moers and other feminist critics have examined feminine traditions in women's writing and discovered that women favour particular genres over others, for example the Gothic and domestic fiction. Although literary women have worked in every available form and style, Moers argues that the genre of Gothic, for example, enabled Mary Shelley to translate her experience of the trauma of miscarriages into accessible and appropriate monster imagery. See Moers (1977). Later critics have gone on to argue that women writers use particular genres, for

example the romance, regarded in the literary tradition as inherently minor, in order to subvert that tradition. See Radway (1984).

Geography

Traditional geography is predominantly economic because it uses paradigms based on capitalism and technology. Feminist geographers argue that these paradigms are patriarchal because they cannot take into account women's needs.

Making a fundamental reassessment of geography, the new feminist criticism focuses on the environment in a search for alternatives to 'alienated labour'. It emphasises the social construction of gendered labour divisions. The main focus of feminist geographical work about gender is on the growing conflict between women's roles in production and in reproduction in the face of a new international division of labour and rapid urbanisation. Feminist geographers prefer to study power in a decentralised form in order to look at regional patterns of the gender division of labour. See Momsen and Townsend (1987).

Feminist theorists have shifted the perspective of geography from its traditional preoccupation with spatial structures to a focus on processes. For example their idea of 'time geography' allows us to examine the constraints of seasonality on rural women's use of time in a new link between ecology, environmental science and feminism.

Gerontology

The study of old people. What feminism and gerontology have in common is that both aim to create a social consciousness, a social theory and a social policy which will improve the chances of a specific group.

Gerontology is the study which furnishes the theory and ideology of anti-ageism movements. It has been heavily influenced by feminist models of social change and it includes many feminist activists. See Reinharz (1986).

Gilligan, Carol

American psychologist and philosopher who argued *In a Different Voice* (1982) that moral reasoning takes quite different forms in men and in women. Because women are concerned with the activity of care and children's moral development they define morality as the understanding of responsibility and relationships. Men claim that morality is defined by fairness which leads men to think of rights and rules.

Gilman, Charlotte Perkins

American writer who is considered to be the leading theorist of 'first wave' feminism. Gilman used the theories of social Darwinism to argue, in *Women and Economics* (1898), that women's subjugation was an unnatural aberration which would impede the progress of the race. Gilman welded feminism with the anarchist idea, from Kropotkin, that the race is evolving into a cooperative phase. Gilman argued that the feminine virtues of altruism are those most needed in this phase of development. In particular she believed that the power of maternal energy is a socially cohesive force.

Gilman's most original contribution to feminist theory lies in her discussion of the ideological pressures on culture, education and politics imposed by an androcentric perspective. In *The Manmade World or Our Androcentric Culture* (1911) Gilman argues that androcentrism is destructive and should be replaced by a mother-centred world. That matriarchal vision is embodied in her utopia *Herland* (1915) and in *The Home* (1903). Here Gilman's thesis is that the home, as an institution, is an antiquated system which restricts women and retards social evolution. Gilman's writing is the most clearly articulated piece of radical feminist theory about the domestic sphere. Dolores Hayden calls Gilman a 'materialist feminist' because she was concerned to transform the material conditions of women's lives. See Hayden (1980a).

Goddess

Feminist theologians argue that Goddess symbols can counter the repressive patriarchy of monotheistic religions. Mythologists claim that the rule of a great goddess is reflected in matriarchy and that the elimination of the Goddess religion was part of a general devaluation of women in culture. See Stone (1976). Mary Daly describes how Christianity dismembered the original Goddess religion by turning female symbols into male symbols, for example the rebirth of the Son of God simply repeats the myth of Demeter and Persephone. See Daly (1973).

During periods when women's fertility was thought to be a primal power, Goddess religion was part of a gynocentric perspective. See Rich (1976). Rich describes the symbolic evocations of this female power.

Some feminists suggest that women's social position could be enhanced by Goddess worship and that belief in a female deity would give religion more meaning. See Goldenberg (1979). In this sense 'Goddess' could stand for the expression of communitarian and ecological values, enabling religion to stress female symbolism and immanence. A Goddess religion would emphasise the continuity of natural phenomena and the interdependence and mutual aid of female power. See Christ and Plaskow (1979).

Goldman, Emma

In *The Traffic in Women* (1911) Goldman set feminist theory in the context of anarchism – both of which are theories of organic growth. Like Charlotte Perkins Gilman and Margaret Fuller, Goldman envisioned an ideal society to be an organic community of people living and working in mutual harmony.

Goldman adapted Kropotkin's anarchist view that society could be motivated by 'mutual aid'. She argued both for the liberation of the human mind from the domination of religion and for the liberation of women's bodies from the dominion of property. See Goldman (1970).

Gossip

A method by which women explore our lives. 'Through gossip, women both express and find reinforcement for their thoughts, which then influence what they do' (Kaplan 1982, p. 58).

Gossip is a way of solidifying female bonds and communal consciousness in small communities and is relevant to feminist theory. For example Sheila Rowbotham cites gossip along with giggling and old wives' tales as three characteristics especially associated with women and often regarded by men as marks of women's inferiority. These characteristics, she argues, can provide women with important ways of perceiving and describing the world – a relation of experience to theory. See Rowbotham (1983).

Greenham

The name of the women's peace camps established in September 1981 on Greenham Common outside the gates of the United States Air Force Base housing nuclear weapons. As the only all-women peace camp, Greenham came to symbolise positive uses of feminist theory in women peace campers' constructive programmes for women's action. Support for the 'squatting' Greenham women united women across classes, generations and countries who wanted to demonstrate for peace. Greenham camps created new feminist ways of organising, using holistic analyses based on peace which moved beyond socialism.

Women at Greenham put into practice many ideas from feminist theory such as collective decision-making and the identification of warfare with patriarchy, and generated feminist forms of non-violent action using aspects of feminist culture and art, for example web imagery, mirrors and women's chants. See Finch *et al.* (1986).

Greer, Germaine

Australian writer and English academic whose first book, *The Female Eunuch* (1970) played an important role in encouraging media consciousness of women's oppression. Greer made an ideological analysis of aspects of misogyny in culture rather than creating a method or agenda for feminism. In *Sex and Destiny* (1984) she moved away from current feminist theories of the family and the sexual division of labour to advocate a return to large and extended families. See Greer (1970 and 1984).

Griffin, Susan

American philosopher who identifies 'female' with nature. In *Woman and Nature* (1978), *Rape: The Power of Consciousness* (1979) and *Pornography and Silence* (1981) Griffin created a theory about global violence. Arguing that rape and imperialism had common elements, Griffin connected the crime of rape at home with American crimes in Vietnam. Both rape culture and imperialist ideology are socially produced and Griffin thinks that both stem from a profound contempt for, and fear of, women. Similarly pornography shares with the Western Christian tradition, Griffin argues, a hatred of the flesh in the way both associate women with the body, with the evocation of desire. What Griffin termed 'the pornographic imagination' is the desecration of the female. The imagery of pornography has taught women silence and self-annihilation which is now a cultural norm.

Griffin advocates a feminist metaphysic in which women would be reunited with themselves and the environment as natural beings. See Griffin (1978, 1979 and 1981).

Grimké, Sarah

In *Letters on the Equality of the Sexes and the Condition of Women* (1838) Grimké attacked women's subordination and argued for women's rights. Grimké's overall analysis is similar to that of Mary Wollstonecraft, but Grimké takes a more radical direction by arguing that men as a class keep women as a class in a subordinate position because it is in men's interest to do so. Grimké also made the first major feminist attack on domesticity and argued that men are tyrants in the domestic sphere. See Grimké (1838).

Gynaesthesia

A term invented by Mary Daly in *Gyn/Ecology* (1978) to describe the new form of perception and understanding which develops in women when they become feminists. This is 'gynaesthesia' or the ability to perceive the interrelatedness of disparate phenomena.

With gynaesthesia women have a more holistic response to the environment. The term is similar to 'synchronisities' coined by Susan Griffin to describe forms of knowledge which lacked critical vocabulary.

Gynarchism
Feminist anarchists believe that if a 'gynarchy' created by women replaced patriarchy it would not replicate the same forms of hierarchy. The term is sometimes elided with 'matriarchy', and Charlotte Perkins Gilman used one version of the term — 'gynaeocracy'. See Ehrlich (1979).

Gyn ecology
A term invented by Mary Daly, in her book of the same name *Gyn/ Ecology* (1978), to refer to the new 'bodies' of knowledge which would be created in women-only collective relationships. A deliberate pun on gynaecology, Daly's term defines a holistic environmental process of knowing which would replace, for women, the patriarchal medicalisation of our bodies into objects of science.

Gynergy
A term invented by Emily Culpepper and taken up by Mary Daly to refer to the strength of feminist ethics. The development of women's collective consciousness would produce a new faculty and process of valuation. See Culpepper (1975).

Gynocentric
The sharing of certain kinds of women-centred beliefs and women-centred social organisations. Gynocentric activities involve a set of women's strengths which could be explored and cultivated, for example the strength of women's eroticism. There are several different uses of gynocentric in feminist theory. It is an important concept in feminist myth and anthropology, for example in Adrienne Rich's writings, in the literary criticism of Elaine Showalter and in the philosophy of Susan Griffin and Mary Daly.

Gynocritics
This is the study of women writers and of the history, styles, themes, genres and structures of writing by women. Gynocritics includes the psychodynamics of female creativity; the trajectory of the individual or collective female career and the evolution and rules of a female literary tradition. Feminist literary critics who use the term gynocritics share a 'second wave' approach to literary criticism which concentrates on texts written by women. The 'first wave'

feminist critics, known as resisting readers, analysed the misogyny of books written by men. See Showalter (1979) and Humm (1986).

Gynomorphic

A term coined by Mary Daly to describe a 'whole' new woman's language. Gynomorphic represents, according to Daly, a rejection of the reductionist language of patriarchy; a rejection not simply by women replacing term for term, but by women involved in a *process* of knowledge creation. See Daly (1978).

Hag-ography

A term invented by Mary Daly to describe the 'living/writing' process of women's new history. Hag-ography (a pun on hagiography or the biography of saints) will re-establish the power of hags or witches. See Daly (1978).

Hartmann, Heidi

American economist and critic whose essays 'Capitalism, patriarchy and job segregation by sex' and 'The unhappy marriage of Marxism and feminism' describe the way patriarchy produces and reproduces job segregation. Hartmann criticises dual labour market theory and Marxist theory for paying insufficient attention to gender divisions. Men maintain power by controlling organisations, through the exclusionary power of male unions and by denying women training. See Hartmann (1976, 1981).

Health

Feminism argues that the everyday role of women in our society is regarded as 'sick' rather than healthy. The behaviour and attitudes of women are often falsely characterised as neurotic and women's experiences (of double work in the home and in occupations) lead to ill-health. See Chesler (1972).

Feminist attacks on existing health care for women come from many political perspectives but all share a general aim which is to change the definition of women's health and to change the ways in which women's health is managed. Feminists point out how the methods and discipline of modern medicine prefer mechanistic and technological techniques inappropriate to most of women's needs (particularly for reproduction). There is sexism in medical education, and discrimination against women health workers. See Doyal and Elston (1986).

Feminist theories of health care in the 1970s described the history of medical misogyny. See Ehrenreich and English (1979). These theorists supported self-help processes in women's health groups by offering accounts which integrated medical information with examples from women's experiences. See Boston Women's Health Collective (1971).

Recent research continues to examine the relation between women's health and sex discrimination, for example by looking at the relationship between health and safety at work and in the home in relation to gender. See Kenner (1985).

Herstory
Women's history.

The theory of, and documentation about, past and contemporary lives, groups, language and experience of women. 'To live with herstory is to . . . find patterns both in our oppression and in our responses' (Nestle 1984, p. x).

Heterosexism
This term refers to the unconscious or explicit assumption that heterosexuality is the only 'normal' mode of sexual and social relations. Feminist theorists agree that heterosexuality, as an institution and as an ideology, is a cornerstone of patriarchy. For example heterosexism implies the suppression and denial of homosexuality and assumes that everyone is, or should be, heterosexual. Second, heterosexism relies on the fallacious superiority of the dominant male, passive female pattern. See Darty and Potter (1984).

Other critics point out that heterosexist values and norms legitimise the sexual division of labour. See Ferguson *et al.* (1982).

A feminist sensitivity to homophobia is part of the ongoing attempt to free women's studies from heterosexism. The assumption of heterosexuality both reflects and reinforces ignorance about lesbian perspectives. Writers Adrienne Rich and Elly Bulkin, in particular, are making feminist theory more truly inclusive from a lesbian perspective.

Heterosexuality
A sexual relationship between members of the opposite sex. At issue in feminist theory is whether heterosexuality in human society has a 'natural' basis or whether it is socially produced. For example feminist anthropology focuses on the way human heterosexuality is falsely conceptualised from primate behaviour.

Anne Koedt's essay 'The myth of the vaginal orgasm' demystified heterosexuality by arguing that heterosexual relations, and in particular penetration, had no necessary connection with female orgasm. Koedt identified the heterosexual norm as a means by which patriarchy divides women from each other (Koedt 1973). Feminist psychoanalysts point out how, in Freud's model of female identity, heterosexuality has Victorian characteristics that include the notion of women's passivity and the subordination of sexuality to procreation. See Chodorow (1978).

The argument that heterosexuality is a social not 'natural' institution was made by Charlotte Bunch and other lesbian writers in the 1970s as a critical response to Chodorow and Dorothy Dinnerstein. Bunch believes that heterosexuality is basic to women's oppression (Bunch 1975). Adrienne Rich went on to charge feminist theorists with the responsibility of looking as carefully at heterosexuality as they did at motherhood, the family and other social institutions. Rich argues that feminist analysis is weakened by a failure to treat heterosexuality as a political institution and she proposes we use a concept called 'compulsory heterosexuality'. Compulsory heterosexuality, according to Rich, is a key mechanism perpetuating male dominance, which inculcates and then enforces a heterosexual preference in women by a variety of mechanisms. See Rich (1980).

In this way radical lesbian theory extends a feminist analysis of sexual politics to an analysis of sexuality itself as an institution. Rich's concept 'lesbian continuum' provided a background against which various strategies of resistance could be evaluated. Often, heterosexual women use heterosexual relations to escape or to avoid other mechanisms. See Ferguson *et al.* (1982).

The French theorist Luce Irigaray points out that heterosexuality constructs an 'artificial' femininity. She defines heterosexuality as man's relation to his imaginary Other. See Irigaray (1974a).

Liberal feminists like Betty Friedan attacked this direction of feminist theory and claimed that it alienated ordinary women. Heterosexual socialist feminists are now creating theories which could provide heterosexual feminists with a way of enjoying heterosexuality while understanding the contradictions of the system. See Haber (1979). But all feminist theory agrees that the abolition of *compulsory* heterosexuality would have an enormous impact on the system of male domination. It would disrupt the way gender is imposed on the infant psyche (as described by Freud).

Hidden curriculum
Sometimes called the partial curriculum. Feminist theory describes how education includes not only clearly defined subjects but also a hidden curriculum. This transmits to girls a collection of messages which reinforce sexual stereotyping and sustains a sexual division of labour in the social process of schooling. See Byrne (1978).

Shocked by evidence of girls' underachievement in schools, a number of writers are now focusing on how the hidden curriculum creates gender divisions. Not only is there 'artificial' sex segregation in the curricula, for example in physical education, but evidence is growing that sextyping of curricula 'choices' in secondary schools has roots in the primary years, for example in girls' rejection of the 'masculine' areas of physics; and of course girls' 'underachievement' is itself in question. See Frazier and Sadker (1973). The sex bias in subject choices continues *within* subjects when women's invisibility leads to a misleading view of society.

Classroom dynamics are an important part of the hidden curriculum and contain implicit messages about the importance of men in society. A number of structural and attitudinal constraints give girls a minority status in classrooms which affects their performance and commitment to subjects. See Spender (1982a). Boys and girls are handled in very different ways and girls are specifically discouraged. It is difficult to tease out the interrelated facets of sex differences in classroom practices, school organisation and girls' achievement, but feminist writers draw attention to language as a medium of control and to how even school uniform is used to suggest an appropriate gendered behaviour to girls. See Stanworth (1981).

The hidden curriculum can be undermined, feminist theorists suggest, by women-only classes, the insertion of more information about women into subjects, abandoning concepts of objectivity and validating the diverse experience of women as part of any curricula.

Hidden women
A term used by feminist historians to describe the virtual exclusion of women, their lives, work and struggle from research. Although women's contribution to history is now being recorded, women's contribution to historical science is still not acknowledged. See Lerner (1978).

Hierarchical theory
Feminists draw attention to how terms such as 'patriarchy', the 'family' or 'bureaucracy' name hierarchical ways of organising what people do rather than the real human activities under these institutions' supposed control. They are not neutral terms, feminists argue, because assumptions about hierarchy are part of a social order constructed by men. Indeed feminist theorists question whether hierarchical concepts like 'the family' refer to reality at all. See Ferguson *et al.* (1982).

Hispanic

Cherríe Moraga calls Hispanic theory a 'rite of passage' because it comes to terms with community, racism and internal colonialisation See Moraga and Anzaldúa (1981). Hispanic writers are now creating a collective cultural history in essays about the myths of women in Hispanic culture, for example the myth of female purity; and in essays about the taboos surrounding the feminine functions of contraception and maternity. Hispanic writers are replacing these myths by information about women's power and spirituality.

Hispanic theory is affected by the specific history of colonialisation in the Americas and also by differences within feminism. Calling Hispanic theory a 'theory in the flesh' because it must deal with the physical reality of skin colour, writers also write about the restrictions imposed on their language, for example the way Spanish composition follows a zig-zag rather than the straight linear prose of English. The question of Hispanic Spanish is one of renovation. See Castellanos (1973).

History

Gerda Lerner argues that the key to understanding women's history is accepting that it is the history of the *majority* of humankind. Feminists writing women's history have a dual goal: to restore women to history and to restore our history to women. This writing revitalises theory because it shakes the conceptual foundations of historical study. The fundamental category of feminist historical thought is the social relationship of the sexes.

There are three ways in which feminist historians have altered our perceptions of the past. First, feminist historians redefine methods and categories – in particular the concept of periodisation. For example the Renaissance scholar Joan Kelly-Gadol constructed a new theory of social progress by noting the human costs paid by women in a period previously thought of as progressive (Kelly Gadol 1976). Nancy Cott's studies of nineteenth-century Europe and America similarly reconstructed our ideas of capitalist culture by presenting new information about the importance of the male/ female cultural dialectic of Victorianism (Cott 1977). Second, feminist historians focus on sex, along with race and class as a category of analysis, to reject platitudes about woman's nature. They substitute instead questions about the position and function of women in particular times and places. Finally, feminist historians transformed our understanding of social changes and of how, as domestic and public spheres diverged, women lost control over production, property and their own persons.

Optimistically, feminists propose that a subjective appropriation of our history will lead to a collective women's consciousness. See Mies (1983). Marcia Westkott suggests that a study of the history of women, especially if it is recorded through the *consciousness* of women themselves, will join psyche and history (Westkott, 1983).

Holism
An important term in radical feminist theory. Holism involves the rejection and abolition of dualistic divisions and the creation of nonexploitative, nonhierarchical, reciprocal relationships between parts of our bodies and between women and nature. Holism helps women regain autonomy and reject the idea of infinite progress — since the aim of work is the production of life itself. See Griffin (1978).

Homophobia
The fear of homosexuality in oneself or others. Lesbian theorists suggest that aspects of white feminism are homophobic because early 'second wave' writings referred exclusively to heterosexual feminist women. See Bulkin (1980).

Homosexuality
Although most known societies have homosexual practices, contemporary theorists (influenced by theories of Michel Foucault) now argue that the development of a distinctive homosexual *identity* is a socio-historical phenomenon which is *not* applicable to all societies and all periods of history. Homosexual identity is an ideological concept and homosexual practices may, or may not, be *themselves* sufficient or definitive constituents of a homosexual identity. See Ferguson *et al.* (1982).

Hooks, Bell
Gloria Watkins the American radical writer who in *AIN'T I A WOMAN : Black Women and Feminism* (1981) and *Feminist Theory : From Margin to Center* (1984) attacks the racism of white feminist theory, for example the endless analogies in white feminist theory between 'women' and 'blacks'. Hooks calls for a new feminist theory which would define all aspects of domination and reflect the needs and experiences of nonwhite and working-class women. See Hooks (1981, 1984).

Hormones
Feminists refute studies that base definitions of emotional differences on hormonal differences, with counter-studies which indicate that when changes in body chemistry are artificially induced,

individuals continue to behave on the basis of what they perceive are the social expectations of any given situation. See Weisstein (1970).

Horney, Karen
The American psychoanalyst who dissented from Freudian theory in the late 1930s and provided the first full critique of Freud's theory of female psychology. Known primarily for her essay 'The dread of women', Horney describes the resentment harboured by all men towards women, which expresses itself in phallocentric thinking, in the devaluation of motherhood and in a generally misogynist civilisation. See Horney (1967).

Housework
Feminist theory is the first social theory to recognise that housework is a crucial issue in gender and social relations. Feminist sociologists describe the repetitive nature of housework and argue that housework is analogous to the routines of factory work because both involve a division of labour. However, housework in addition involves women in maintaining men as well as in maintaining capitalism, and therefore housework is a key example of the sexual division of labour and women's specific oppression. See Oakley (1982).

Liberal feminism argues that housework is unjust because there is no legal recognition of the value of domestic work. Marxist feminists describe housewives as a reserve army of labour and radical feminists argue that since housework is always women's work we need to question the whole institution of marriage and heterosexuality. See Delphy (1984).

All feminist theories agree that housework is a key mode of patriarchial production. For example, Pat Mainardi argues that men refuse to share housework because they recognise its essential nature: repetition and drudgery. See Mainardi (1970).

The housework debate, then, has focused on concepts of productive and unproductive labour. Some theorists argue that housework can be analysed in its own terms as productive labour and others, for example Dalla Costa, argue that housework contributes directly to *reproductive* labour. See Dalla Costa and James (1973). Dalla Costa claims that her campaign − Wages for Housework − could solve the problem of housework. Other feminists disagree and argue that paid housework would isolate women, solidify the nuclear family and do nothing to solve the sexual division of labour. See Lopata (1971).

The issue of housework is a major part of feminism's social theory. The arguments range in a continuum from de Beauvoir's negative account in *The Second Sex* (1953) to other accounts of housework which describe housework as the site of a continuing feminine culture.

Howe, Florence

A pioneer practitioner of women's studies in America whose essays in *Women and the Power to Change* (1975) raised questions about the tensions between the academic and political goals of women's studies and its responsibility to the women's movement. Howe calls on women's studies to break the disciplines. According to Howe disciplines create a fragmented academy that is antithetical to the holistic view and problem-solving intention of women's studies. The essential characteristics of the new scholarship would be its historical perspective, critical approach and empirical practice in a women-centred education. See Howe (1975).

Hysteria

Characterised in the nineteenth century as a female disorder, feminist theorists now prove that this definition was part of the sexual politics of sickness. See Ehrenreich and English (1979).

Feminist historians explain that 'hysteria' was often a rebellious outlet for the domesticated nineteenth-century woman. For example Carroll Smith-Rosenberg suggests that hysteria was an alternative role option for middle-class women faced with conflicting expectations about their behaviour. See Smith-Rosenberg (1972).

Since Freud's definition of hysteria in psychoanalysis depends on the idea that the hysteric transfers her desire to seduce her father onto her analyst, feminist psychoanalysts are particularly concerned to redefine hysteria more positively. Hélène Cixous argues that the role of the hysteric is ambiguous since she is both heroine and victim. She is a divine spirit operating at the edge of culture as an unorganisable feminine construct. See Cixous (1981).

Iconography

Pictorial representation.

In art women are always differentiated iconographically from men. Iconographical analysis is a valuable tool of feminist art theory. Feminist art historians use it to show how heroines, for example Delilah, are compromised or distorted by traditional iconography because heroines are defined almost exclusively in erotic terms. Historians reveal how women artists, for example Artemisia Gentileschi, were able to break with a conventional iconography of female protagonists. Feminist critics also deconstruct avant-garde icons revered as *master*pieces of modernism, for example Matisse's nudes. See Broude and Garrard (1982).

First wave feminists created alternative icons of strong women, for example the image of Joan of Arc was adopted by the suffragettes. Contemporary feminist artists are developing a whole new feminist iconography of biomorphic imagery, for example Judy Chicago's *The Dinner Party* (1979) and *The Birth Project* (1985). Marina Warner has made an extensive analysis of female icons. See Warner (1981).

Identity

Feminist theories of identity have moved on from neo-Freudian psychoanalysis and current poststructuralist theory. Feminists argue that identity is not the goal but rather the point of departure of any process of self-consciousness. They suggest that women's understanding of identity is multiple and even self-contradictory. See Bulkin *et al.* (1984).

The contemporary debate about identity politics was initiated by feminist psychoanalysts who described sources of female identity other than penis envy. For example Nancy Chodorow suggests that the first task of individuation women undertake is the discovery of the ego boundaries between ourselves and our mothers. See Chodorow (1978). Feminists have gone on to argue that a rejection of the mother, and hence of a true identity, is responsible for the anti-feminism of some adult women. See Flax (1980).

Ideology

A feminist ideology is a body of ideas which describes the sexism of any particular society and describes a future society in which sexist contradictions would be eradicated. Sexist ideologies of domesticity are those most attacked by feminist theorists since these ideas depict a static and conservative image of women's societal condition. By accounting for ways in which women's social conditions evolved historically and how male defined social ideologies perpetuate women's inferiority, historians can recommend prescriptions for change. See Cott and Pleck (1979).

Marxist critics argue that the economic function of a social institution, like the family, needs to interact with an ideological function in order to produce a stable patriarchal unit. The task of sexist ideology, they argue, is to capture and preserve the institution across changes in economic production. Ideology has, then, an autonomy from economic formations. See Barrett (1980). The task of feminism is to expose the contradiction between the two.

Other definitions of ideology, for example Althusser's concept of ideology as the way we live in the world, have encouraged feminist theorists to explore psychoanalysis. Juliet Mitchell describes how this concept of ideology helped her understand the family from *within*, and therefore understand its relative autonomy in the ideological superstructure of society. See Mitchell (1971).

A consistent theme in all feminist writing about ideology is that the values and goals of women's ideal social condition must form the basis of any feminist ideology. Some feminists, however, are concerned about the *project* of theorising ideology itself. Susan Griffin argues that no matter what feminist ideology is constructed, it will always presume the idea of the Other and hence the possibility of domination. See Griffin (1982b).

Illegitimacy

The concept of a child born out of wedlock which, according to Adrienne Rich, is used by patriarchy to institutionalise motherhood in the heterosexual couple. Rich describes how behaviour which threatens institutions like the family, for example abortion or illegitimacy, is falsely defined as deviant or criminal. Rich claims that definitions of illegitimacy are ways of channelling property to the male in Western patriarchy. See Rich (1976).

Imaginary

A concept in French feminist theory which stands for female strength and identity. Luce Irigaray claims that the imaginary can transform ideology because its source is the erotic memory of the pre-oedipal mother. See Irigaray (1974a).

Imperialism
Usually the control of one State or country by another, or the economic and ideological control of Black people by white. Bell Hooks argues that this condition applies internally in America, which was colonised by white patriarchal men who institutionalised an imperialistic social order in America not just in the Third World. See Hooks (1981). Black feminists have identified ways in which a particular white Eurocentric and Western view established itself in all theory, including that of feminism. See Amos and Parmar (1984).

Incest
A sexual relationship between parent and child. Rules prohibit sexual relations in order to preserve the integrity of the family and access to women. Feminist theory argues that 'incest' extends the male sense of entitlement to women they annex. See MacKinnon (1982).

Individualism
This term in feminist theory usually stands for nineteenth-century liberalism and the Enlightenment tradition stemming from Mary Wollstonecraft's *A Vindication of the Rights of Women* (1789). In contemporary feminism individualism is associated with reformist or bourgeois positions, for example in the writings of Betty Friedan. Marilyn Frye describes a more positive concept of individualism. She argues that an individualism of interests can see the interests of each self as distinct from those of others but can also see them to be part of a contractual model of human relationships. See Frye (1983).

Inequality
A social model of female inequality has been outlined by Michelle Rosaldo. She defines inequality as a state where women are universally subordinate to men; where men are dominant due to their participation in public life and their relegation of women to the domestic sphere. The differential participation of men and women in public life gives rise not only to universal male authority over women but to a higher valuation of male over female roles. See Rosaldo and Lamphere (1974).

Integrationist
A feminist who thinks that acts of convincing, informing and

consciousness-raising within the academy and existing disciplines will transform education. Opposed to this view are the autonomists who believe in the separateness of women's studies as a study in its own right and believe that the structure of knowledge can be changed only by radical, innovative feminist scholarship. See Duelli Klein (1983).

Intelligence
The ability to deal with ideas and circumstances. Intelligence is measured by tests which are normed as Intelligence Quotients or IQ. Feminists argue that these tests are inherently biased because they are produced by members of the white male middle class and are based on the concepts of that group. Dale Spender calls 'intelligence' a convenient concept and the ultimate justification for stratification, since intelligence in patriarchy is supposed to represent an inherent and natural quality over which human beings supposedly have no control and which is used to explain inequality. See Spender (1983).

Interactionist theory
Used by many lesbian theorists to show that the development of sexual orientation and sexual identity is an ongoing life process. They argue that people have a varying capacity for sexual experiences, defined and limited by both a personally constructed and a socially constructed idea of sexuality. Interactionists argue that the development of sexual orientation is a process that emerges through interactive encounters. See Darty and Potter (1984).

Interdisciplinary
A collaboration between disciplines. The term and its uses are a source of debate among feminist theorists of women's studies. Gloria Bowles argues that interdisciplinary suggests an integration of disciplinary perspectives and she prefers the term transdisciplinary which means going beyond disciplines altogether. See Bowles and Duelli Klein (1983). Sandra Coyner rejects interdisciplinary as an approach in favour of creating a new discipline of women's studies. See Coyner (1983). Barbara Smith claims that Black women's literature is inherently interdisciplinary because you find accessible in it Black women's culture, music, politics, history and sociology. See Smith (1978).

Intersubjectivity
Marcia Westkott defines this as a dialectical relationship between the subject and object of research. Intersubjectivity allows the

researcher to compare and share her own experiences as a woman and as a researcher with those of the researched. See Westkott (1983).

Intertextuality (*intertextualité*)

A French term introduced by Julia Kristeva. She defines it in *La Révolution du language poétique* as the transposition of one or more systems of signs into another, accompanied by a new articulation of the enunciative and denotative positions. Any signifying practice is a field (in the sense of space traversed by lines of force) in which various signifying systems undergo such a transposition. Intertextuality is a common feature of women's writing. See Kristeva (1974a).

Intuition

One of the faculties that radical feminists think is women's unique source of knowledge. Through intuition women can have direct, noninferential, access to the feelings of others. The claim is problematic because there is no precise evidence that women, more than men, have innate faculties of perception. However, women, as subordinates, are likely to develop a special sensitivity to behavioural cues since intuition is indicative of the objective position of any oppressed minority. The power of intuition which involves the mental exercise of placing fragmented details is glorified and called deductive intelligence when done by members of a dominant group. When this faculty appears in women it is immediately devalued by those in power and called metaphysical. See Guillaumin (1983b).

Irenics

A neologism coined by Moira Ferguson to describe a feminine nonaggressive polemics. Irenics is a suitably feminist style which enables women to write lovingly to and about other women but also enables us to be indirectly confrontational when social constraints demand. See Ferguson (1986).

Irigaray, Luce

A French philosopher and psychoanalyst whose general enterprise in *Spéculum de l'autre femme* (1974) and *Ce sexe qui n'en est pas un* (1977) is to explore analogies between female sexuality and women's language. Irigaray articulates 'fables' about sexuality and criticises the phallocentric premisses of Freud and Lacan. Irigaray defines '*différence*' as being in the female body and in women's capacity for a decentred, multiple sexuality. She makes a direct homology between feminine sexuality and feminine language. The two female labia, Irigaray argues, contrast with the unitary penis and it is this duality which permits women uninterrupted autoeroticism. By affirming the double morphology of the genitals women can relate to otherness. The continual diffuse *'jouissance'* which results will generate a different mode of libidinal functioning for women.

Irigaray's own writing shifted from a theoretical to a more fluid language and her style is characterised by fluidity and simultaneity. Irigaray concludes that liberating women's desire will require a total re-evaluation of the existing cultural system which is founded on the exchange of women. Her strategies for dismantling phallocentric language are mimetism, disturbance and excess. Irigaray reaches for an 'other side' — a conceptual realm beyond and outside masculine phallogocentrism. See Irigaray (1974, 1977).

James, Selma

An American activist who, with Mariarosa Dalla Costa, wrote *The Power of Women and the Subversion of the Community* (1975) about the division of labour in marriage and the function and significance of housework. The book is now a classic of the women's movement and helped James begin the Wages for Housework Campaign and other radical initiatives on issues of rape and prostitution. See Dalla Costa (1975).

Janeway, Elizabeth

American critic who, in *Man's World, Woman's Place : A Study in Social Mythology* (1971) traces the origins and persistence of the notion 'woman's place is in the home'. Janeway explores the power discrepancy between the sexes and the subordination of women to men. She argues that the strength of sex role differentiation derives in part from male propaganda and is internalised by women. Janeway transformed the meaning of sex roles from a 'value free' description into a critique.

Jewish feminism

Defining Jewish feminism is difficult for feminists both because the language available to describe Jews as a racial group is inadequate and because implicit anti-Semitism is no less part of the women's movement than any other movement. Characterising Jewish feminism as a narrow version of identity politics has limitations because anti-Semitism is not only an attack on identity, nor does it only affect Jewish women. Women stand in a particular relationship to Jewish culture. Adrienne Rich points out how Jewish women suffer a double disadvantage by being both a target of biological determinism and also invisible in Jewish history. See Rich (1986).

Jewish women in the USA were active in the women's movement since its inception, though often not identified as Jews. The earliest feminist papers about Jewish identity are critiques of the patriarchal and misogynist elements of Judaism. For example articles in *Davka* magazine (1971); the creation of *Ezrat Nashim* (1971); and the *Off Our Backs* (1972) special issue on Jewish women.

The aims of Jewish feminism are to examine Jewish history and its progressive and reactionary aspects in relation to women; to distinguish between forms of oppression and the connections between racism and anti-Semitism and to develop an analysis of Jewish identity and anti-Semitism within a feminist context. See Heschel (1983). Evelyn Torton Beck addresses the lesbian dimension in *Nice Jewish Girls* (1984). Elly Bulkin argues that, for Jewish feminists, the choices both of political priorities and of strategies are influenced by communities and also by the need to transcend communities. See Bulkin *et al.* (1984).

Jouissance

A term in French theory which means a totality of enjoyment — sexual, spiritual, physical and conceptual. *Jouissance* exists outside of linguistic norms in the realm of the poetic. Julia Kristeva defines *jouissance* in a similar way to Jacques Lacan but where Lacan speaks of *'jouissance sexuelle'* and *'jouissance phallique'*, Kristeva defines sexual pleasure as *'plaisir'* and *'jouissance'* as total joy or ecstasy. See Kristeva (1980).

Michele Montrelay and Luce Irigaray both contrast a sublimated phallocentric orgasm with unmediated concentric *jouissance*. Female sexuality is a *jouissance* enveloped in its own contiguity. See Montrelay (1977) and Irigaray (1977b).

Jung, Carl Gustav

A Swiss psychiatrist who broke with Freud in 1913 to develop the theory and techniques of Analytical Psychology. Jung's concepts of myth, archetypal symbols and the collective unconscious have been utilised by feminists working in anthropology and cultural history.

Archetypes are the collective beliefs and myths of a race which are represented in dreams. Feminists use Jung's theories to account for female archetypes which can be feminist paradigms. For example the Jungian therapist Nor Hall in *The Moon and the Virgin* (1980) documents a variety of feminist symbols suggested by the archetype of the moon which include witches and mirrors.

Kelly-Gadol, Joan

American historian who contributed to the new feminist historio-graphy by reconstructing the theory of social progress. Noting the human costs paid by women (loss of social autonomy and cultural regard) in periods previously thought progressive, for example the Renaissance, Kelly-Gadol extended existing histories of the State to include gender as well as class relations. See Kelly-Gadol (1974 and ed. 1984).

Kinship

Family and inheritance relationships on which depend agreed social rights and taboos. The theory of kinship most associated with feminism is that devised by Claude Lévi-Strauss. In *The Elementary Structure of Kinship* (1949) Lévi-Strauss described a system of marriage exchange which depended on the patriarchal relationship of a son to his uncle. Underlying this exchange system is a universal taboo about incest which imposes a need for exogamous intercourse. See Lévi-Strauss (1969). The primary form of exchange was that of women in marriage. Juliet Mitchell uses this theory to argue that the systematic exchange of women is definitional of human society. See Mitchell (1971). Feminist anthropology points out that the meaning of kinship ties varies enormously, for example it is only recently that households in Western Europe have been based on ties of kinship.

Gayle Rubin argues that kinship is a widely prevailing empirical form of the sex-gender system and one based on the subordination of women. In order for this system of wife exchange to work, a norm of heterosexuality must be imposed. See Rubin (1975).

Klein, Melanie

A psychoanalyst who created a theory of childhood development, arguing that a child learns pleasure *and* aggression from its relation to the mother's breast. Klein's work is not explicitly feminist but current feminist theory claims that aspects of her work are important to feminism. Klein extended Freud's theory and practice about hysteria, neurosis and sexuality to the treatment of the depressive anxieties associated with aggression. These are anxieties which often inhibit feminists when fighting women's social subordination. See Sayers (1987).

Sayers argues that to work through paranoid and depressive anxieties enables us to gain a realistic sense of mothers, of women generally, and of ourselves as whole and independent beings. Kleinian therapy is effective for oppressed groups whose aggression is vetoed by society and who deal with that social oppression in fantasy.

Knowledge

The traditional organisation of ideas which is attacked by feminists in all disciplines. See Spender (1981). Feminist theory pays attention to women's different ideas especially the way in which feminist knowledge is constructed through the interaction of the self and the natural world. See Stanley and Wise (1983). Within feminism social knowledge and self-knowledge become mutually informing and Marcia Westkott suggests that feminist knowledge begins with an awareness of our relationship to the historical context in which we live. See Westkott (1983).

Socialist feminism characterises knowledge as a practical construct shaped by its social origins. Many feminists working in the sociology of knowledge argue that disciplines are social phenomena with male-defined objectives and male-defined environments. See Bernard (1975). Other feminists argue that the methods of sociology itself, its conceptual schemes and theories, are built up within a male social universe. See D. Smith (1974). Mary Belenky's *Women's Ways of Knowing* (1986) argues that women acquire knowledge through a different process than do men and thus, that the learning process demanded by academic institutions place women at a major disadvantage.

Radical feminism argues that knowledge does not grow in a linear way, through the accumulation of facts and the application of the hypothetico-deductive method but resembles 'an upward spiral'. Mary Daly uses the image of spiralling to describe the growth of women's knowledge and recommends that feminists spin a new web of ideas like a spiral net. See Daly (1978). In this way radical feminism has been able to create its own epistemological standards, and argues that women have sources of special knowledge, for example in Susan Griffin's concepts of nature. Radical feminism sees the world as a structure of relations in process, a reality constantly in evolution. See Hartsock (1975).

Koedt, Anne

An American radical who edited many collections of feminist writings from the women's movement. In 'myth of the vaginal orgasm' (1973) Anne Koedt demystified heterosexuality by proving that only a *clitoral* orgasm is the source of female sexual climax, and that all orgasms are extensions of sensations from this area. Penetration is unnecessary for female orgasm. The theory helped contemporary feminists to rethink the whole terrain of heterosexuality. See Koedt (1973).

Kollontai, Alexandra

The Russian socialist feminist who was Commissar for Public Welfare in the Bolshevik government of 1917. In *The Social Basis of the Women Question* (1908), *Society and Motherhood* (1916) and *Communism and the Family* (1926) Kollontai developed an equal rights theory for women. Kollontai's avocation of the importance of motherhood and child development brings her ideas about women's experience close to the American feminist Perkins Gilman. See Kollontai (1977).

Kristeva, Julia

French semiotician and psychoanalyst whose work focuses on theories of writing and subjectivity. Her theories about signification influenced much of contemporary feminist theory, although Kristeva rejects the label feminist.

Kristeva's key concepts are the 'semiotic chora' (the pre-verbal psychic/biological 'pulsations' that generate an infinite number of signifiers); the 'thetic' or 'symbolic' (a domain of meaning that identifies the subject); the 'mirror' stage (a term for a threshold between semiotic and the symbolic); and *'jouissance'* which is subversive of the symbolic domain. Kristeva claims that modern linguistics has ignored the (female) semiotic in favour of the (male) symbolic. She argues that subjects operate at once in two levels of articulation: the conscious, socialised or symbolic level, and the pre-linguistic, pre-oedipal instinctual or semiotic level. There is an inextricable link between a subject's linguistic and her psychic processes. This double process underlies all signification. Kristeva claims that these linguistic functions are inherent to all social systems (the State, the family and religion). Women's identification with the mother in the pre-oedipal or semiotic stage, which is different from men's, therefore propels them away from 'socialist realism', and leads to society's devaluation of the semiotic. See Kristeva (1974a, 1980).

Labour

A feminist theory of labour defines the goal of work as the production of life. The theory uses a different concept of time: one in which time is not segregated into labour and leisure. A third element in a feminist theory of labour is the definition of work as a direct and sensual interaction with nature, organic matter and living organisms where work retains its sense of purpose. See Mies (1983).

Labour force

The increasing number of women in the labour force has made it necessary for feminism to address the needs of wage-earning women and the redefinition of women's working lives. Feminist economists argue that the labour market is responding to changes in the family and that women's participation could lead to an erosion in the patriarchal structure of labour. See Eisenstein (1982). Feminists have been able to modify existing definitions of the labour force by addressing the needs of Third World women who do not work for wages in the subsistence economy but do have a great impact on total agricultural production.

Labour market

An example of the sexual division of labour.

There are several feminist theories about women and the labour market. Feminist scholars have produced evidence about protective legislation and women's exclusion from male-dominated trade unions as examples of the collaboration between capitalism and patriarchy. The 'dual' labour theory describes how industrial societies create two levels of work. It is the secondary level (which is technologically less advanced) which involves aspects of female employment – especially in the way it discriminates against training and creates job insecurity. This theory does not account for why *only* women should be restricted to secondary labour. In Marxist feminist theory women are characterised as a 'reserve army of labour', able to be called up into the labour force but not central to it. This theory does not address the sexual division of labour in work nor why only women have two 'labour markets' – the home and the industrial environment. See Kuhn and Wolpe (1978).

Lacan, Jacques

French psychoanalyst whose contribution to feminist theory lies in his idea that Freud's hypotheses must be interpreted symbolically; his claim that language structures the social subject; and his concept of the 'mirror-phase'. This concept replaces 'penis-envy' as a source of female identity with the idea that a subject knows itself when it perceives itself in a mirror.

But in Lacan's theory difference is foundational. The unconscious, like language, signifies by means of binary oppositions but difference in the guise of the Other controls the mind. The Other and desire are sexualised. Lacan distinguishes between desire which is masculine and *jouissance* which is feminine. *Jouissance* exists outside of linguistic norms in the realm of the poetic and therefore women might be seen as constituted outside of society. See Lacan (1966).

Language

Feminist theory takes language to be an index of patriarchal attitudes, and the sexual distribution of social roles and status. See McConnell-Ginet (1980). The relationship between language and cultural categories was an issue in the sociology of knowledge before contemporary feminism. For example Basil Bernstein relates variations in language to class, status and education codes. However, language, its uses and powers, has been of foremost concern to feminists. As early as 1946 the feminist historian Mary Beard declared that the ambiguity of the generic masculine was a fundamental social problem. Dale Spender thinks that the power of language is basic to patriarchy and Shirley Ardener argues that 'women's speech' exists because men have labelled it 'women's'. The debates about language characterise contemporary debates in social and political theory. For example Sheila Rowbotham argues that language is so part of political and ideological power that its meanings need to be changed and cannot simply be annexed. See Rowbotham (1973b).

Feminist theory first analyses the several forms taken by sexism in language. These include the male generic, terms of address, and idioms. It aims to reinvent language. Barbara Du Bois suggests that poetic prose can be one of the ways in which writers withdraw consent from a patriarchal construction of reality (Du Bois 1983). The problem is both one of concept formation within an existing male-constructed framework of thought and one of creating a language which can articulate an authentic understanding of the world. Radical feminism, understanding that language is a weapon which diminishes the range of women's thought, argues that the liberation of women is rooted in the liberation of language. Mary Daly in particular creates a feminist vocabulary. (Daly 1978).

Toril Moi claims that this Anglo-American criticism depoliticises theoretical paradigms. See Moi (1985). The issue of re-creation involves some feminists in rejecting the language of theory altogether and others in investigating women's body language. See Henley (1977). Even if staying within a definition of language which involves verbal communication, some feminists, for example Hélène Cixous, argue for an essentially feminine mode which arises from women's sexual difference. Linguists, for example Robin Lakoff, define language difference as one of semantic usage in women's 'genderlects'. All theories agree however, that some language is specifically, if not essentially, characteristic of women and that feminist theory must move beyond the examination of domination *in* language to the emancipation of women *through* language.

Law

Feminists are asking new questions about the function of law in society. They point to particular features of law which help patriarchy regulate the family and to the way in which legal rights help the male head of the household to exercise power and authority. In effect, by assuming that women should belong to a 'private' domestic sphere, men who make and interpret laws act on assumptions that make women less than full citizens. See O'Donovan (1981).

Diane Polan argues that the whole structure of law – its hierarchal organization, its adversarial format, and its underlying bias in favour of rationality, is essentially patriarchal (Polan 1982).

Leadership

From the British Women's Co-operative Guild to the American Redstockings, women's groups have doubted the value of formal leadership. Consciousness-raising groups in the early 1970s were leaderless in a deliberate desire not to repeat the sterile bureaucracy of much of left male politics. Charlotte Bunch points out that, although these groups were models of power sharing, leaderless groups manifest a feature of women's oppression – the fear of responsibility – and are often too internalised. See Bunch (1976).

More positively, feminist theory describes new ideas of feminist leadership whose special qualities, for example their educational nature, distinguish them from male leadership, which is one of political inequity between leader and constituents.

Drawing on a concept devised by Paulo Freire of 'revolutionary leadership', feminist leadership similarly involves a leader in dialogic education. Another alternative is 'horizontal leadership', which is one based on individual skill and time commitment. Feminist leadership is an active form of leadership, one of a process where leaders are stewards or carriers of experience. Its aim is to maintain the spirit of the women's movement and create spiritual bonds among women. Feminist theorists argue that women have special experiences as 'leaders' in everyday life, for example as mothers or carers. These roles are models of good leadership, for example mothers have to learn to 'let go' of power over children. The motherhood model of leadership is particularly suitable for small groups. Taking responsibility for what one does, whether in a leadership function or not, is the first step towards framing a concept of feminist ethics. See Bunch *et al.* (1976).

Left

Although a broad view of the history of feminist theory would show important connections between the left and feminism, contemporary feminism has an uneasy relationship to left-wing politics. In Britain Sheila Rowbotham and other socialist feminists argue that it is essential for feminism to organise in a more democratic and less authoritarian way than the traditional male left. When feminism contributes to the left, they argue, radical organisations are more effective and democratic. See Rowbotham (1979). In America socialist feminists have worked for an 'unhappy marriage' of Marxism and feminism feeling that only the combination of these theories can account for women's oppression, and that it would be naive to move feminist issues outside of left politics. See Eisenstein (1979). However, any analysis of the issue of pornography, for example, would need a different set of axes from those defining traditional politics.

Radical feminist theory is hostile both to the political left and to Marxist theory. Adrienne Rich claims that the word 'revolution' is tainted and is a 'dead relic' of leftism (Rich 1979b). Radical theory grew out of, and in opposition to, the male New Left, claiming that women's condition was ignored or trivialised in Marxist theory. Leah Fritz and Mary Daly, in particular, dismiss the possibility of any further connection between feminism and the political left.

Lenin, Vladimir Ilyich

Leader of the first Bolshevik government, Lenin made revolutionary changes to Russian marriage, divorce and abortion laws. His contribution to feminist theory lies in his concern for the emancipation of women and his argument that the cause of socialist construction must unite with the struggle against women's oppression. Some 'first-wave' feminists made connections between their feminism and the Russian revolutionary movement. See Rowbotham (1973a).

Lerner, Gerda
American historian.

In *The Women in American History* (1971) and subsequent texts Lerner developed a new feminist historiography which starts from the premiss that until recently women were studied and written about largely by men and that women's experience was treated as secondary. 'The key to understanding women's history is in accepting – painful though it may be – that it is the history of the *majority* of mankind' (Lerner 1978, p. 12).

In a pioneering account of the experiences of Black women in America, Lerner helped to correct historical stereotypes by revealing, in particular, Black women's access to education. See Lerner (1972).

Throughout her work Gerda Lerner describes female experiences of work, childhood, marriage and politics in an exciting analysis of female culture. See Lerner (1986).

Lesbian continuum
The best known term of radical feminism coined by Adrienne Rich in 'Compulsory heterosexuality and lesbian existence' (1980). Lesbian continuum means a range of women-identified experience embracing all forms of intensity between women, not simply the fact that a woman has had or consciously desires to have genital contact with other women (defined as 'lesbian experience'). Lesbian continuum is a political term since it incorporates the giving and receiving of practical and political support between women. Opposed to it is 'compulsory heterosexuality' which, Rich argues, perpetuates itself by rendering lesbian experience invisible.

Rich built on the deconstruction of the institution of heterosexuality made by Charlotte Bunch and others in the early 1970s, and wrote her essay as a critical response to the feminist theories of psychoanalysts like Jean Baker Miller and Nancy Chodorow. Rich argues that the institution of compulsory heterosexuality is the key mechanism underlying and perpetuating male dominance. By expanding the meaning of women-centred resistance, the idea of the lesbian continuum brings into focus a new quality of resistance, qualitatively different from previous attacks on patriarchy because it includes a sexual component. Rich defines lesbianism, as it exists under patriarchy, as women-centred politics. Lesbian continuum will be a source of power and knowledge for women outside of any particular historical movement because it releases women from false continuities. Marxist feminists argue that Rich's term artificially poses a subject outside the social. See Kaplan (1986).

Lesbianism

The condition of emotional and sexual relationships between women or between self-identified lesbians. The term comes from Lesbos — the name of the Greek island home of the sixth-century poet Sappho. Lesbianism is used as a scare term and policing mechanism by patriarchy, and feminist historians and others are annotating a fuller tradition of lesbianism in order to counter sexist stereotypes.

In *Surpassing the Love of Men* (1981) Lillian Faderman uses the term lesbianism to describe women writers and thinkers throughout Western history who had feelings of love for, emotional attachment to, or sexual attraction to, other women. Few of the writers she examines explicitly identified themselves as lesbians but Faderman argues that in any case there is a continuum between exclusive heterosexuality and exclusive homosexuality (Faderman 1981). Other theorists are also developing feminist categories which describe sexual identities more carefully. Ann Ferguson distinguishes three aspects of lesbianism: a clear term of clinical description which is often used pejoratively; a socio-political self-definition of lesbian culture and a transhistorical tradition connecting lesbian women. See Ferguson *et al.* (1982).

Broad definitions of lesbianism have come to dominate feminist revisionist scholarship with the development in the 1970s of the idea that women-to-women relationships were models of egalitarian bonding. The politics of intimate relations assumed great importance in the radical feminist community. Writers such as Charlotte Bunch, the Furies and Ti-Grace Atkinson argued that heterosexuality was the cornerstone of male supremacy, and moved into an agenda for lesbian feminism and lesbian separatism.

Lesbian feminism

A belief that women-identified women, committed together for political, sexual and economic support, provide an alternative model to male/female relations which lesbians see as oppressive. The theorists Charlotte Bunch, Ti-Grace Atkinson, Adrienne Rich and collectives such as The Furies argue that lesbian feminism involves both a sexual preference and a political choice because it rejects male definitions of women's lives. In statements like 'feminism is the theory, lesbianism is the practice' the Furies and others made lesbian feminism a primary force in a radical women's culture. Lesbian feminism attacks both the institution and the ideology of hetero-sexuality as being the centre of patriarchy. See Bunch (1975). Radicalesbians were the first lesbian feminists to suggest that the concept lesbian should be reconstructed, but theories of lesbian feminism differ in their emphasis on sexual or on political goals.

Ti-Grace Atkinson argues that women can refrain from hetero-sexual relations. Lesbians are the radicals of the feminist movement because only lesbians can think radically about social change and gender arrangements by virtue of their freedom from conventional heterosexuality. See Atkinson (1974). Mary Daly, on the other hand, argues that lesbian feminism (by which she means separatism) means choosing an erotic community of women. Radicalesbians agree that until women make a 'primal' commitment to each other which includes sexual love, they would be affirming their second-class status. See Radicalesbians (1973). Whatever political position lesbian women take on the lesbian feminist continuum their development of a woman-centred perspective created new definitions of female identity. For example Adrienne Rich argues that women are fundamentally attached to other women because women maintain an infantile connection to the mother. Expanding the definition of lesbian, Rich describes lesbian experience as the whole historical and contemporary existence of lesbians and lesbian continuum as all women-identified women. See Rich (1980). Lesbians of colour provide a valuable corrective to lesbian feminist separatism by pointing to the difficulties facing Black women who need to struggle together with Black men against racism, while also struggling with Black men about sexism. See Combahee River Collective (1981).

Lesbian nation
A term coined by Jill Johnston in her book of that name. *Lesbian Nation* is a pioneering argument for lesbian separatism. Johnston claims that all heterosexual relationships are shaped by male prerogatives and that only through identification with other women will women reclaim their 'virgin' status, that is, to be unowned. See Johnston (1974).

Liberal feminism
The theory of individual freedom for women. Liberal feminism is one of the main streams of feminist political and social theory and has the most long-term history. Mary Wollstonecraft's *A Vindication*

of the Rights of Women (1789) is the first full statement of liberal feminism. Wollstonecraft describes women as rational agents whose 'inferiority' is due primarily to inferior education. Wollstonecraft argues that this can be redressed by equality of opportunity for women. Contemporary liberal feminism shares Wollstonecraft's optimism that the roots of women's oppression lie simply in our lack of equal civil rights and educational opportunities. At the heart of liberal beliefs about sexuality is the view that one's private life should not be subject to regulation by society. Liberal feminism therefore accepts the public/private dichotomy which radical feminism attacks. Liberal feminism argues for individual fulfilment free from the strictures of highly defined sex roles. It limits itself to reformism, seeking to improve the status of women within the system but not fundamentally contesting either the system's operation or its legitimacy. Contemporary liberal feminists espouse women's rights in terms of welfare needs, universal education, and health services. For example, liberal critics of science point to unfair employment practices rather than attacking the institution as a whole. Jean Bethke Elshtain claims that liberal feminism reduces human motivation to a utilitarian calculus of self-interest. See Elshtain (1982b).

Similarly, Shulamith Firestone characterised liberal feminism as exemplified by NOW, the National Organization of Women which Firestone claims concentrates only on the more superficial symptoms of sexism. See Firestone (1970).

Zillah Eisenstein argues that liberal feminism is a radicalising force if only because mainstream feminist demands derive from liberal ideology – particularly feminist campaigns for freedom of choice and equality before the law. See Eisenstein (1982).

Liberation

The liberation of women is the chief goal of feminist theory. Contemporary women's liberation, or feminist action, is consciously revolutionary. It breaks with reformism, it is internationalist and it simultaneously attacks the State, cultural ideology and the economy. See Mitchell (1971).

Feminist liberation is inspired by liberation theology, for example Paulo Freire's belief that liberation must be rooted in the concrete experiences of oppressed groups.

From the mid 1970s feminist theory described women's liberation in terms of women's differences from men. Jo Freeman refers to this as the liberation ethic. In her view, it is not sufficient to have both women and men participate in liberation action but in addition men and women's actions themselves must change. See Freeman

(1976). For example women's liberation includes reproductive self-determination which is a category devalued in male politics. Sheila Rowbotham argues that this is the value of women's liberation, that is, the recognition that the organisation of the family oppresses women as much as the sexual division of labour and that change in both areas is inconceivable without revolution. See Rowbotham (1972). Nancy Hartsock argues that liberation must pervade all the aspects of life which were not considered politically important in the past. See Hartsock (1981). Radical feminism therefore calls on women to reject the reformism and cooption of the women's movement in order to embark on a journey to liberation. See Daly (1978).

Libertarianism

The political theory of anarchism which argues that since governments have no legitimate moral authority, social groups (like anarchists) should not imitate existing forms and practices but instead work to establish models of a utopian society. Libertarian theory is analogous to feminist theory. Both describe the educative value of small groups and ecological communities. Carol Ehrlich argues that feminist definitions of women's autonomy and our rejection of 'vanguard' forms of leadership in the women's movement are libertarian forms of the politics of daily life. See Ehrlich (1979). 'Second wave' consciousness-raising groups and Adrienne Rich's woman-centred university are examples of feminist libertarianism. See Rich (1979b).

Life history

A record of a person's life in letters, diaries and autobiography. Life histories play an important role in the production of feminist knowledge, particularly that of Third World and minority women in the West. Anthropology, history, sociology and psychology all use life histories which reveal the content of women's lives and can also provide a feminist and deeper understanding of women's culture by linking experience and consciousness. Life histories avoid universalism and can deal with the specifics of women's oppression as it relates to colonialisation, industrialisation or liberation. In this way life histories correct an androcentric historical record by linking a woman's individual history to the overall social history of a period. See Geiger (1986).

Feminist sociologists describe how life histories are action oriented because collectively they can help women understand the similarity of women's experiences. For example we become aware of the sociological and historical roots of our suffering in documenting and analysing our life histories. By making our stories public, women acknowledge that our own experiences have social origins. Life history makes women subjects of our own histories and is a method of conscientisation. See Mies (1983).

Literacy

The ability to read and write. Definitions of literacy and illiteracy are often used to discriminate against minority and Third World women. Charlotte Bunch describes a feminist politics of literacy as involving: a means of conveying ideas and information for pleasure; access to interpretations of reality in order to increase a capacity for thought; a violation of the norms of culture and perception of social alternatives in order to act politically. See Bunch and Pollack (1983).

Literary criticism

See Criticism.

Feminist literary criticism rejects traditional standards of criticism and of literary history. Feminists use literary criticism to help them deconstruct the politics of patriarchy as it is represented in language. For example Kate Millett's *Sexual Politics* (1970) analyses the ideological implications of the depiction of sexual behaviour. Carolyn Heilbrun traces a history of androgyny through Western literature in order to validate androgyny as an alternative to patriarchy (Heilbrun 1973). Mary Daly also uses literary criticism, in her synthesis of history, philosophy and radical politics, to demand from the reader a detailed attention to language.

Feminist critics have: revealed the misogyny of male writers regarded as 'great masters', for example D.H. Lawrence; created a literary history of women writers; described women's 'different' writing modes and 'different' reading strategies; and broadened the definition of literature by including genres like science fiction. Marxist feminism analyses how literature historically represents categories of gender while deconstructive critics challenge the very notion of gender categories and poststructuralists refuse the coherence of self and author altogether. See Moi (1985). Feminist literary criticism is a major challenge to the institution of 'literature'. See Humm (1986).

Literature

See Canon, Criticism.

Defining what is literature is the work of literary criticism, and feminist critics describe the relation between literature and ideology. Julia Kristeva argues that literature reveals the truth about an otherwise 'repressed, nocturnal, secret and unconscious universe' and that women need the 'potency of the imaginary'. See Kristeva (1982).

Feminist critics aim to revise the entire institution of literature. This involves changing ideas of literary value, for example the notion of *avant-garde*, changing the list of literary texts, for example by including Black or lesbian writing; and changing the methods of literary analysis, for example by including reader reception techniques.

The new, feminist, model of literature is based on women's culture and history. Myra Jehlen argues that women's literature begins to take its individual shape before it is properly literature in the anterior act by which women create their creativity. See Jehlen (1982).

Women's literature is called 'gyno-criticism' by Elaine Showalter and a 're-vision' by Adrienne Rich.

Logos

The Word, and the power to create language. Feminist myth critics claim that the Goddesses Kali and Hecate are the female originators of languages and alphabets. These feminine versions of logos enable myth critics to argue that there has always been a feminine language and a feminine theory and mode of creation. See Pagels (1979). Jacques Derrida labels Western thinking logocentric because it privileges the Logos and Hélène Cixous's theoretical project is to undo this logocentric ideology. See Moi (1985).

Lorde, Audre

Black American poet and theorist.

In 'An open letter to Mary Daly' (1984) and other essays, Lorde attacks the false universalism of much contemporary feminist theory. Lorde argues that without a women's community there can be no liberation but that such a community must not involve a shedding of our differences.

In 'Uses of the erotic' (1984) Lorde connects civilisation's fear of the associative and musical language of poetry with its fear of Black skin, of the female, of darkness, the dark Other. Lorde states that feminism can only produce a new analytical framework if it sees the experiences of women of colour as a source of wisdom not just as examples of victimisation. See Lorde (1984).

Love

Second wave feminism takes the concept of 'love' to be a key element in the way patriarchy trains women to think of eroticism only in terms of heterosexual concepts of romance. Kate Millett, Andrea Dworkin and Germaine Greer argue that the emotion of love is socially constructed and not innate. Shulamith Firestone, in *The Dialectic of Sex* (1970) goes further to claim that women are taught to develop an emotional need for men, which is called 'love' by patriarchy and that this emotion is corrupted by its power context — the sex class system.

Madness

Feminist psychoanalysis helps us understand that madness, or insanity, is defined by culture not by biology. Phyllis Chesler, in her pioneering work *Women and Madness* (1972), argues that 'madness' is a label used for people whose behaviour radically departs from what is socially prescribed. What we consider madness, she suggests, is either the acting out of the devalued female role or the total or partial rejection of one's sex role stereotype. Women's madness is an intense experience of female biological, sexual or cultural castration. Chesler argues that society expects women to have mental illness and that this is part of the definition of what and how women are. Feminism argues that sex-role stereotyping is a prescription for women's failure and, therefore, for subsequent mental illness. Women who do not conform are labelled mentally ill or deviant.

Madness is often represented in feminist writings, as in other writing, as a form of 'truthful' perception. For example Doris Lessing in particular incorporates the insights of R.D. Laing the radical psychotherapist into *The Golden Notebook* and subsequent novels.

Feminist critics argue that male writers give madness a different aesthetic function because male writers make 'madness' into a philosophy, while women writers use 'madness' to define their own lives in the conventions of the literary text. See Gilbert and Gubar (1979). Gilbert and Gubar suggest that the madwoman is a mirror image of the woman writer – a character who vividly projects an author's rebellious feelings and can subvert patriarchy in fictional form.

Mainstream

A term for the public expression of liberal feminism. In America, the National Organization of Women represents a mainstream approach to politics because it is concerned with legal and social reforms for women. Mainstreaming is the term defining an integrationist approach to feminist studies. The mainstreaming of women's studies involves the integration of women's studies into the university curriculum. This can subvert the traditional disciplines but mainstreaming can also be an obstacle to the development of women's studies in its own right. As Gloria Bowles and Renate Duelli Klein point out, why is there always 'this impetus to tell "them" rather than to develop "us"?' (Bowles and Duelli Klein 1983, p. 10).

Maitland, Sara

British writer who describes the relationship of feminism to Christianity in *A Map of the New Country* (1983). Unlike her American counterpart Mary Daly, Sara Maitland is not writing to create an alternative mythic religion for women but in order to describe feelings about spirituality from within the women's movement. See Maitland (1983).

Male dominance

The word 'male' itself represents dominance, many feminist writers argue, because it has institutional force, for example in the Constitution of the United States of America. Socialist feminists argue that male dominance is part of a system of dual or multiple systems of dominance: capitalism, patriarchy, heterosexism, racism, imperialism. These are the several mechanisms of State, political and economic power involving discrimination based on class and race which support and perpetuate male dominance.

A social ideology of male dominance depends on the idea of legitimate male power and the idea that males construct reality for women in order to confirm their own way of being and their own vision of truth. See MacKinnon (1982). Adrienne Rich selects compulsory heterosexuality as the key mechanism of male dominance and Catharine MacKinnon argues that a strategy of male hegemony is 'aperspectivity' or the power to create the world from one's point of view.

Man

The practice of using 'man' to refer to persons of both sexes is a focus of feminist concern. Feminists agree that to use 'man' (or the generic masculine) to refer to people is iniquitous, ambiguous and exclusive. See Martyna (1980).

Feminist philosophers point out that the genderisation of language plays an important, and therefore oppressive part in self-identity. See Beardsley (1977). For example Simone de Beauvoir in *The Second Sex* (1953) argues that the use of man in language shows us how woman is defined as Other in our culture.

Feminists counter the generic masculine in many ways: there are dictionaries of alternative feminist definitions. See Kramarae and Treichler (1985). Feminists advocate the use of neutral terms like Chairperson to replace Chairman, and are creating a new women's language. See Daly (1978).

Manual/mental

Feminist theory argues that this distinction controls and exploits women because women are associated with the body and men are associated with the mind. See Ortner (1974). In general the distinction rationalises not just a hierarchical division of labour but a division of labour which is sexual. Labour divisions are generic, not a specific result of industrialisation, and one of the areas into which women are segregated is the 'manual' economy of catering in work which is like housework. The distinction is most explicit in medicine which has historically created a manual/mental sexual division of labour. See Ehrenreich and English (1979).

Marcuse, Herbert

German American Marxist critic whose theories of repression and liberation greatly influenced the New Left and subsequent feminist theory. In *Eros and Civilization* (1955) Marcuse argues that, historically, civilisation embodies the reality principle carried to an extreme, which he calls the performance principle, and that this behavioural code expresses the values of a male capitalist society. Socialism will provide an antithesis and, Marcuse suggests, women express the values and behaviour required by such a future society. The liberation of women, Marcuse argues, would bring the release of otherwise repressed feminine characteristics which Marcuse calls life instincts, or Eros. These will subvert the performance principle governing patriarchal society.

Feminist critics point out that Marcuse fails to analyse the specific conditions of women's existence because he describes an idealised, abstract female essence. They argue that a patriarchal organisation of sexuality entails, not only the repression of Eros, but also the specific displacement of Eros onto women. See Ferguson *et al.* (1982).

Marginality

Sometimes called *les marginaux*, this term describes the social and material reality of many women. It is also a philosophic construct meaning the irrational and the margins.

Where Marxist writers argue that marginality is functional to capitalism, feminist theory argues that marginality is a relational concept not a reified category since what is perceived as marginal at any time depends on the position one occupies. See Moi (1985).

Political theorists draw on the work of Robert E. Park and others about the 'marginal man', a concept developed to describe migrants and ethnic minorities. For example the similarities in marginality between Blacks and women help to explain attitudinal obstacles to the advancement of women in politics. See Githens and Prestage (1975).

Sociologist Elise Boulding calls for a more positive interpretation of marginality. She argues that the marginality of women and our key leverage points in the family and the community provide hope for social transformation (Boulding 1977).

Market place
Feminist theories about the market place argue that the growth of service and retail trade sectors at the expense of the industrial sector reflects the market's response to changes in the family, as well as to changes in the relation between the State and the family. See Eisenstein, 1982.

Eisenstein argues that increases in State welfare and the secretarial service sector reflect changes in women's place within the family, for example work once done in the home has been increasingly shifted to the market and many responsibilities of the family now belong to the State. The challenge by wage-earning women to the patriarchal organisation of the market has led to the New Right's attack on women's rights.

Marriage
The institution which traditionally provides women with a social identity. Second wave feminists introduced the term Ms to enable women to avoid being labelled by marital status. Feminist theory addresses several aspects of marriage: as the site where categories of gender are reproduced; as the site of the sexual division of labour and women's subordination; and as the model for other social institutions of a sexual 'norm'.

Marxist feminism deals in the main with the sexual division of labour. Christine Delphy in *The Main Enemy* (1977) argues that marriage is a labour contract in which the husband's appropriation of unpaid labour from his wife constitutes a domestic mode of production and a patriarchal mode of exploitation. Other critics argue that this theory isolates domestic production and that it does not enable us to raise questions about historical variations. Michèle Barrett and Mary McIntosh argue that we need to distinguish between the ideology of marriage and particular historical arrangements. See Barrett and McIntosh (1982). Their argument is a useful contribution to the sociology of knowledge since it addresses how marriage is represented as a universal, or natural, event in a heterosexual relationship and in the variety of its forms.

The ideology of marriage is a major area of feminist enquiry because this ideology is embedded in the operation of other institutions like the State. For example the State institutions of social welfare and taxation operate on the false criteria that women are economically dependent on men. See Wilson (1977).

Rather than focusing on the economic aspects of marriage and household arrangements, feminist anthropologists and historians point to the way marriage is a means by which families are reproduced from one generation to the next. They suggest that what might be seen as a simple social contract is part of historical relations through the reproduction of children. See Harris (1984).

A different concept of marriage has been developed by feminists using discourse theory who argue that economic theories about labour divisions in marriage or social theories about marriage and the State need to be linked to an analysis of objectivity *within* marriage. A psychoanalytic analysis of social practices looks at how the universal use of women in marriage as exchange objects constitutes the basis of patriarchy. See Mitchell (1974).

This research has enabled feminists writing about violence in contemporary marriage to describe the patriarchal underpinning of an institution in which men can claim both domestic service *and* sexual exclusivity from women. See Dobash and Dobash (1980). Violence against women by their married partners stems from the perceived challenge to men's possession of women and the power that men have in marriage.

These issues lead radical feminists to define marriage as a form of compulsory heterosexuality whose main aim is to control women's sexuality by tying her to her husband. This, combined with men's control over women's labour in housework, makes marriage *the* central source of women's oppression under patriarchy. See Rich (1980).

Martineau, Harriet

English political economist who matched her activism about the issues of slavery and the 'Woman question' to her arguments for equal political, economic and social rights for women. In *Illustrations of Political Economy* (1832-34) and *How to Observe, Morals and Manners* (1838) Martineau gave a clear account of women's need for self determination. The works are pioneering examples of social observation methods and institutional analysis.

Marx, Karl

German philosopher and economist.

Several of Marx's theories have had a major impact on contemporary feminism. Of particular relevance is his idea, in the *German Ideology* and *Capital* (1867), that the natural division of labour in the family created the first form of ownership of one person by another. Marx understood that the enslavement of a wife and children by her husband was the first form of private property. Other theories of Marx which are relevant to feminism are his concepts of 'exchange value', 'use value' and 'surplus value'. (See Marxism.) Contemporary feminists point out that although Marx sought to abolish the alienation of labour, he does not deal with reproduction in a dialectical way. See O'Brien (1982).

Marxism

The theory and practice of revolutionary class politics. Marxism is a system of philosophical, economic and social beliefs about human nature and society. The main elements of Marxism which guide feminism are dialectical materialism and the labour theory. Catharine MacKinnon states: 'feminism stands in relation to marxism as marxism does to classical political economy: its final conclusion and ultimate critique' (MacKinnon 1982, p. 30).

Shulamith Firestone 'transubstantiates' Marxism into a new materialist theory of history based on sexuality. She agrees that the historical basis of patriarchy is 'material' but argues that this should not simply define economic conditions. The material basis of history, Firestone claims, is the physical reality of female and male biology and reproductive biology. See Firestone (1970).

One continuous element in radical feminism is a hostility to Marxism, for example the writings of Adrienne Rich and Mary Daly. Rich and Daly make a fundamental challenge to Marxism by raising issues which are trivialised in Marxist theory, for example the issues of rape and lesbianism.

Marxist-feminism

Feminist theory is crucially different from Marxist theory because feminism must focus on gender and sexuality rather than on material conditions in any ideological construction. Many feminists argue, however, that only a synthesis of Marxism and feminism, even if it is 'an unhappy marriage', can emancipate women. The aims of Marxist-feminism are: to describe the material basis of women's subjugation, and the relationship between the modes of production and women's status; and to apply theories of women and class to the role of the family.

In *Woman's Consciousness, Man's World* (1973b), Sheila Row-botham shows how the separation of work (production) from leisure (consumption) is a separation which exists for men only. The social concept of the home as a refuge from the world of work masks a sexual division of labour. It mystifies women's work in the home, obscuring the fact that domestic labour helps reproduce capitalist and patriarchal society.

American Marxist-feminists are similarly creating a unified theory about women's social inequality. For example Nancy Hartsock argues that the material basis of women's unequal existence is a constituent of women's consciousness. Only Marxist-feminism, she suggests, has a distinctive theory of the relation between the construction of woman's inner experience and her social experience. Marxist-feminism is based on a praxis which links conscious being and social causality. See Hartsock (1979). Although there are many varieties of Marxist-feminism, radical feminists argue that none of these deal with 'the woman question' on its own terms, because such theories inevitably have to incorporate a feminist analysis *within* Marxism. See MacKinnon (1982).

Masculinity

Abstract masculinity, according to Nancy Hartsock, is a mode of conceptualisation that emphasises mutually exclusive dualities. She suggests that this accounts for hierarchical dualisms in social institutions which underpin gender domination. See Hartsock (1981). Masculinity is not constructed on the basis of man's *real* identity and difference but on an *ideal* difference constituted most essentially in the cultural differentiation of Man from his Other. Nancy Chodorow describes these aspects of masculinity in Western culture. She offers a plausible psychoanalytic explanation for the male characterisation of woman as 'Other'. This occurs, Chodorow argues, because men learn to define themselves as not woman, not the mother, so that masculinity is inevitably negative identity. Chodorow claims that there could be a conscious break in the con-struction of masculinity (and femininity) if patterns of mothering changed. See Chodorow (1978).

Marxist-feminists argue that the ideology of masculinity has played a crucial role in the division of labour as it has developed historically and that definitions of masculinity (and femininity) that pervade our culture are pre-eminently constructed within the ideology of the family. Barbara Ehrenreich and Deirdre English talk of a transition from patriarchy to what they call 'masculinism'. They characterise patriarchy as a pre-capitalist social order organised around household production and 'masculinism' as the industrial capitalist system itself. Feminist theorists believe that these concepts can highlight the complex importance of gender in differentiating public and private spheres of activity. See Interrante and Lasser (1979).

A particular focus of feminist analysis is on the educational processes by which masculinity is defined and constructed. See Deem (1978). For example feminist critiques of science point to the fallacious congruence between rationality, knowledge and masculinity. Evelyn Fox Keller suggests that masculine connotes autonomy, separation, distance and particularly objectivity. Hence, she argues, masculinity in science is located in the very concepts of science and also in the way science separates subjects from objects. See Keller (1978). Currently the reappraisal of masculinity in men's studies treats masculinity as a more problematic construct. See Kimmel (1987).

Materialism

Second wave feminism expanded Marxist concepts of materialism to include sexuality together with other social divisions. In *The Dialectic of Sex* (1970) Shulamith Firestone substitutes sex for class in a dialectical analysis of biological materialism. Firestone defines the material basis of history as the physical characteristics of men and women. Juliet Mitchell in *Woman's Estate* (1971) criticised Firestone for not dealing with the historical specificity of women's condition. A materialist analysis of the oppression of women, Mitchell argues, must include actual examples of reproduction *and* production.

Other feminists draw attention to additional absences in the Marxist theory of materialism. For example 'objectification' in Marxist materialism describes the way a person is part of a work process and its products. A feminist analysis has to deal with the way women as commodity objects are sexually fetishised and how *sexual objectification* is the primary process of women's subjection. See MacKinnon (1982).

Maternal thinking

A term coined by Sara Ruddick to describe the capacities and achievements women display or recognise in the task of mothering. Making a cross-cultural analysis of maternal practice, Ruddick argues that maternal thinking connotes pacifism and the virtues of preservation, growth and acceptability learned through childcare.

Maternal thinking is available to all women, whether or not they are mothers, because it is a residual power accruing from women's capacity to bear and nurse infants. Ruddick's work enables feminism to bring a transformed concept of the maternal into the public realm. See Ruddick (1980).

Maternity
The practice of bearing children. 'Maternity' is used as a theoretical concept by feminist philosophers who link the material and biological practice of mothering to women's consciousness. See O'Brien (1983). O'Brien and others argue that women do not have to overcome alienation from others, or from the race because women's labour or 'maternity' assures our integration. This argument assumes that 'maternity' represents a form of dialectical relationship.

Matriarchy
A form of society in which mothers are leaders and operate a women's descent line. Ideologically a matriarchy assumes that the power of maternal energy and mother love is a socially cohesive force.

Evelyn Reed argues that matriarchy preceded patriarchy. Using Engels' *Origin of the Family* (1884) as her authority, Reed describes the superiority of women. Reed adopts a basically evolutionist perspective which assumes that patriarchy could only occur with the development of sedentary agriculture (from J.J. Bachofen). See Reed (1975). Helen Diner, Merlyn Stone and Elizabeth Fisher do not envisage matriarchy as the *opposite* of patriarchy but to be a system based on very different principles from those of male dominated systems. See Diner (1932).

A matriarchy is a nonalienated society in which women define the conditions of motherhood and the environment of the next generation; where childrearing creates trust; and where all relationships are modelled on the nurturant relationship between mothers and children. See Love and Shanklin (1983).

Feminists have reinterpreted archaeological evidence and the oral evidence in Greek Goddess myths to prove the existence of matriarchies. See E.G. Davis (1971). Adrienne Rich doubts the existence of periods of female *rule* but agrees with Davis about the possibility of a gynocentric period. In the worship of the Great Goddess and women-centred beliefs we encounter the female as primal power (Rich 1976).

In addition, feminists have often described utopias as matriarchies. For example Charlotte Perkins Gilman incorporated powerful visions of matriarchy into her fiction and essays.

Matrilineal
Societies in which inheritance is from the mother not the father.

Matrilineal clans existed until the ninth century in Britain. Feminist anthropologists describe many cultures, including Amerindian and African tribes, which have matrifocal marriages and a matrilineal ownership of the home. See Washbourn (1979).

Mead, Margaret

American anthropologist who found in her field work among different societies in the South Pacific that 'masculinity' and 'femininity' are culturally, not biologically, determined. In *Sex and Temperament in Three Primitive Societies* (1935) and *Male and Female* (1949) Mead argued that in many societies, characteristics we think of as typically female are assigned specifically to men and others, typically 'male', are assigned to women in arbitrary fashion. Her work set the foundation for feminist research into the cultural and social contexts of men and women's gender development.

Media

Women's Movement campaigns in Britain and America encouraged feminist theorists to question the way in which media images and representations of women are constructed within a patriarchal system of production and reproduction. See Women's Studies Group (1978).

Feminist research takes concepts from semiotics and psychoanalysis and the methods of the social sciences. It has four main aims: to make a content analysis of sexism and female stereotyping; to deconstruct the 'reality' of representation and the mechanisms which construct meanings of femininity; to describe the relationship of the media to its viewers and cultural readings; and to analyse the media as a socio-economic system in terms of women's employment. See Williamson (1978) and McRobbie and Nava (1984).

Helen Baehr describes how feminist scholarship both redirects the central questions of media studies and creates its own specialised area of study (Baehr 1981). Feminists also draw attention to the objectification of women in advertisements and pornography and the extent to which familial assumptions – that a woman's 'natural' role is that of housewife and mother – pervade the media. A body of work is also defining and creating alternative feminist media, particularly feminist film and video and film theory. See Kaplan (1983).

Medicine

Feminist critics question the content of medical knowledge, the form in which it is reproduced, and the institution of medicine. Barbara Ehrenreich and Deirdre English argue that medicine could be a strategic site for women's liberation because it is the most powerful source of sexist ideology in our culture. See Ehrenreich and English (1979). They show that, in the historic relationship between women and medicine, women have been continually denigrated by male doctors. Medicine defines sickness as part of women's general condition and treats women's health issues as irrelevant.

The sexist medical model is at its most explicit in the institutional control of women's reproduction. Medical reproductive technology and practices rely on machine metaphors, technological intervention and chemical engineering. See Petchesky (1986). Medicine fits natural processes such as childbirth, fertility control and infant care into an inappropriate biomedical model.

Feminists also draw attention to how the organisation of medical practice is built on a misogynist morality and ideology. Medicine discriminates against women entering the profession except as lowly paid workers. See Elston (1981). There are feminist health practices. The Women's Health Movement and women's clinics have developed women's own medical skills and knowledge. See Boston Women's Health Collective (1971). The feminist challenge to medical practices and beliefs has played a major part in society's more critical understanding of health care.

Memory

Given the particular forms of repression in Western culture which women experience, feminist psychoanalysis has a special interest in investigating how memory structures concepts of the self. It argues that memory preferences are gendered. For example Mary Jacobus claims that women's memory is a revision or representation of an ultimately irretrievable past – our memories of our mothers (Jacobus 1987).

Feminist historians read the memories recorded in women's diaries in order to reclaim the personal and communal histories of women. See Smith-Rosenberg, 1985. Because much of Black history comes through an oral tradition, memory plays a pivotal role in Black culture enabling Black women to be both subjects *and* sources in their own worlds. The memories of rural Black women are changing scholarship. See Darling (1987).

Many women artists are constructing an aesthetic of memory. The writer Maxine Hong Kingston describes 'reverse memory' which is a memory of the future not the past and the artist Mary Kelly made her *Post Partum Document* an archaeology of memories of family life.

A feminist politics of memory would prevent women denying aspects of female experience and would be, what Adrienne Rich calls, a feminist Re-vision.

Menstruation

Feminist myth critics describe how, in Tantric and other traditions, menstruation is associated with powers of longevity, authority and creativity. Menstrual blood represents the life of a clan and occupies a central position in matriarchal theologies. Only later did the church and early medical authorities classify menstruation as pollution. See Spretnak (1982).

Patriarchal societies describe menstrual blood as both the source of pollution and as the promise of conception, as simultaneously sacred and accursed. Taboos of exclusion and contact, especially about sexual intercourse, focus on women's contaminating potential. See Douglas (1966). These myths are the basis of current day menstrual taboos, particularly those of orthodox Jews. Feminist theory welds together the single disciplines of anthropology and psychology in its focus on the crippling psychological effect on women of patriarchy's characterisation of the female body as a polluting and dangerous object. Adrienne Rich suggests that the menstrual cycle is yet another aspect of female experience which patriarchal thinking has turned inside out and rendered sinister. See Rich (1976).

Feminist theory points to the absence of menstrual-cycle research as a prime example of science's masculine bias. The lack of attention to the topic reveals a bias both in the choice of, and definition of, problems in the health sciences. See Keller (1982). The most serious effect of women's sense of uncleanness is to deny that female power is body centred and that this can be celebrated.

Mental health

Psychologists R.D. Laing and Thomas Szasz and the historian Michel Foucault have described the way society uses definitions of mental health as a form of social control. Building on this work, feminist theory shows how these definitions take different forms for men and for women. Contemporary society operates a double standard of mental health. The 'normal' woman, according to Phyllis Chesler in *Women and Madness*, is thought to have a limited mental health because femininity is a negative quality in a society which values aggression. See Chesler (1972).

Historically women were made mentally ill by the social construction of pathology in the home and family. See Smith-Rosenberg (1972). Feminist literary critics draw attention to the relationship between definitions of mental health and portraits of women in literature. See Rigney (1978).

Sociologists show how women's mental health is damaged by sex discrimination which structures women's lives into low status jobs and isolates mothers in the home. See Brown and Harris (1978). Feminist psychoanalysis argues that because definitions of mental health derive from feelings of well-being which depend on a positive self concept, the internalisation of the female role denies women the possibility of full mental health. See Bart (1971). The medical model gives more diseases associated with depression and anxiety to women than men.

Feminist psychotherapy is now creating a new feminist mental health therapy. It mixes techniques from *Gestalt* or psychodrama in a group context, and explores specifically gendered aspects of mental structuring, for example mother–daughter relationships. See Eichenbaum and Orbach (1982).

Metaethics
The metaethics of radical feminism is the subtitle of Mary Daly's *Gyn/Ecology* (1978). She defines a feminist metaethics as a deeper 'intuitive' type of ethics than male metaethics, which Daly claims is the study of ethical theories. In contrast a feminist metaethics functions to affirm the deep dynamics of 'female be-ing'.

Metaphysical feminism
Feminist theory which believes that one woman's experience can be all women's experience. Metaphysical feminism takes an extreme woman centred perspective and encourages women to make spiritual journeys rather than political ones. See Clavir (1979).

Methodology
Shulamit Reinharz argues that feminist methodology is experiential analysis, based on a communal approach, because it has subjective, and qualitative elements. See Reinharz (1983). Few other feminists propose that feminist theory should have a single methodology. All agree, however, that feminist methodology must be *for* women, that it should be useful in improving the daily lives of a diversity of women, and that all methods must allow conscious subjectivity where women study women in an interactive process without the artificial object/subject split between researcher and researched. See Duelli Klein (1983).

Mary Daly warns of 'the tyranny of methodolatory' which hinders new discoveries. This tyranny, she claims, has been institutionalised as 'good' scholarship by the male academy (Daly, 1973). Catharine MacKinnon suggests that method makes a positive contribution to feminist theory since method organises, determines what counts as evidence and defines what is taken as verification. The task for theory, she claims, is to explore the conflicts and connections between the methods. See MacKinnon (1982). Evelyn Fox Keller adds that method and theory may constitute a natural continuum. See Keller (1982).

Midwife

Originally a wise woman or ancient priestess. Feminist accounts of midwifery both argue for the right of women to 'choose' a female midwife and document the historical and material conditions which devalue that choice. Feminist historians describe how healing was women's work until the eighteenth century and how changes in childbirth practices displaced women healers. See Ehrenreich and English (1979).

The development of obstetrics–gynaecology and a masculine medical science contributed to the elimination of midwives in America. In contemporary Britain midwives in particular have experienced a de-skilling process in which their knowledge has been downgraded. Feminist accounts of reproductive history and the growing number of women's groups and cross-generational networks encourage women to choose midwives rather than hospitalisation. See Boston Women's Health Collective (1971).

Militarism

Feminist theory identifies the sources of women's compliance with, and resistance to, militarism and the gendered nature of military values. Feminists have highlighted the masculinism of war, particularly the way in which armies locate militarism in a masculinist ideology based on sexual metaphors devaluing women and celebrating the male. See Enloe (1983). However, women's peacefulness cannot be sentimentalised as inherently anti-militarism since women are, and have been, militaristic, for example in the Israeli army. Feminist theory therefore focuses on the *prima facie* opposition between maternal and military thinking and has articulated a maternal ethics of nonviolent action. See Ruddick (1980).

Mill, John Stuart

English philosopher and social critic whose argument for women's rights in *The Subjection of Women* (1869) is a classic of English liberalism. Using the utilitarian ethic of the greatest good for the greatest number, Mill claimed that the reason women were in a state of subjection stemmed from traditional roles and men's interest in the stability of those roles. Mill does not seriously question the role of women within the family as sustainers of the domestic sphere and remains therefore within a reformist rather than a radical perspective.

Miller, Jean Baker
American psychologist who devised a 'new psychology' for women based on 'affiliation': the sense of a self acquired from the early symbiotic bond with the mother. In *Toward a New Psychology of Women* (1976) Miller argues that aspects of women's psychology now regarded as inferior, for example our emotions, would become the building blocks of a more humane culture.

Millett, Kate
American writer and activist who in *Sexual Politics* (1970) provided a broad theoretical base for the ideas of the contemporary women's movement. In this and subsequent writing Millett widened the concept of politics to refer to power structuring in general and shows how patriarchal power creates a sexist society. She argued that sexual politics grounded in misogyny results in women's oppression both institutionally and in private. Millett made a devastating and very influential analysis of the modes in which patriarchy operates – biology, sexual violence, class and education and transformed contemporary thinking about women's roles.

Minority group
A term coined by Helen Hacker in 1951. She argues that women, although the majority, display many of the psychological attributes of a minority group, for example self hatred, a tendency to denigrate other group members and an acceptance of the dominant group's stereotyping. Hacker's is the first feminist theory in contemporary sociology about gender role stratification. Hacker reveals how impossible it is to isolate women's issues within sociology in terms of orientation or numerical studies. See Hacker (1951).

Mirror
In *A Room of One's Own* Virginia Woolf describes how women act as mirrors reflecting back to men an enlarged view of masculinity rather than acting for themselves. Contemporary feminist psycho-analysis argues that this narcissistic use of woman defines her as Other.

The French psychoanalyst Lacan defines the mirror phase as the moment when a child, seeing himself in a mirror, is enabled to a unitary body image. The screen (*écran*) between the subject and the real is part of a specular structure that constitutes the subject. Luce Irigaray questioned the status of this 'identity' and describes what mirror theory omits. For example aspects of women's bodies (vaginal lips) give women more self-identity than the static spectacle of themselves (Irigaray 1977). Julia Kristeva argues that the mirror phase makes individuals detach themselves from the semiotic – the mother – which is more representative of femininity than the symbolic and specular. See Kristeva (1980).

Misogyny

Feminist psychoanalysts argue that misogyny, or hatred of women, is rooted in the infant's primitive rage towards the mother because society allocates childrearing to women. Only the full participation of men in infant care, they argue, can eradicate the deep roots of misogyny. See Dinnerstein (1976) and Chodorow (1978).

Feminist literary criticism began with an analysis of misogyny in the work of male authors. See Fetterley (1978). The analysis of psychosocial aspects of misogyny is an important part of radical feminist theory beginning with *Sexual Politics* (1970). Susan Brownmiller and Andrea Dworkin describe the links between misogyny and men's sexual violence towards women, and Susan Griffin describes the further links between these features of misogyny and militarism. Adrienne Rich has characterised misogyny as organised, institutionalised, normalised hostility and violence against women. See Rich (1986).

Mitchell, Juliet

British psychoanalyst who in *Psychoanalysis and Feminism* (1974) pioneered the feminist revision of Freudian psychoanalysis. Mitchell argued that Freudian theory, rid of its biologism by Lacan and reworked from a feminist theoretical perspective, can provide a theory of the construction of sexed subjectivity. In *Woman's Estate* (1971) and her subsequent writings, Mitchell linked radical feminism to historical materialism. The book was a blueprint for the new field of Women's Studies, pioneered by Mitchell who was the first British feminist to teach Women's Studies at London's Anti University in 1968.

MLF

The *Mouvement de Libération des Femmes* was at first a general term for French feminism and later became the publishing trademark of one feminist group Psych et Po. Founded in 1970, the MLF is a women only movement which conducted abortion, childcare and equal rights campaigns.

The MLF has moved to a more radical feminism, paying more attention to the subjective and to collectivity. For example the group now refuse to use the term *la femme* and favour *les femmes*. The movement brought together at some point all the major French feminists including Simone de Beauvoir. See Duchen (1985).

Modernisation theory

A theory which analyses the economic and cultural changes accompanying industrialisation and, at the same time, provides ideas for future social policy. The landmark feminist theories are those of Ester Boserup, June Nash and H. Safa who challenge existing modernisation theory and argue that industrialisation is more likely to exacerbate sexual subordination than to weaken it. See Boserup (1970) and Nash and Safa (1975).

These writers found that a shift from subsistence agriculture to machine-based economics, rather than liberating women, often changed women's oppression by intensifying it. The process of modernisation tends to remove women from productive labour and increase sexual stratification.

Moers, Ellen

American literary critic who in *Literary Women* (1977) wrote the first annotated guide to a female tradition in literature describing the links between women's socialisation and literary forms. Moers celebrated a woman-centred approach to the study of British and American women writers.

Moon

In myth the moon represents women's spirituality and biological strengths. Many ancient calendars are based on moon phase and menstrual cycles. Feminist anthropologists analyse moon symbols and imagery in fairy tales, in witch folklore and in psychic paradigms. See Hall (1980).

Moraga, Cherríe

American Chicana theorist and writer.

In *This Bridge Called My Back* (1981) co-edited with Gloria Anzaldúa, the first anthology of writing by women of colour, and other writings Moraga outlines a feminism which accepts the realities of race, ethnic and class differences, and develops an analysis making race and class integral with gender to explain the multiple oppressions of women of colour.

Morality

Feminists argue that moral theory is based on male experience because morality is defined as a public realm rather than as private or concrete and particular; moral theory uses terms like 'deviance' which is particularly suspect to lesbian theorists. Carol Gilligan claims that males and females also differ in forms of moral reasoning. She argues that women have a moral development distinct from, but parallel to, that of men and that moral perspectives derive from the distinctively different life experiences of each sex. See Gilligan (1982).

Gilligan's theory converges with the findings of the feminist psychoanalysts Nancy Chodorow and Jean Baker Miller that a female perception of morality is connected with responsibilities to others (from a female embeddedness in relationships), while male perceptions relate primarily to the balancing of rights. Gilligan speaks of a possible 'marriage' between male and female 'moralities' making an analogy to the androgyny school of feminist psychology. Gilligan's theory caused much debate in moral philosophy. Kathryn Pyne Addelson draws on the different technique of symbolic interactionism to argue that moral decision-making is a 'career' not a gendered development. See Addelson (1987). Virginia Held argues that women have a different morality from men because we draw on the paradigm of the mother child relationship. See Held (1987).

All feminist moral theories agree that women share a unique morality of care based on women's needs and experience.

Morgan, Robin

American writer and activist whose *Sisterhood is Powerful* (1970) is the first comprehensive collection of second wave writings. By arguing for the autonomy of the Women's Movement, Morgan helped prepare the way for its development. In *Going Too Far* (1977), which includes her angry manifesto about leaving the New Left, Morgan argues that radical feminism must go beyond previously known forms of cultural transformation.

Mother

Feminism distinguishes 'woman' from 'mother' in order to examine the psychological dynamics in our culture that absorb femininity into maternity. French theory provides helpful concepts of the mother which recognise the complicated and sometimes contradictory social categories. Julia Kristeva describes 'mother' as a maternal body which is both a site of subjugated socialised 'feminine' and is also the un-socialised 'pulsionistic' female subject with female power. (Kristeva 1974a).

Hélène Cixous argues that women's texts are metaphors of the protective mother. Both Kristeva and Cixous question the representation of the mother in the symbolic order, that is in patriarchy, and both locate the 'mother' in the semiotic as a part of women's discourse.

Motherhood

The definition and value of motherhood is a source of debate in contemporary feminism. Firestone and de Beauvoir argue that to abolish motherhood in its current form would change society and social reproduction. Other feminists argue that it is not motherhood itself which is the problem but the way that society has institutionalised motherhood. For example Charlotte Perkins Gilman's fantasy novel *Herland* (1915) depicts a world in which motherhood can be gratifying but not oppressive in a society without men.

Margaret Mead revealed that the behaviour, attitudes and feelings that different cultures attribute to, or expect from, motherhood changes with different social conditions. See Mead (1949). Sociologists point to the development in Western culture of diverse forms of family life that will have important repercussions for the institution of motherhood and economic and technological change. See Bernard (1974).

The re-examination of motherhood was a major development of the women-centred analytical work of the 1970s. Firestone's axiom that motherhood and freedom were in diametrical opposition was challenged by Adrienne Rich, Dorothy Dinnerstein and Nancy Chodorow. They claim that motherhood is a social construction, subject to cultural imperatives and changed by a decreasing birthrate, women's participation in production and the isolation of the nuclear family. Dinnerstein argues that women's monopoly of motherhood leads to human malaise. Rejecting the idea that women are suited by nature for mothering, Chodorow argues that girls want to become mothers by means of a profound process of psychological character formation which is composed of differential object-relational experiences from those of boys. Women are impelled to recreate their infantile experience by having an infant of their own.

Feminist psychoanalysis, however, dovetails with Firestone, Ortner and Rosaldo by agreeing that women's responsibility for mothering is a primary cause of the sexual division of labour and of the continued domination of women by men. For example motherhood and fatherhood are not symmetrical roles because fathers are less committed to the home. The project of French psychoanalytic theory is to dismantle this unity of the symbolic order and draw on attributes of plurality. Both French and American schools of psychoanalysis stress the particular continuity between mothers and daughters.

Liberal feminism takes the 'problem' of motherhood to be its socially constituted and sanctioned role. Socialist feminism argues that motherhood is problematic because it occurs in a context of male economic power.

Radical feminism argues that motherhood is both a source of women's special values and characteristics, the basis of a female culture, and that it is institutionalised by patriarchy into a form of women's oppression. Adrienne Rich, in *Of Woman Born* (1976), gives a complete and complex account of motherhood as an institution in patriarchy, and motherhood in history and its evolution from antiquity to the present. Rich divides the concept motherhood into two: 'experience' and 'institution'. The experience of motherhood is the potential relationship of any woman to her powers of reproduction and to children and it is the institution of motherhood which keeps that potential under male control. Once the institution is dismantled, Rich argues, motherhood would be a transforming experience for woman. All feminists agree with Rich that if the nature and status of women's ties to socially prescribed reproductive roles could change, then that freedom might be more revolutionary than any social revolution.

Multiple depth conversations

A method of feminist research created by Shulamit Reinharz. She characterises the method as involving open-ended meetings between researcher and subject, or subjects where meaning is constructed rather than information simply given, and topics in a partnership are flexibly defined and redefined. See Reinharz (1983).

Multiplicity

An important concept in French feminist theory which describes multiplicity as the base of feminine alterity. Multiplicity begins at the level of woman's anatomy, libido and *jouissance* expressed in certain styles of writing and in women's homosexuality. See Cixous (1976). On a philosophical level multiplicity means resistance to organisation, to the unicity of phallogocentrism. It challenges the values and concepts of masculine discourse from a position distanced from it. On a political level multiplicity means resistance to organisation and the hierarchy of structure and a commitment to a plurality of voice, style and structure. The concept of multiplicity is used by French feminists as a way of defining women's difference.

Music

Feminist theories of music argue that the discipline of musicology is inherently conservative because it locates women in the reproductive sphere as singers and not in the active area of composing. See Rieger (1985). Rieger suggests that the very concepts of music are built on essentially masculine cultural attributes. For example the concept of the autonomous work of art and the isolated artistic genius are masculine. In addition the syntax of music is gender stereotyped, for example in the way it uses 'dominant male' themes.

Feminist critics are retrieving a history of women's music. See Pool (1977). A feminist music aesthetic is expressed through collective women's groups and centres on women's experiences.

Muslim

Muslim women face the social contradiction that they have the opportunity to participate in productive work, while Muslim ideology reinforces the family as a patriarchal unit. The impact of capitalism has been differential for Muslim men and for Muslim women. For example women's work is longer and harder and more connected with subsistence production. The position of Muslim women is highly dialectical in that industrialisation has brought women into low paid jobs but also fostered factory and maternity laws. However, Muslim women's legal and customary status is often precarious. Where Islam is particularly patriarchal is the degree to which matters relating to women's roles are legislated by religion, especially the Quran, in terms of women's obedience to men, and in the strength of Islam as an ideological system.

Fewer women are educated in the Muslim world than in other cultures but advances have come among urbanised women. The success of women's organisations in revolutionary South Yemen suggest what can be done by governments and women's movements. Muslim women also play an important part in leftist movements in the Sudan, among the Palestinians and in Oman. Muslim feminists reinterpret traditional forms. For example Muslim women use the veil as a way of resisting the outside world while being pulled into it in order to gain a distinct identity. Another example is the way Muslim women use solidarity networks in traditional neighbourhood associations and kinship ties as a potential form of women's power. See Beck and Keddie (1978).

Muted groups

The theory which explains the discordance between what men expect women's behaviour to be and what women actually do is called the theory of muted groups. According to Shirley and Edwin Ardener every society has a dominant ideology which describes all social behaviour. That dominant ideology shapes thinking about social norms and expectations, supplies the vocabulary used by, and reflects the image of reality held by, the dominant group. Suppressed subgroups who have different views may lack the language to express their views or conceptualise their differences. According to the theory of muted groups the dominant male perception may provide a model of the world whose existence and pervasiveness impede the creation of alternative models. See Ardener (1981).

Women who are trained in academic disciplines whose theoretical models correspond to a male perception of reality may also find it difficult to discover a conceptual framework and vocabulary which expresses our own perception of reality. See Smith (1974).

Mysticism

Mary Daly argues that feminism has a long history of mysticism and that the branch of feminism most intent on reviving mystical cults – usually of Jungian inspiration – is powerful. See Daly (1983).

Myth

Little can be said with certainty about what myths, or verbal, visual and ritual expressions women have held, as opposed to the way women are represented in myth by men. But feminist critics, in particular Mary Daly, Adrienne Rich, and Cathy Davidson, think myths are keys to defining women's experience. Departing from the Graeco-Roman misogyny of male myths, Adrienne Rich and Mary Daly collect psycholinguistic evidence of women's mythical superiority and unite this with contemporary autobiography. Cathy Davidson, Annis Pratt and Marta Weigle range through native American myths, the polytheistic myths of the ancient Near East, Jewish ritual and Jungian archetypes to offer women critical structures in which we can locate our private needs. See Davidson (1980), Pratt (1982), Weigle (1982).

Myth criticism reveals how literature represents the psychological dilemmas of women in mythical figures. For example Virginia Woolf wrote about Isis iconography to reject Greek patriarchal myths. Weigle argues that in literature written by Chicana, Black and Jewish women myth enables minority women to express social hardships through metaphor or mask. The recreation of *new* myth in lesbian and science fiction novels, as Joanna Russ says, represents an uncharted territory of women's psychological and physical potential. See Russ (1973).

'Myth of the vaginal orgasm'

A pioneering essay by Anne Koedt which radically redefined contemporary thinking about women's sexuality. Koedt's essay encouraged the American and British women's movements to see connections between women's sexual oppression and women's political oppression. Koedt argued that male power is based on the myth that for women to achieve 'true' orgasm they must experience penetration by a penis. Koedt claimed that women's liberation must involve women's independent sexuality. See Koedt *et al.* (1973).

Naming

Radical feminists call the task of redescribing reality a process of 'naming'. Mary Daly argues that women have had the power of naming stolen from us and she describes ways in which women can reclaim this power through linguistic invention. See Daly (1973).

Feminist social scientists also point to the way naming is the first order of interpretation in science in the naming of the question and the naming of one's observations. The power of naming defines the *quality* and value of that which is named and denies reality to that which is not named – often women's lives and experience in our own terms. See Du Bois (1983).

Susan Griffin argues that naming can freeze women's experience and keep apart things which knew each other without names. For example she describes how hand and breast know each one to the other. See Griffin (1982b).

Narcissism

Sandra Bartky describes how the organization of contemporary heterosexuality encourages the development of feminine narcissism. Narcissism separates a woman's mind from her body and produces a duality in feminine consciousness. See Bartky (1982).

Audre Lorde replaces narcissism with the concept of 'self-love' which she describes as a way in which Black women can regain a sense of identity. See Lorde (1984b).

Nature

Since the exploitation of nature is a major feature of patriarchal capitalism, defining a feminist concept of nature is a central task for feminism. Feminists argue that a new definition of nature will provide the rationale and impetus for social or political strategies and goals. See Jaggar (1983).

Feminists share a concern about the thwarting of women's natural potential and a concern about ideas of women's nature which consign women to subordinate roles. But there are differences within feminism about political strategies and proposals. In *The Second Sex* (1953), Simone de Beauvoir claims that nature is transcended by culture and that women, partly because of biological constraints, have not been allowed to achieve transcendence. Socialist feminism defines woman's nature in terms of social values. Chief among these is the value of productive work since socialist feminism thinks that women are constituted essentially by the social relations they inhabit. To change those relationships would change woman's nature.

Radical feminists, on the other hand, argue that woman's special power lies in her closeness to nonhuman nature. This concept of nature informs the work of Susan Griffin. She claims that patriarchy fears woman's body and has created a dualism between culture and nature, intellect and emotion, spirit and nature. See Griffin (1982a). Griffin draws parallels between men's attitudes towards women and men's attitudes towards nonhuman nature. Women's closeness to nature gives women special ways of knowing and conceiving the world. (Griffin 1978).

Other feminists add that women have a reciprocal interaction with nature because our bodies are productive and creative in the same way that nature is productive and creative. As producers of new life, women are the first subsistence producers and inventors of the first, natural, productive economy. See Mies (1983).

Nature/Culture debate

This is an important issue in feminist theory inspired by Sherry Ortner's essay, 'Is female to male as nature is to culture?' and in subsequent responses to the essay. Ortner argues that women are universally considered to be secondary to men. This is because, she claims, there is a universal and symbolic identification of women with nature, while men are universally associated with culture and its products. Woman's body, Ortner suggests, being more involved than man's in 'species life', places her closer to nature. See Ortner (1974). Ortner's claims have not gone unchallenged. Nicole-Claude Mathieu argues that the sexes are a social product of social relations. We have to discover, Mathieu suggests, what women are in *each* society and in *each* discourse. See Mathieu (1978). Other feminists argue that what cultures make of sex differences is almost infinitely variable so that biology cannot determine women's roles. See Brown and Jordanova (1981).

Nonaligned feminism

A term coined by Charlotte Bunch to describe the perspective of *Quest* contributors and what she thinks should be the aim of the women's movement. Nonaligned feminism involves a genuine commitment to cross-cultural, and cross-political analysis. Bunch is careful to distinguish nonaligned feminism from liberal feminism. For example she does not advocate the airing of *any* view but only those which can contribute to the development of a strong feminist movement. See Bunch (1976b).

Nonverbal
There is a coherent body of feminist research about nonverbal sex differences in group communication. Researchers find that differences in social interaction reflect the sex role demands of conventional society. For example in mixed groups capable women fall to the level of less capable men. See Aries (1976). In research focusing on body orientation, eye contact, movement and touch, researchers show that females make more eye contact than males do, and maximise closeness. Women's nonverbal cues are consistent with sex role stereotyping. See Henley (1977).

More positively, recent studies show that women are better readers of other people's nonverbal communication (of facial expression, body language and tone of voice) than are men, and women are more easily read. See Hall (1984).

Novels
The rise of the novel and the rise of women to professional literary status are interlinked. From the beginning, women were associated with the sentimental novel both as readers and writers. Novel writing became an occupation of middle-class women because it did not require the classical training from which women were debarred. See Moers (1977).

Feminist critics of the novel look at the institutional practice of novel writing; patterns of consumption; the designation of novels as literature; the internal practices of novels as texts; and the conventions and modes of women's writing. Critics describe how literary history is based on gender-related assumptions which are masculine. For example Judith Fetterley examines how male novelists misrepresent women. See Fetterley (1978).

Women's novels are an undercurrent in the mainstream of literature. Looking at how womanhood shapes novel styles, Elaine Showalter describes four theoretical models: the biological, the linguistic, the psychoanalytic, and the cultural. The biological, she suggests, looks at metaphor in the novel as a source of female imagery; the linguistic looks at stylistic devices, for example indirection; the psychoanalytic looks at gender identity and the relations of women characters; and cultural analysis looks at women as a muted group. See Showalter (1986).

Ros Coward provides a dissenting argument. She points out that women's experience in women's novels, even if centralised, is not necessarily feminist. The question to answer, she asks, is how we relate the representative experience of women in novels to feminist politics (Coward 1980).

All feminist critics agree that gender plays a characteristic role in women's novels. Writing about developmental fiction by women, critics describe recurrent narrative structures and thematic patterns which are gendered. For example female growth is depicted as brief epiphanies, which is very different from the masculine *Bildungsroman*. See Abel (1983). Arguing that narrative tensions reveal social tensions, critics show that women's novels (in particular the feminist lesbian novel of development) can be paradigms of women's communities.

Nude

The representation of the nude women in the media and in art is of increasing concern to feminists. Feminist criticism mapped out the shifts and changes in the representation of the nude and developed a critique of cultural misogyny. Women artists were excluded from nude life classes, which debarred them from essential training just as the female nude became *the* erotic spectacle in art history. Women are objects of 'the gaze', itself a form of male voyeurism. For example in the 'classic' image of the nude the address is to a male spectator through the way that the female body is displayed for his aesthetic and erotic enjoyment. In many of the powerless nudes of the twentieth century woman is merely a universal type. See Berger (1980).

Since traditional art makes the female nude be 'nature' opposed to male culture, the first issue in feminist cultural production is to reclaim the female body and find new imagery to escape the oppressive codes of representation. There has been much interest in women artists like Frida Kahlo or Suzanne Valadon who represent the female nude as the site of different meanings from those embodied in the masculine iconographic tradition. For example Suzanne Valadon avoids timeless nudes by giving attention to individual women in relation to their female companions. See Betterton (1987).

When women artists represent the nude they are challenging fundamental assumptions about the gendered nature of creativity. For example for women to paint the male nude is to break with tradition. Since the 1960s many artists, such as Sylvia Sleigh, depict male nudes in order to question the invisible bias of art. However, a feminist form of sexual self-expression is problematic both because such expression can perpetuate the exclusive identification of women with their biology and, too, because male nudes may be placed in a feminine position but always remain dominant. See Parker and Pollock (1981).

Nurturance

The work of nurturance is both imposed on women and a source of women's special power. A feminist ethic of nurturance, using the transformative power of mother–daughter relationships is based on two principles: that the power of the nurturer must be healing and creative and that the relation should be mutual and reciprocal.

In *The Reproduction of Mothering* (1978) Nancy Chodorow explores the psychological dimensions of the fact that women nurture and men do not. She argues that the qualities for successful nurturance are embedded in female personality. Forms of nurturance can be a new way of organising society in order to transcend patriarchal dualisms. Socialist feminists argue that nurturance is a type of labour ignored by the traditional political economy. The social relations of women's nurturance account on the one hand for our oppression and on the other hand for our potential strength as bearers of a radical culture. See Ferguson *et al.* (1982).

Dolores Hayden describes the work of 'materialist feminists' who transform architecture and the environment in terms of nurturing. See Hayden (1980a).

Radical feminism argues that women must nurture themselves as well as nurture others. For example Sally Gearhart defines lesbian as a woman who seeks out her own self-nurturance. See Gearhart (1978). Susan Griffin argues that women who nurture embody feelings and eros in a world located outside of existing language. Luce Irigaray suggests that this world would support life-affirming emotions. Women will be psychologically empowered if the nurturance of children is undertaken in women's spaces like matriarchies or in a new body politics. See Trebilcot (1983).

Oakley, Ann
British sociologist whose books *Sex, Gender and Society* (1972), *Subject Women* (1982) and *Taking It Like a Woman* (1984) cover a range of issues from housework and pregnancy to autobiography. Oakley describes the conflicts involved for a feminist researcher engaging in social science research. For example her description of housework in terms of industrial labour was a radical departure in sociology.

Objectification
Sexual objectification is the primary form of the subjection of women, Catharine MacKinnon argues. It is the male epistemological stance. There is no distinction, for women, between objectification and alienation. See MacKinnon (1982).

The objectification of women in art and literature goes along with our objectification in pornography, claim feminist critics, since pornography is merely a simplified version of general objectification. Within culture, women are a generic object whose subject is the male gender. Culture is itself predicated upon the aestheticisation and objectification of women. See Kappeler (1986).

Women have a double objectification in pornography where we are the objects of men's action in scenarios and the object of representation with no correspondence to, or reference to, any real objects. MacKinnon argues that this process is hard to refute empirically because it acts as a barrier to consciousness. When women *experience* objectification we can evolve feminist methods which in turn can overthrow the distinction between subjectivity and objectivity. MacKinnon thinks that sexual objectification has its own periods, forms and technology but that it might, potentially, have its own revolutions.

Objectivity
The apparently value-free or neutral detachment of a researcher from a subject. It is normally polarised to subjectivity. It is a contentious concept in feminist research. Many feminists argue that objectivity

is the method of traditional disciplines because they all deny the personal experiences and emotions of women. The quest for objectivity and the tendency towards isolation are now part of a masculine professionalisation because the rhetoric of objectivity has influenced concepts of professionalisation and academic style. See Furner (1975). Others argue that since no research can be objective, feminists can use the *appearance* of objectivity as a powerful tool for changing public opinion. For example a good research method can be objective while the researcher can still subjectively identify with her topic. See Jayaratne (1983).

The most thoroughgoing critique of objectivity has been made by feminist critics in science. They argue that the need for objectivity, which is the need to dominate, has shaped the form of scientific research and is part of scientific culture. The association of science with objectivity, Evelyn Fox Keller argues, is based on its association with maleness. She defines the separation of subject and object and the objectification of nature as a masculine mode because part of the way boys acquire their gender identity is by objectifying their mothers. Keller attacks the arguments which assert an eternal opposition between (male) objectivity and (female) subjectivity as being nihilistic. She claims that if the mythological connection between (male) gender and science is dissolved, this will benefit both the practice of science and social attitudes toward maleness and femaleness. See Keller (1982). Chodorow, Dinnerstein and Fox Keller echo male writers of the 1960s like Marcuse who similarly questioned the apotheosis of scientific objectivity, but what their feminist perspectives contribute is the realisation that objectivity is linked to patriarchy not just to capitalism.

Object relations theory

A crucial paradigm of object relations theory is the primary attachment of infants and mothers. This paradigm, with its heavy stress on the value of the maternal, is attractive to feminist theory. Feminist psychoanalysis uses object relations theory to help it develop a causal account of gender difference. Gender differences originate in infantile developmental processes. Male and female infants have different struggles to separate from the mother. As a result men become objectifying personalities and women become relational because women are closer to their mothers. Nancy Chodorow describes how our personality develops in terms of both innate drives and relations with other objects. Evelyn Fox Keller adds that one result of gender difference is the entrenchment of an objectivist ideology and a corresponding devaluation of female subjectivity. See Chodorow (1978) and Fox Keller (1982).

Although critical of some *principles* of Freudian analysis, feminist psychoanalysis now uses object relations theory in relation to Freudian theory to encourage women clients to better express their emotional demands. See Eichenbaum and Orbach (1982).

O'Brien, Mary

North American philosopher whose overview of feminism and political theory in *The Politics of Reproduction* (1983) is the first thorough analysis of the politics, conditions and status of biological reproduction.

Ontology

A description of the nature of existence. A feminist ontology has at its core a conception of a self–other *relation* that is significantly different from the self–other opposition in traditional Western thought. A feminist ontology is a society organised around the practice of mutual realisation whose paradigms come from mother–child relations and the practice of mothering and family living.

Radical feminism, for example in the writings of Adrienne Rich, Sara Ruddick and Carol Gilligan, claims that ontology and epistemology imply each other. A radical feminist ontology is one where everything is connected to everything else. See Whitbeck (1983). Nancy Hartsock claims that women's relationally defined existence, experience of boundary challenges and activity of transforming both physical objects and human beings would result in a world-view in which dichotomies would be foreign. See Hartsock (1981).

It is the standpoint of women which generates an ontology of relations and of continual process.

Oppression

Women's oppression is the experience of sexism as a system of domination. Christine Delphy makes the point that the use of the term oppression is crucial to feminist theory because it places feminist struggle in a radical political framework. See Delphy (1980).

Contemporary feminists are united in opposition to women's oppression, but differ not only in their views of how to combat that oppression but also in their ideas of what constitutes women's oppression in contemporary society. Liberal feminists believe that women are oppressed because we suffer discrimination; Marxists believe that women are oppressed in production; while socialist feminists characterise women's oppression in the home as similar to the oppressive experience of wage labour. Distinctions between the so-called public and private spheres obscure the fact that the subordination of women is part of the foundation of society. The apparent universality of women's oppression has encouraged radical feminism to conclude that this is *the* primary or fundamental form of domination. As Ti-Grace Atkinson pointed out, the oppression of women has not changed significantly over time or place. Susan Griffin, Andrea Dworkin, Susan Brownmiller, Robin Morgan and Shulamith Firestone all agree that women's oppression is primarily due to a universal male control of women's bodies and sexuality. Firestone's distinctive, biologically-based theory, influenced by Marxism, attempts to provide an account of women's oppression that is both historical and materialist. Firestone argues that biological imperatives are overlaid by social institutions. For example sexual and child rearing practices reinforce male dominance. (Firestone 1970).

Radical feminism argues that since only patriarchy defines women by their sexuality, women's oppression must be located in the institutional practices of sexuality. For example motherhood and rape reinforce the innate and unchanging oppression of women by men. See Koedt (1973). In other words, where idealist definitions of women's oppression involved the idea that patriarchy was an ideology negotiated through interactions, feminists now think women's oppression is derived from phallocentrism. See Stanley and Wise (1983).

Adrienne Rich argues that when women both take oppression as an object of understanding, (that is, reflect on its history) and feel oppression in a deeply personal way, we can assert ourselves against it. See Rich (1976).

Organisation

Feminist forms of organisation make a radical contribution to contemporary politics. Rita Mae Brown claims that women-identified collectives are nothing less than the next step towards a women's revolution. See Brown (1976).

Socialist feminists suggest that women's organisations help us restructure how we come to know ourselves and others. Feminist politics must reach those institutions which most forcefully bear upon sexuality – the family and community. To restructure personal relations and peer relations feminism needs to transform the social organisation of work, property and power. See Kelly-Gadol (1979).

Internal organisation is an important political issue for feminism. Nancy Hartsock describes how the internal organisation of women's activities must grow out of the tensions between using our organisations as instruments for taking and transforming power and using our organisations as models (Hartsock 1979).

Ann Foreman sums up the feminist approach to organisation by arguing that only separatist organisations can prevent the traditional exclusion of women in both its crude and more sophisticated forms (Foreman 1977).

Orgasm

Feminist theory's major contribution to contemporary sexual politics is to demolish the Freudian theory of orgasm and to describe women's sexual potential. Where Freud believed in the primacy of a vaginal orgasm, Anne Koedt in 'The myth of the vaginal orgasm' argues that women's orgasms are clitoral. The essay demonstrates how men control women by means of control over the sex act (Koedt 1973). This control, Koedt argues, depends on the myth that women need penetration by a penis to achieve orgasm. Koedt argued that psychoanalytic literature failed to describe women's greater orgasmic capacity. Mary Jane Sherfey and other feminists built on Koedt's work to describe women's multiple orgasmic potential and the possibility of a biologically-based, inordinate sexual drive in women. Sherfey suggests that this drive could be one source of man's fear of female sexuality (Sherfey 1976).

Radical feminists have developed a theory of sexuality which describes a great range of women's pleasure. For example Adrienne Rich describes how women experience orgasmic sensations while suckling and while giving birth (Rich 1976).

Origins

The search for feminist origins, for example in prehistory matriarchies, is a constant theme in feminist anthropology and myth criticism. Elaine Morgan and Elizabeth Gould Davis argue that matriarchies precede patriarchies in a relation of linear causality. Rayna Reiter, on the other hand, believes that the aim of feminist scholarship should be to look for evidence of the flexibility of gender roles and their variability in different contexts. She believes in critical junctures in which gender relations changed quantitatively. See Reiter (1975).

Ortner, Sherry

American anthropologist whose essay 'Is female to male as nature is to culture' made an important contribution to feminist theory. The essay contributed to the debate about definitions of nature and universality in relation to women's condition. In the essay Ortner argues that women's devaluation grows out of the (male) association of women with nature since nature is seen as inferior to culture (the masculine area), which in turn controls and transforms the natural environment. Ortner based her argument on the observation that every society recognises a distinction between 'culture' and 'nature'. See Ortner (1974).

Other, The

A crucial concept developed by Simone de Beauvoir in *The Second Sex* (1953) to explain how, in patriarchal culture, woman is set up as the negative, the inessential, the abnormal to the male. Women are Other because they are defined by men as inferior. De Beauvoir adopted a notion from Sartre about the basic conflictual nature of human relations, arguing that woman as Other was a metaphysical idea, a myth on which men had built society. The concept is pervasive, de Beauvoir reveals, because woman accepts her Otherness, her inferiority. In her later writings de Beauvoir expressed second thoughts about her formulation of this theme but not about her articulation of feminism in terms of existentialism.

In French theory the concept has two meanings: 'Other' as in relation to a speaking subject and 'Otherness' as *outside* the conceptual system. Lacan, for example, describes the unconscious of the subject as the discourse of the Other. By being a conscious 'Other', woman affirms man in his manhood. See Lacan (1966). The feminist critics Hélène Cixous and Luce Irigaray argue that Otherness, if defined as the feminine, opens up new possibilities for women because by *celebrating* difference women achieve immanence.

Outsiders Society

Virginia Woolf invented the Outsiders Society in *Three Guineas* (1938) to describe feminist separatism. Features of her organisation resemble many second wave feminist groups. For example the Outsiders Society celebrates the private, is nonhierarchic and promotes women's education, peace, freedom and equality. A very close analogy can be made between Virginia Woolf's society and Adrienne Rich's plan for a woman-centred university. See Woolf (1938) and Rich (1979b).

Pacifism

There are several concepts of nonviolence and ideas about the relation of militarism and gender in contemporary feminism. For example feminism both campaigns for a demilitarised world and argues that military practices depend on degraded definitions of womanhood – definitions based on women's second-class citizenship and sexual exploitation.

Cynthia Enloe shows how a gender analysis can expose the contradictions of militarism, for example by revealing the misogyny of military training and the exportation of that misogyny to the Third World (Enloe 1983). Other radical theorists, notably Sara Ruddick and Jean Elshtain, argue that women are peaceful because women are relational nurturers.

Radical feminism claims that women are innately more peaceful than, and thus morally superior to, men. It draws support for this view from a matriarchal past. Virginia Woolf's *Three Guineas* (1938) is one early example of radical feminism. Sara Ruddick's theory of pacifism is based on the concept of 'preservative love', and Jean Elshtain borrows elements of Ruddick's work to construct a conservative feminist pacifism that might encourage mothers to fight militarism. This concentration on the maternal is reflected in the anti-militaristic practice of feminist groups like Greenham women and activists like Helen Caldicott who make extensive use of maternal imagery in their campaigns. See Ruddick (1984).

Whether or not individual feminists believe in an *innately* pacifist woman, in general feminist theory argues that social and political priorities must be restructured so that pacifism can serve human needs on a global scale.

Paradigm

A term for a scientific perspective coined by Thomas Kuhn in *The Structure of Scientific Revolutions* (1962). Paradigms are problem solving 'exemplars' shared by a scientific community. Scientific revolutions, according to Kuhn, involve shifts in paradigms.

Much of the literature about feminist scholarship which assumes an isomorphism of feminist studies and traditional disciplines is couched in terms of paradigm shifts. Feminist thinking is not discipline based but cuts across psychology, sociology or economics and integrates them within the framework or paradigm of the feminist writer. For example Ruth Hubbard suggests that what we perceive or see as relevant when constructing theories depends to a great extent on our histories, roles and expectations, or paradigms. See Hubbard (1983).

The goal of radical feminist analysis is to change consciousness through paradigm shifts which redescribe reality. The use of paradigms cannot answer all the needs of feminist scholarship because differences in feminist theory are not analogous to the paradigms of Kuhnian science. For example by emphasising how paradigms set *limits* for groups of scientists, Kuhn uses a masculine cognitive discourse. Some feminist writers argue that feminist theories cannot be reduced to single positions, or competitive conceptual frameworks, and therefore are not amenable to paradigm shifts. See Strathern (1987).

Paranoia

A term used by radical feminists to describe how women feel after they become conscious of sexism. Sandra Bartky argues that this consciousness leads to inner confusion (paranoia) about how to interpret one's own and other behaviour. She distinguishes between valid and invalid paranoia in terms of whether one is justified in reading people's behaviour differently. Valid paranoia, she suggests, is based on a notion of 'truth', that one can make accurate perceptions of social reality in a phenomenological account of personal transformation. See Bartky (1978). Mary Daly adds that paranoia is an appropriate term for the kind of feminist thinking required by a feminist revolution. See Daly (1978).

Parthenogenesis

The theory that women can reproduce without fertilisation from a male. Parthenogenesis is an important idea in radical feminist thinking about sexuality and reproduction and is a continuing theme in women's science fiction and women's utopias, for example Charlotte Perkins Gilman's *Herland* (1915). Jill Johnston argues that parthenogenesis is central to a feminist eros. Parthenogenesis implies autonomy and individuality within a community of equals. Johnston claims that the order of the day for all women is *psychic* parthenogenesis. See Johnston (1974).

Passionate scholarship

A term coined by Barbara Du Bois to describe feminist theory. It is a form of our science-making rooted in, animated by, and expressive of our values, empowered by community. Passionate scholarship, Du Bois claims, can integrate subjectivity with objectivity, substance with process, passion with responsibility and the knower with the known. See Du Bois (1983).

Paternity

The concept of fatherhood and descent by the male line on which patriarchy depends. Feminist theory argues that the process of paternal reproduction (or the lack of it) is interdependent with a male historical praxis. Paternity is not, like maternity, an *experienced* relation to the natural world but an idea dependent on cause and effect. Mary O'Brien suggests that it is paternal uncertainty which forces men to institutionalise marriage and create a private realm. See O'Brien (1982).

Men have to create social substitutes for their own lack of a biological continuity.

Patriarchy

A system of male authority which oppresses women through its social, political and economic institutions. In any of the historical forms that patriarchal society takes, whether it is feudal, capitalist or socialist, a sex-gender system and a system of economic discrimination operate simultaneously. Patriarchy has power from men's greater access to, and mediation of, the resources and rewards of authority structures inside and outside the home.

The concept 'patriarchy' is crucial to contemporary feminism because feminism needed a term by which the totality of oppressive and exploitative relations which affect women could be expressed. Over and above this particular characterisation, each feminist theory finds that a different feature of patriarchy defines women's subordination. The two ends of the feminist continuum might be represented on the one hand by Gayle Rubin who argues that if we use the term sex-gender system patriarchy would be only one form, a male dominant one, of a sex-gender system. See Rubin (1975). The other approach is that of Kate Millett or Shulamith Firestone. Millett argues that patriarchy is analytically independent of capitalist or other modes of production and Firestone defines patriarchy in terms of male control of women's reproduction.

Socialist or Marxist feminists prefer to locate patriarchy in a materialist context. They argue that the capitalist mode of production is structured by a patriarchal sexual division of labour.

Capitalist class relations and the sexual division of labour are mutually self-enforcing. For example Heidi Hartmann defines patriarchy as a set of social relations with a material base operating on a system of male hierarchical relations and male solidarity. She denies that patriarchy is universal and unchanging and claims that its intensity changes over time. See Hartmann (1976). Zillah Eisenstein suggests that an erosion in patriarchy begins to occur with structural changes in the market place and changes in wage structures. Such conflicts between capitalism and patriarchy, she claims, will undermine liberalism and the Welfare State. See Eisenstein (1982). Still within this materialist perspective, Ann Ferguson argues, more positively, that the weakening of the patriarchal family during capitalism created the material conditions for the growth of lesbianism. See Ferguson *et al.* (1982). Ferguson builds on the economic theories of Mirra Komarovsky who describes the distinction in economic theory between masculine privilege (sanctioned advantage) and patriarchal authority (sanctioned domination) in different segments of the class structure. See Komarovsky (1964).

Radical feminism, on the other hand, equates patriarchy with male domination. It is a system of social relations in which the class 'men' have power over the class 'women' because women are sexually devalued. Radical feminism is sometimes attacked as being ahistorical because it argues that patriarchy cannot be periodised like the Marxist modes of production. For example Mary Daly argues that patriarchy is itself the prevailing religion of the entire planet. Radical feminism relies on feminist psychoanalysis to provide explanations for this construction of patriarchy. The psychoanalyst Dorothy Dinnerstein claims that patriarchy, or women's exclusion from history, stems from the gender formation of males and females and the double standard that this entails. Patriarchy, in other words, unites psychic and property relations. According to radical feminists patriarchy is characterised by divisions and dualisms. For this reason they claim that hierarchy is built into the fundamental ontology of patriarchy. Robin Morgan argues that the either/or dichotomy is inherently and classically part of patriarchy. See Morgan (1977). In contrast to patriarchy, radical feminism conceives of the world as an organic whole. See Griffin (1978).

Some feminist theory argues against describing patriarchy as 'universal'. For example Sheila Rowbotham expresses concern about the ahistorical character of the concept. See Rowbotham (1983). Feminist anthropologists, for example Michelle Rosaldo, refuse to abstract patriarchy from the specific social practices through which men dominate women. Feminist theory describes many different ways of resisting patriarchy which include socialist feminism's attack on the sexual division of labour, Adrienne Rich's replacement of patriarchy with a lesbian continuum and Mary Daly's symbolic constructions and new language.

Peace

A feminist theory of peace is the basis of women's environmental campaigns about reproduction, about nuclear war or power, and about the aggressive misuse of the natural environment through drugs or pesticides. Sometimes known as New Framework Scholarship or New Social Order Perspective, peace theory argues that the technology of war and the technology of social exploitation are equally destructive. See Capra and Spretnak (1984).

Feminist theory consistently argues that the main issues in disarmament are not only technical or political but also social and psychological. Common to all feminist peace theories is a focus on women's specific role in reproduction politics. For example feminists wish to replace society's technological conquest of nature with symbols and language which can procreate life. See Griffin (1978). Women at Greenham and other peace camps identify peace with mothering. See Ruddick (1984). Some socialist feminists are concerned about an ahistorical identification of women with peace. See Barrett and McIntosh (1982). Others argue that only feminism can utilise the values and symbols of women's reproductive rights and experiences to provide an alternative to a nuclear society. Feminist theory, by examining the similarities between violence at interpersonal, interracial and international levels, shows that the use of violence is rooted in a masculinist ideology which defines violence as active and daring. A feminist ideology of peace replaces violence with empowerment through consciousness-raising. See Elliott and Walden (1984).

Penis envy

Freud's theory that a girl's biological lack of a penis leads her to penis envy and to her subsequent need for children as penis substitutes. Feminist theory argues that females envy male *social* status and freedom not male biology. For example de Beauvoir in *The Second Sex* (1953) describes penis envy as representing women's resentment of male privilege.

Kate Millett claims that Freud devised his theory of penis envy in order to stigmatise women who tried to escape socially correct feminine behaviour by shifting their daring to a biologically impossible state. See Millett (1970). Feminist psychoanalysis rejected Freud's idea that girls turn to their fathers from penis envy.

For example Nancy Chodorow suggests that girls only turn to fathers because girls are unable to have the *total* love of a mother – the primary attachment. See Chodorow (1978).

Periodisation

A framework of time used by historians. Joan Kelly-Gadol, in an influential article, demonstrated how periodisation takes male experience to be a norm for humanity. The traditional markers for conventional periodisation, she reveals, are wars, political events and transitions in rulers, which are only changes in men's status and do not represent women's moments. See Kelly-Gadol (1976).

Personal is political, The

A phrase first coined by Carol Hanisch, and published in *Notes from the Second Year* (1970), which became the main slogan of second wave feminism. See Hanisch (1971). Radical feminism used the slogan to argue that distinctions between the personal and the public realms are fallacious. Males dominate women in the public sphere in the same way they dominate women in the home. In addition, radical feminism argues that women's personal experience, revealed in consciousness-raising groups, could provide the inspiration and basis for a new politics.

'The personal is political' stresses the psychological basis of patriarchal oppression. Catharine MacKinnon argues that the phrase makes a direct relation between sociality and subjectivity so that to know the politics of women's situation is to know women's personal lives. See MacKinnon (1982).

Personality

There are few agreed definitions of personality (or individuality); neither about what are personality's appropriate constituent parts nor by what methodology personality should be studied. Some writers take personality to be a collection of general psychological processes (the Id, Ego, Superego of Freud); others define it as traits or attitudes (Allport). Since aspects of personality are used by sociologists to explain sexual differences in behaviour, feminist focus on the deficiencies of, and disagreements about, conceptions of 'masculinity' and 'femininity'.

Margaret Mead questioned the concept of universals in personality development. By comparing adolescence in different societies Mead concluded that it was the socialisation of human development that shaped personality rather than biologically-determined universals. Mead proved that the traits 'masculine' and 'feminine' were culturally determined, not inherent in sexual difference. See Mead

(1935). Juliet Mitchell awakened interest in Freudian theory and in how his descriptions of personality could be regarded as accounts of his own culture rather than empirical descriptions of personality attributes. See Mitchell (1974). Political theorists connect the development of a 'feminine' personality with a patriarchal society that devalues women. Jane Flax argues that only a radical transformation of society can bring about changes in the family relationships that stereotype the personalities of women. See Flax (1980).

Phallocentric

A term in feminist theory used to describe the way society regards the phallus or penis as a symbol of power, and believes that attributes of masculinity are the norm for cultural definitions. The phallocentric fallacy in disciplines is the assumption that 'person' stands for male and therefore that women's experience has made no contribution to disciplinary methods or content. This perspective (sometimes known as androcentric) makes women unknowable. See Du Bois (1983). Feminists argue that phallocentricism is a source of women's oppression in education. See Stanley and Wise (1983). Feminist literary critics also draw attention to how phallocentrism in literature establishes the idea that artistic creativity is a masculine quality. See Gilbert and Gubar (1979).

Phallogocentrism

A concept devised by Jacques Derrida to describe the meeting of phallocentrism with logocentrism. Phallogocentrism is how patriarchy models its thought and language. Because phallogocentrism is the name of the everyday discursive world, French feminists are determined to replace this ideology with an alternative women's language, or *écriture féminine*. The writings of Hélène Cixous and Luce Irigaray, in particular, contain new forms of expression using attributes of female sexuality (of *jouissance* and multiple pleasure) to replace phallocentric (male) pleasure which is singular (the phallus). See Cixous (1981) and Irigaray (1977b).

Phenomenology

The analysis of consciousness which is an important part of feminist research. In feminist analysis 'consciousness' includes both the consciousness of the observer as well as that of the observed. Phenomenological researchers try to use first-hand, immediate and intimate contact with their subjects, through reflective analysis, drawing on their own experiences (for example their feelings or fantasies) as well as on observations of what women say and do. In this way the subjective relates to the objective. See Reinharz (1983).

One technique of phenomenology is epoché. This is a term for the way phenomenologists attempt to suspend preconceptions about the people they are about to study in order to enter into a more subjective relationship with them.

Philosophy

Feminist philosophers argue that the fundamental categories of Western philosophy, the same categories that define the basic problematics of Western epistemology and political theory, stem from a masculine preoccupation with separation and domination. See Hartsock (1975).

Jane Flax suggests that the apparently insoluble dilemmas within philosophy reflect distorted or frozen social relations. She argues that a feminist philosophy, by focusing on social relations, can analyse the influence of patriarchy on both the content and process of thought (Flax 1983).

Feminists are making connections between feminist thinking and morality. They argue that philosophy's morality of rights gives inadequate explanations of the moral issues that concern women, particularly those of pregnancy and abortion. Carol Gilligan argues that the basic categories of Western moral philosophy about rights, categories such as rationality, autonomy and justice, are drawn from and reflect the moral experience of men, rather than the experience of women. Gilligan defines a feminist morality as one of care. See Gilligan (1982).

Adrienne Rich characterises the major dualism of Western philosophy as the 'mind-body' split and she argues that this split is a product of a masculine objectification of women. In male culture women are subjected to artificial dualisms, for example the alienation of consciousness from physical reality. See Rich (1976).

Feminists argue that, because dualistic thinking is so fundamental to political philosophy, only by merging the public and private worlds in a new feminist philosophy can progress be made.

Photography

Feminists writing about photography use feminist theory to demystify photographic practices. Feminist critics and photographers have used theories of signification to analyse how media photographs position women as erotic or domestic objects in networks of family and gender divisions. By rethinking the nature and role of photography feminists hope to eliminate the practice of women being presented as objects for men, for example in pornography. See Holland *et al.* (1986).

Addressing the question of the medium of photography itself, critics and practitioners are reinterpreting and using photography for feminism. The feminist movement has created new distribution networks, feminist journals enthusiastic about photography (*Spare Rib*) and contributed to a resurgence of interest in photography as an art form. Feminist photographers have created a new tradition of studio portraiture (Jo Spence). They have demystified militarism in a new iconography of feminism (for example Raissa Page's Greenham photographs); and they have created a new form of documentary based on empathy between the photographer and her subjects (for example the Hackney Flashers). See Williams, 1986. Feminist photographers use new photographic techniques in order to disrupt and re-use traditional imagery. By mixing graphics, advertisements, high art and cinema, feminist photography and theory has subverted media stereotypes and visually reframed women's experience. For example Jo Spence and Rosy Martin developed the technique of photo therapy (which deals with taboos of breast cancer and family trauma) in order to overcome the notion of women as sexual spectacle. See Spence (1987).

Feminist photographic theory, by mixing practice and analysis, private and public, is, in itself, a medium of sexual politics.

Pizan, Christine de

A French writer who, in *The Book of the City of Ladies* (1404) and *The Treasure of the City of Ladies* (1405), wrote the first accounts of feminist theory in the West. Pizan rebuffed misogyny with the revolutionary idea that received wisdom about women stemmed from particular psychosexual experiences which were masculine. Pizan turned Boccaccio's *Tales* into a compelling case for the female origins of culture and civilisation. The historian Joan Kelly-Gadol calls Pizan the advocate of women. See Pizan (1983).

Pleasure

Descriptions of pleasure are an important part of feminist theory because the *meaning* of pleasure is a site of contradictions bisected by class, race and sexual preference. The juxtaposition of pleasure and danger engaged the attention of feminist theorists and activists in both the nineteenth and the twentieth centuries, for example in prostitution campaigns and work on family violence. See Du Bois and Gordon (1984).

Radical feminism argues that women need the positive possibilities of pleasure – in explorations of the body, sensuality, human connection and the infantile and non-rational. See Griffin (1978). Lesbian theorists argue that we cannot create a body of knowledge that is true to women's lives if sexual pleasure cannot be spoken about safely and completely. See Webster (1984).

French feminism describes a geography of pleasure that is diversified and multiple in its differences. For example Luce Irigaray claims that women experience pleasure almost everywhere in a more complex and subtle way than is imagined (Irigaray 1977b).

Black feminism describes new languages of pleasure because, as Ntozake Shange suggests, to 'take pleasure in ourselves is subversive' (Shange 1987, p. 178). A feminist theory of pleasure requires women to make the political decision to allow ourselves the freedom to feel.

Poetry
The aim of feminist poetry is what Adrienne Rich calls 'the dream of a common language'. Women poets, from Aphra Benn onwards, have always tried to subvert received theories of poetry. Feminist critics describe the way women poets, for example Robin Morgan, can use and revise myths and fairy-tales to connect subjectivity and art. They can make a revisionist use of gendered imagery to assert intimacy against fixed concepts of the poetic subject, for example the poetry of Ann Sexton. See Ostriker (1986). Janet Todd claims that some contemporary critics erroneously find subversion in early writing. See Todd (1988).

There are several tasks in current feminist poetry theory. First, critics are writing about the history of women poets to create an alternative women's tradition. This focuses on gynocentric writing, for example Sylvia Plath's 'Three voices', and what Mary Daly terms a 'ludic celebration'. See Gilbert and Gubar (1979). The second task is to construct poetic meanings which can free women's discourse from masculine or androgynous forms. This has been the most generative task both theoretically and creatively. For example Marge Piercy and Adrienne Rich constantly connect women's bodies, politics and poetic form.

There is now a new language of the self/other boundary in poetry of maternity which enables the intensity of mother–child relations to be described. These maternal relations are symbolised in women's poetry about war. Another form of revisionist poetry records the experience of meeting one's mother within oneself. See A. Walker (1983).

Some images stress female power, for example Audre Lorde in *The Black Unicorn* (1981) creates a mythological world of women to provide an alternative to racist America. With the dismantling of a logocentric conception of poetry, there are now a variety of poetic forms used by writers who are dissolving genre boundaries. For example Erica Jong and Sandra Gilbert both use diaries and quilting imagery.

Women critics and poets describe new relationships between consciousness and the natural order. They use our rootedness in nature to reverse a patriarchal division of nature from culture. See Montefiore (1987). But perhaps one of the chief contributions women writers are making to the repertoire of poetic culture is developing new kinds of reading practice, for example minimising distances between poets and readers in women's writing collectives. In addition poetry is now part of feminist theory itself, for example Mary Daly synthesises history, diatribe, poetry and philosophy in *Gyn/Ecology* (1978).

Political theory
Traditional political theory is the theory of forms of government and methods of social organisation. By focusing on the structure of relations within institutions, it often ignores the experiential quality of political groups. Feminist political theory on the other hand, describes the role of feelings and emotions, and attributes of care and respect in relationships. Feminists attack normative arguments about the nature of a good society with a vision of women's liberation. Hence feminism constructs a complicated political theory built around conceptual, normative, empirical and methodological claims. See Love and Shanklin (1983).

Hester Eisenstein suggests that contemporary feminism draws on three streams of political theory: eighteenth-century political rights, nineteenth-century socialism and the continuing battle for sexual rights. See Eisenstein (1984). Not surprisingly then, feminist political theory is not homogeneous because it mixes such different theories of human nature and different views of the role of the State. One common theme is feminism's commitment to the personal and to domestic issues. Fundamental to feminist political theory is the conviction that concepts of care and responsibility stem, not from abstract principles of right or justice, but from the social contexts of sexuality, the family and education.

Politics
Kate Millett defined politics as any power-structured relationship in which one group of persons is controlled by another. Contemporary feminists refuse to use traditional political concepts, for example the concept of political delegation, or vicarious politics, and prefer a concept of personalised politics. See Mies (1983).

Liberal feminism is based on a politics of antidiscrimination and opposes laws that establish different rights for women and for men. Liberal feminism accepts that many established political procedures such as universal suffrage, free elections or freedom of assembly, are adequate to eradicate discrimination. The goal of socialist feminist politics, on the other hand, is to abolish these socially constituted categories and develop a form of political practice which can link the personal with the political. Socialist feminism criticises the ways centralised forms of political organisation replicate sexual and other divisions in the larger society. One alternative to centralised politics is participatory democracy where decisions are made by everyone. However, Sheila Rowbotham, and others, suggests that this form of politics is problematic unless everyone has a respect for the other's experience. See Rowbotham (1979).

Structural functional analysis shows that political socialisation, or the process by which a person acquires a political repertoire, occurs through sex roles and childhood experiences with father figures and authority patterns. Hence the goal of radical feminist politics is for women to deconstruct this past and gain control over our own bodies. A radical feminist politics will build a feminist culture in a new society of women-centred spaces. However, the politics of separatism, Black feminists claim, ignores the way working-class and Black women have political interest in common with men. See Combahee River Collective (1981).

Feminist concerns are difficult to place in a traditional political spectrum. Some feminists attempt a *rapprochement* with the Left and others, for example Mary Daly, retreat from political struggle as it is normally constituted. Summarising the political theory of the contemporary women's movement in the USA, Hester Eisenstein has described its move from debates about individual rights, to debates about difference and finally to a politics of mutuality. See Eisenstein (1984). Feminist politics can be summed up as a politics based on an ethics of caring. Citing political movements that appealed to an ethics of care, for example the women's suffrage campaign and the antipornography movement, feminists argue that an ethics of care can be conjoined with a progressive feminist politics. See Katzenstein and Laitin (1987). More simply and satisfactorily, Adrienne Rich describes feminist politics as a politics of asking women's questions.

Popular culture

The term 'popular culture' includes both spontaneous amusements created by women for themselves and 'mass entertainment' created for women by the State or commercial interests. Discussions about popular culture before contemporary feminism, for example those by Walter Benjamin and Theodor Adorno, ignore the issue of gender.

Feminists writing about popular culture focus on woman as signifier. In the 1970s feminists began to study romance novels, magazines and television soap operas as examples of a 'feminine' popular culture. Critics analyse textual contradictions and how women audiences subvert the overt messages or codes in each text. Feminist theory moved from criticising stereotypes and representation to questions of cultural production and cultural readings, focusing on the dominant theme of gender in contemporary cultural practices.

Analysis revealed how popular culture operates with a very restricted range of gender stereotypes, for example women in advertisements are usually set domestically in a rigid sexual division of labour. See Williamson (1978).

Marxist and socialist feminists write about the social context of popular culture in order to challenge the hegemony of literature and form a ground from which new forms of popular culture might develop. See Barrett (1979).

Feminist theory also uncovered in popular culture important developments and shifts in sexual ideologies and forms of resistance to them, for example in adolescent girls' culture. See McRobbie and Nava (1984).

Using psychoanalytic theories about pleasure, Tania Modleski describes the interaction between female readers and texts and proves that popular culture often provides an outlet for women's dissatisfaction with male–female relationships and domesticity. See Modleski (1982).

If a feminist reworking of popular culture often comes close to celebration rather than to appropriation, it has enabled cultural studies to rethink concepts of production. By creating new areas of enquiry and new techniques of analysis, feminist theory has altered the terrain of popular culture and made a cultural milieu in which a feminist popular culture can exist.

Pornography

Feminists and conservative moralists both define pornography as sexual material depicting and encouraging violent and coercive sexual degradation. Where feminist theory diverges from conservatism is in defining pornography as a *political* phenomenon rather than simply a moral one. Contemporary feminist theory about pornography developed alongside the formation of feminist groups (for example Women Against Violence Against Women) and feminist campaigns (for example Take Back the Night).

Feminists argue that pornography has two major characteristics: the representation of women's degradation through sexual violence or compulsion; and the institutionalisation of patriarchal sexuality. Robin Morgan claimed that 'pornography is the theory and rape is the practice'. See Lederer (1980).

Feminist theory takes the view that pornography does not in fact violate the norms of heterosexuality but operates to sustain them. Pornography expresses and reproduces the hierarchical difference between masculine and feminine which is part of culture. Both the form and content of pornography mutually determine and constitute women as objects available for the use of, or contemplation by, the male subject. All feminists agree that pornography is the ultimate objectification of women but there are two divergent arguments about pornography within feminism. One focuses on male violence, the other develops a woman's perspective which calls into question the universality of male values. An example of the first position is Andrea Dworkin who describes pornography as a quintessential expression of the belief men have in their right to sexual power over women. Dworkin thinks that this power is endemic to male nature. See Dworkin (1981). Susan Griffin agrees with Dworkin that pornography teaches women self-annihilation and expresses the psychosexual needs of Western masculinity to annihilate the female. But Griffin represents a divergent line in feminist theory by preferring to look for scientific and historical reasons for the apparent 'universality' of male violence. See Griffin (1978, 1981).

Andrea Dworkin, together with Catharine MacKinnon, has designed an antipornography law which defines pornography as a violation of women's civil rights. Susan Griffin, on the other hand, defines pornography as expressing fundamental themes of Western Christianity and Western science – domination over nature and a hatred of the flesh. Ellen Willis argues that obscenity laws suppress feminism and sexual dissidence. See Willis (1984).

A common theme in feminist analysis is the view that pornography is sadistic and that pornographic values are also racist. But where Dworkin, Griffin, MacKinnon and others extended the critique of masculinity begun by Nancy Chodorow to argue that sadism is part of a male desire to hurt and exploit others, lesbian theorists argue that sadomasochistic pornography *within* lesbian practice, could be a creative use of fantasy. See Califia (1981). Underlying this discussion is the disagreement about woman's 'true' nature and the correct direction for feminist politics.

Positive discrimination

Positive discrimination (and its successors, affirmative action and comparable worth) is defined by governments in terms of social and legal provision designed to eradicate areas of sexual inequality, for example the Equal Pay Act (1970) or Sex Discrimination Act (1975), in Britain. Feminist theory argues that this definition is based on the inadequate belief that sexual discrimination is individual rather than systematic. Further, feminist researchers reveal that governments use their positive discrimination legislation to institutionally contain women's demands for full economic, political and social equality. See Hartmann (1976).

Since institutional approaches are limited by the possibilities inherent in existing political structures, feminist theory argues for a necessary, and major, political and economic revolution.

Power

There is now a large body of writing in feminist theory about the nature of power, where power is located and whether there can be a feminist form of power. Second wave feminism began by defining power as sexual politics, arguing that the balance of power in society lay with men. See Millett (1970). Female power has usually existed only within a framework of male authority. For example Jean Bethke Elshtain talks of 'unintentional' power, which is how a group possesses power because of its position in society. She argues that the benefits of privilege will belong to such social groups even though the possession of power may be personally unintentional to any one of them. Elshtain claims that males are the sole possessor of unintentional power which has any public meaning with political consequences. See Elshtain (1979).

Feminist anthropologists distinguish between power, authority and influence. They describe how, cross-culturally, women are not without certain forms of power in social decision-making. But throughout cultures, anthropologists claim, the source of legitimacy in the exercise of power lies with men since male activities are the locus of cultural value. This is because men maintain a distance from the domestic sphere. See Rosaldo and Lamphere (1974).

Other feminist theorists locate the source of power in consciousness and language. For example Elizabeth Janeway argues that one of the most significant forms of power held by the weak (that is women) is the refusal to accept the definition of oneself that is put forward by the powerful. Women's power is the power to disbelieve. See Janeway (1981). Sheila Rowbotham argues that power is part of the nature of language and that language is itself one of the instruments of domination. See Rowbotham (1973b).

Radical feminism argues that these theories about power are inadequate if they do not take women's domination as a central theme and do not see this as a model for all forms of interpersonal domination. Radical feminism argues that the psychology of male power is expressed in cultural artifacts like pornography and in the sexual violation of women. For example Catharine MacKinnon claims that sexuality is a form of power because it is the linchpin of gender inequality. See MacKinnon (1982). Julia Kristeva suggests that women's attempts to gain political power in existing society, cannot change the status quo. Feminist theory, she argues, must challenge myths and radically pinpoint women's potential power, for example in mother imagery. See Kristeva (1982).

Feminist models of power are an important issue in feminist discussion. Women's groups reacted against the power of leaders and tried to define power in a way which did not require domination patterns. Judith Newton defines women's power as 'ability' where women are active agents. See Newton (1981). However, Nancy Hartsock claims that until society can be reconstructed in such a way that domination is not basic to it, feminists need power *within* society, rather than creating alternatives to social power. See Hartsock (1981).

Praxis

Feminist theologists define praxis as the struggle to unite theory and practice in action and reflection upon the world in order to transform it for women. Socialist and Marxist feminists claim that women's subordination is due to existing praxis, in the way that societies organise to produce and distribute goods. They describe the relationship between women's inner lives and social praxis by connecting concepts of masculinity and femininity to the sexual division of labour. Socialist feminism argues that women can recreate themselves through historically specific forms of praxis. See Rowbotham (1979).

Feminist praxis comes in small group consciousness-raising which connects personal experience to social structures. Feminist praxis promises a new cooperative social order beyond the principles of hierarchy and competitiveness. See Reuther (1974). This entails a new definition of theory which will not depend on the application of certain methodological principles and rules but on its potential to orient the process of praxis towards women's emancipation. See Mies (1983).

Primatology

Theories of primatology or the study of primate behaviour, have been a fruitful target for feminist critics. Women working in the area have extensively examined existing theoretical concepts and proved that scientific language biases theoretical formulations. Theorist Jane Lancaster and biologist Jane Goodall argue that the scientific theory of male primate dominance results from the predominance of men in the field of primatology. In reality, primate groups do not depend on male aggression for maintenance if environmental conditions are such that the male role can be minimal. See Lancaster (1975). The groundbreaking scholarship of Donna Haraway revised primatology to a focus on matrifocal groups and social cooperation rather than on social aggression. See Haraway (1979).

Privacy
Feminist philosophers define women's privacy as the right to bodily integrity, and freedom from mental distress and coercion. See Thomson (1975).

Other feminists, rather than basing a right to privacy on ultimate values, advance a 'functional' analysis of privacy. They argue that women have social interest in anonymity and solitude because women frequently suffer unwarranted losses of privacy (of information or our bodies) at the hands of employers, the State or violent men. See Gavison (1980). Women's privacy lies essentially in our freedom of choice in marital, sexual or reproductive concerns. See Gould (1976).

Procreation
The bearing of children. Feminist psychoanalysis argues that women's subordination is grounded in the organisation of procreation. For example Nancy Chodorow suggests that this organisation creates small privatised family units in which women have a major responsibility for young children. See Chodorow (1978). Hence the transformation of procreation, Firestone claims, would be unlike any other transformation of production, if procreation would cease to be defined biologically. See Firestone (1970).

Radical feminism defines procreation as a cross-cultural, universal biologically-determined event and argues that women's subordination is rooted in the fact that women in all societies are childbearers. See Rich (1976).

Socialist feminism insists that procreation and production are mutually determining parts of the economic foundation of society. Procreative activities are deeply affected by the prevailing system of market production, for example in the switch from breast feeding to bottle feeding. In this way feminist theory agrees that systems of procreation have a significant and determining influence on the organisation of nondomestic production. Ann Ferguson and Nancy

Folbre relate economics to procreation and to male dominance by developing the concept of 'sex-affective production'. Women's specialisation in procreation, they suggest, restricts women's options. See Ferguson and Folbre (1981).

Production

A way of organising labour which was named as one of the four main structures of women's oppression by Juliet Mitchell in 'Women: the longest revolution' (1966). Mitchell describes how the relationships between women and economic production are very complex and how the important changes are in the historic relations between the two over time. Shulamith Firestone radically reinterpreted women's subordination in production to mean our connection to biological reproduction which, she argues, is the root cause of women's oppression. See Firestone (1970). Socialist feminism, on the other hand, identifies types of women's labour that political economy traditionally ignores, for example sex, affection and children. In this sense reproduction both determines the productive needs of society and provides an essential means to those needs being met. Production and reproduction function as limits one upon the other. Christine Delphy defines a family system of production as one which judges the work of married women not in terms of its content but in terms of women's relation to their husbands. Whatever form of domestic labour is undertaken by women, Delphy claims, the proceeds of women's production are always appropriated by husbands. See Delphy (1977).

Property

Radical feminism connects definitions of property to definitions of rape. Susan Brownmiller argues that the use of women as property by men is rape because rape cases were originally brought by one man against another in terms of damage to his property. See Brownmiller (1975). More generally Charlotte Bunch claims that heterosexuality enables every woman to be the property of a man. See Bunch (1981).

Prostitution

In law, prostitution is defined as the hiring out of one's body for the purposes of sexual intercourse. Feminist theory challenges the implicit assumption of free choice in this definition, and argues that prostitution is a paradigm of other interactions between men and women. For example, like rape, prostitution is defined by society as a 'normal' response to female sexual seductiveness and a male sexual drive.

Different periods of feminism pay attention to different aspects of prostitution. Nineteenth-century feminists struggled against the State regulation of prostitution, for example by defeating the Contagious Diseases Act. The struggle encouraged women to challenge male centres of power – the police, parliament and the medical establishment. Contemporary feminism draws strength from this earlier and ideological analysis of prostitution. For example both first and second wave feminism describe the links between sexual violence and the private sphere of the family. See Rubin (1984).

Judith Walkowitz describes how prostitution was transformed at the turn of the century when an interplay of social forces such as ideology, politics and medical practice changed the structure of sexual behaviour. (Walkowitz 1984). The new scholarship about sexual behaviour gives sex a history and constructs an alternative to sexual essentialism by arguing that sexuality is constituted in society and history and that it is not biologically determined.

Radical feminism draws on nineteenth-century models and contemporary research. It argues that prostitution is a paradigm, not only of women's *sexual* vulnerability but also our vulnerability to sexual conditioning and economic discrimination. Radical feminism claims that the economic reductionism of gender issues such as prostitution is one of the most pernicious forms of androcentric thinking. See Dworkin (1981).

Psych et Po

A French group of feminist theorists which was founded in 1973. The group analysed the symbolic nature of women's oppression. It made 'différence' the heart of their definition of woman. See Cixous (1981). The group aimed to radically change conceptual frameworks so that 'the feminine' could be inserted into a new relation between masculinity and femininity. See Duchen (1987).

Psychiatry

The medical treatment of mental illnesses dating from the middle of the nineteenth century. Psychiatry identifies and tries to cure mental and behavioural pathologies. However, because psychiatry relies on behavioural patterns and scientific methods for its explanations, feminist theorists question many of the definitions and techniques of psychiatry which are applied to women.

For example definitions of pathology based on a condition defined as 'hysteria' were applied to single, middle-class, intellectual women (Alice James and Florence Nightingale); and feminist historians show how such definitions are fallacious. See Ehrenreich and English

(1979). Similarly, feminist literary theorists argue that psychiatry gives women stereotypes of irrationality or passivity which depoliticise women's refusal to come to terms with marriage or subordination. See Gilbert and Gubar (1979).

Psychoanalysis

A term invented by Freud (1897) to refer to his theory of the psyche and the methods and techniques he applied to understanding it. Second wave feminists, in particular Kate Millett, challenged the content and definitions of psychoanalysis. They argued that psychoanalysis was inherently sexist because it emphasises biology over social relations and takes masculine characteristics as a psychoanalytic norm. Where Millett and Firestone rejected Freudian psychoanalysis as being inimical to women, Dorothy Dinnerstein drew on the Freudian and *Gestalt* traditions of psychoanalysis in order to theorise gender difference in a universalistic yet radically nonbiological way. Men's fear of women, Dinnerstein argues, is determined psychoanalytically by women's domination of childcare.

Feminist psychoanalysis focuses on how prevailing norms of gender are imposed on infants and how these come to structure the human mind. Often, feminist psychoanalysis is referred to as 'gender theory'. For example, the application of object relations theory by Nancy Chodorow is a significant feminist reconceptualisation of the psychoanalytic concept of gender identity. See Chodorow (1978).

A historicised and feminist version of psychoanalysis requires a new terminology. Socialist feminism turned to other conceptual frameworks. It explains women's apparent acquiescence to male domination by reference to the notion of false consciousness. See Bartky (1979). Juliet Mitchell re-evaluated Freudian psychoanalysis and argues that his critique of constituted subjectivity has important implications for feminism. She explains that the castration complex is not an unavoidable stage in development but required by a culture which needed rigidly enforced sexual differentiation. See Mitchell (1974).

Sandra Harding also uses psychoanalysis to trace back other masculine cultural characteristics. She dates the appearance of these characteristics from the scientific revolution of the sixteenth and seventeenth centuries when the organic conception of nature was replaced by mechanistic causal explanations. See Harding and Hintikka (1983). Nancy Hartsock and Jane Flax agree that, in other disciplines, psychoanalysis can be used to deconstruct masculinity, for example by explaining how philosophical problems came from unconscious attitudes which are typically male. See Hartsock (1981).

Jean Baker Miller claims that psychoanalysis only became necessary because of acts of dissociation and repression by a dominant male culture, but other feminists use psychoanalytic theory creatively to explore the ways in which sexism becomes part of common consciousness and culture. For example feminist film theory uses psychoanalytic ideas to investigate the representation of women within the general organisation of sexuality. See Mulvey (1975) and Coward (1982). Julia Kristeva, Hélène Cixous and Luce Irigaray have reasserted concepts of difference and revalorised femininity and maternity within psychoanalysis. Psychoanalysis is a striking example of an intellectual source shared by feminists of very different disciplinary backgrounds.

Psychology

Most contemporary psychology since Freud adopts sex stereotypes, characterising women as expressive and men as instrumental, rather than analysing the origins and implications of sex-typed behaviour. Feminist theory challenges Freud's definitions of sexuality and shows that sex-role differences are constructed. See Maccoby and Jacklin (1974). Second wave feminism focused first on the damage done to women in psychology. Phyllis Chesler, in *Women and Madness*, showed how psychology was determined to label independent women as examples of deviancy. See Chesler (1972). In addition, Kate Millett defined men's power over women as a social psychology of conditioning.

In the current debate about the psychology of women, feminist theories focus on sex-role socialisation and its impact on personality. For example Gayle Rubin argues that Freudian theory creates the concept of a passive feminine psychology. See Rubin (1975). Dorothy Dinnerstein analyses how psychological inhibitions in men and women prevent changes in social life, and she argued that new gender arrangements in mothering would lead to new psychologies. See Dinnerstein (1976). Nancy Chodorow focuses on the psychological character formation which makes women want to mother. She calls this a 'self-in-relationship' which enables women to grow up with relational capacities. See Chodorow (1978).

An equally important task of feminist theory is to attack the main techniques of psychology, in particular psychology's reliance on experiments. Evelyn Fox Keller describes how the design and interpretation of experiments in psychology is male biased. For example most animal-learning research has been performed with male rats based on the assumption that male rats represent the species. See Keller (1982). Other feminists attack the standardisation of personality tests. As a feminist alternative, Sandra Bem proposed a psychology of androgyny and created an inventory which could set aside sex-role stereotypes. See Bem (1974). Feeling that Bem's concept glossed over issues of social power, other feminists argued that feminism must create a distinct and positive female psychology of nurturance and cooperation. Developing a new model with techniques from consciousness-raising groups, Jean Baker Miller argues that women's condition might have intrinsic psychological value. For example women's emotional skills could create autonomy for women rather than being seen merely as aspects of our social conditioning. See Miller (1976).

Psychotherapy

The method of treatment used in psychoanalysis. Psychotherapy relies on a general theory of human psychology but feminist theory argues that the content and concerns of the human psyche are socially given and vary in time, in place and by gender. Critics of contemporary therapy point to the way the assumed cause of mental illness and the therapy given are very closely related. Therefore the use of causal explanations, for example by tracing psychic disturbance to hormone levels, has meant that women suffer a reductionist form of psychotherapy. They argue that therapy is conservative and encourages individual accommodation rather than structural change. Feminist theory also argues that the historical context in which therapy is used is extremely important because therapy is part of a social process surrounding ill health. See Jordanova (1981a). This feminist critique is summed up by Phyllis Chesler's argument in *Women and Madness* (1972) that men drive women crazy to maintain a male hegemony.

Feminist psychotherapy has its roots in consciousness raising groups and in the women's movement. There are four main similarities between these perspectives: all groups assume that the personal is political and rely on the detail of individual experience; they focus on the family and claim that this shapes women's behaviour and attitudes, and they believe that anger and pain are not pathological but an understandable expression of women's needs; they make explicit the political relationship between women and sexuality. By uncovering the dynamics of mother–daughter relationships, feminist psychotherapy can describe female personality development. In addition the mode, as well as the techniques, of feminist psychotherapy provides an alternative to traditional treatment, in that the feminist therapist reveals her theoretical bias to her client and believes that all therapies are informed by a political perspective. See Eichenbaum and Orbach (1982).

Public/private

Popularly understood to be the separation of work and home in an individual life. In the slogan 'the personal is political' the contemporary women's movement linked public and private. The slogan redefines personal experience as a social process, the product of human activity.

Socialist feminists point out that the public/private distinction is covertly normative and in the nineteenth century functioned to rationalise the exploitation of women. They argue that the distinction must be abolished otherwise an ideology of male dominance will continue. Other theorists who examined the distinction include Jean Bethke Elshtain and Elizabeth Janeway. They show how the ideology of public/private secluded women to the private, or domestic; and that this ideology was being reinforced at a time when large numbers of women were in the labour force. Janeway claims that the social myth that women are powerless depends on the gap between public and private. See Janeway (1971).

Feminist anthropology argues that all cultures assign women to the domestic sphere and men to the public arena. Michelle Rosaldo proposes that there is a direct relationship between the degree of subordination of women in a given society and the degree to which the realms of public and the domestic are separated. Like de Beauvoir, Rosaldo understands that the relegation of women to the private zone is interpellated with biology, for example in the association of women with nature and men with culture. See Rosaldo and Lamphere (1974). While agreeing that what distinguishes women is having to inhabit the world of reproduction, Juliet Mitchell argues that it is only by analysing the *complexity* of the relationship of public and private that feminist theory can transform both structures. See Mitchell (1984).

Radical feminism refuses to recognise a distinction between private and personal relations. For example Joan Kelly-Gadol has suggested that public/private is a false division. Women's personal, social and historical experience, she claims, is shaped by the simultaneous operation of the relations of work and sex, relations that are systematically bound to each other. Public/private is a false division between personal experience and knowledge, between the subjective and the objective. See Kelly-Gadol (1979).

Qualitative research

The method of social science most favoured by feminist theorists who use such qualitative techniques as oral history, experiential analysis, case history and participant observation. In *The Feminine Mystique* (1963) Betty Friedan used qualitative methods to study women's attitudes. Currently, feminist theorists argue that an increase in the use of qualitative techniques would better reflect the nature of women's experience. See Reinharz (1979). This is because qualitative research involves an emotional closeness to the person studied. It allows women to look at more sensitive areas such as sexuality and deals with such concepts as double consciousness.

Although not all feminist critics would agree with Evelyn Fox Keller that opposition to qualitative research reflects a masculine bias in science, they acknowledge that qualitative investigations do reveal power differentials in gender relations. See Keller (1978). For example Christine Griffin, who uses qualitative research in her ethnographic account of young women's lives, argues that the technique helps the researcher better to understand individuality in relation to social forces. See Griffin (1986).

Qualitative research is now a main part of feminist social psychology and helps the discipline make a profound reassessment of existing gender specific theories.

Quantitative research

Analysing data as numerical values. Many feminists argue that this form of research in the social sciences is used to promote a sexist ideology and that it ignores issues of concern to women and feminists. Toby Epstein Jayaratne claims, however, that quantitative research can be used *for* women because more objective means of measurement can endorse our information and beliefs about discrimination against women. Adjustments to the research process, for example in survey research, can enable quantitative research to be more feminist. See Jayaratne (1983).

Questions
Mary Daly calls the 'First Question' of feminism our 'First Philosophy' and the beginning of a feminist ontology. See Daly (1984).

Socialist feminism argues that feminist political theory is distinct from other theories not only because of the answers it gives but because of the questions that it asks. See Reed (1978).

Questions féministes
A radical French journal founded in 1977 by Simone de Beauvoir and other feminists which took the position that women are a class and that women's oppression derives from social stereotypes of biological determinism. The journal therefore made a systematic attack on those feminist theories which celebrate 'différence'.

Race

The term race was first employed by François Bernier in 1684. Due to the Marxist character of Western scholarship about race most research defines race in class reductionist terms rather than in gender terms. See Davis *et al.* (1987). Race is often not mentioned in studies of minority women and the problem is both a research question and a question of theory. For example 'the feminisation of poverty' has different meanings for women, depending on race. In addition feminist symbols of women's equality, Julianne Malveaux argues, may have little meaning for Black women. See Malveaux (1987).

Race is constitutive of the personal and social being of women and race determines the specific context of sexual oppression. Women of colour, especially lesbians, are creating a radical theory and practice that insists on the importance of differences between women and the positive aspects of culture and identity. See Smith (1984). The Combahee River Collective stated that race cannot be separated from class or from sex oppression, basing their argument on the history of the rape of Black women by white men. See Combahee River Collective (1981).

Racism

Second wave feminism grew out of, and was politicised by, the struggle for racial equality by the New Left in the 1960s. However, Black feminists argue that a facile and insensitive comparison between the experience of 'women' and 'Blacks' is a cliché of much white feminist writing in the 1970s. They point to the unconscious racism and false universalism in such feminist theory. For example Angela Davis claims that white feminist accounts of rape omit Black women's history and therefore feed into a racist mythology. She argues that any struggle against sexism must be allied to the struggle against racism. See Davis (1981). Similarly, Audre Lorde took Mary Daly to task for describing women of colour only as victims, not as sources of wisdom. Because white feminism is part of an Anglo–American cultural framework it can be potentially racist and ethnocentric. See Moschkovich (1981).

Voices of women of colour are articulating the historical and cultural differences of race, and making a new feminist theory. This has to be founded, not on the basis of 'correct' politics but on a pragmatic basis of shared beliefs and ethics and a knowledge of particular histories. See Smith (1984).

Radical

Radical has changed in meaning as feminist theory itself has changed from Kate Millett's *Sexual Politics* (1970) to Mary Daly's *Gyn/Ecology* (1978). Second wave feminism first used radical to mean a more revolutionary social theory than the theories of the New Left out of which it had grown. Mary Daly uses radical to mean metaphysical rather than radical as a social or political term. Betty Friedan in *The Second Stage* (1981) argues that radical action must be abandoned when feminists engage in such issues as abortion, rape or lesbianism. See Eisenstein (1984).

Radical feminism

Radical feminism argues that women's oppression comes from our categorisation as an inferior class to the class 'men' on the basis of our gender. Radical feminism aims to destroy this sex-class system. What makes this feminism radical is that it focuses on the roots of male domination and claims that all forms of oppression are extensions of male supremacy. Radical feminism argues that patriarchy is the defining characteristic of our society. The other central thesis of radical feminism is the belief that the personal is political and that woman-centredness can be the basis of a future society. See Eisenstein (1984).

The pioneering radical feminists Charlotte Perkins Gilman, Emma Goldman and Margaret Sanger argued that women must take radical control over their bodies and lives. The main theories of contemporary radical feminism were developed by groups in New York in the late 1960s and 1970s. Ti-Grace Atkinson argued that the politically oppressive male–female role system is the original model of all oppression, and Anne Koedt suggested that women's oppression was primarily psychological not just economic.

Certain issues put radical feminism at odds with other feminist perspectives, specifically a socialist view of the centrality of class and a Black view of the centrality of race. Juliet Mitchell criticised Firestone in particular and radical feminism in general for not speaking of women's oppression in a historically specific way. See

Mitchell (1971). This is because radical feminism, for example in the theories of Adrienne Rich, Mary Daly and Shulamith Firestone, is concerned with sexuality and socialisation rather than primarily with labour. Focusing upon consciousness and culture on the one hand and the unconscious on the other, radical feminists analyse the psychic, sexual and ideological structures which differentiate the sexes in relation to the *lived* inequalities of gender.

One main theme in radical feminist writing is a hostility to the political Left. By arguing, as Robin Morgan does, that sexism is the root, or radical oppression, radical feminism offers a fundamentally different mode of analysis to that of Marxism. A second element which unites radical feminists is their shared attention to the psychology of women. They argue that previous theory fails to analyse the domination of women as a psychosocial form. Radical feminism contributes to feminist theory in several distinctive ways. First, it creates concepts of womanculture where the building of alternative institutions could generate social change, an analogous concept to libertarianism. Second, radical feminism is the first theory to totally reconceptualise reality from the standpoint of women. Third, it reveals that there is a concealed masculine bias in the conceptual framework of much of traditional knowledge and the dualisms that traditional political theory uses to justify the subordination of women. And, more than other theory, radical feminism works to make visible the invisible by bringing into focus the gender structure of society. French radical feminists have added an additional dimension which is the creation of a new women's language, an '*écriture féminine*'. See Cixous (1976) and Irigaray (1977b).

In the 1970s radical feminism gradually abandoned the 'linear', male style of traditional political theory and moved into a poetic and metaphorical mode. Although their concepts are now more difficult to translate into traditional political terms, Susan Griffin and Mary Daly see their first task to be redescribing reality in a new language. See Griffin (1982a). A radical feminist paradigm is still emerging. Radical feminists differ in how they name reality because they use a limited range of concepts, such as rape or slavery, to bring together apparently disparate phenomena such as marriage and prostitution. In addition, radical feminism often presents a somewhat static picture of the world because it does not provide causal explanations. No other mode of feminist theory, however, has centralised issues of rape and sexual difference and, most crucially, has attended to wildness as a quality in, and around, women which should be cherished.

Radicalesbians

A group which was founded in 1970 by women called the Lavender Menace. Radicalesbians argue that theories of lesbianism provide models for any woman seeking her freedom. Radicalesbian theory made a major contribution to politicising feminism, for example by contributing the idea that women ourselves are the sole source of female validity and identity and the idea that women are the prime healers.

Radicalesbians changed the definition of 'womanhood' to that of 'woman-identified-woman', and placed this definition at the core of feminism. Lesbianism in this sense means not only sexual preference but involves a model of female identity appropriate for all women. See Radicalesbians (1973).

Rap group

Sometimes known as a consciousness raising (CR) group, a rap group is one in which women meet in a situation of structured interaction and can speak to each other about individual experiences and analyse them communally. Rap groups aim to alter each woman's perception and conception of herself and society and therefore can function as a medium for social change.

Jo Freeman argues that the recovery of experience begun in rap groups, from a sociological perspective, is probably the most valuable contribution the women's liberation movement has made so far to social change. See Freeman (1973).

Rape

Feminist theory defines rape as an act *and* a social institution which perpetuate patriarchal domination and which are based *on* violence, rather than specifically as a *crime of* violence. This definition is a major contribution to social theory. Feminist analysis proves that rape is the logical conclusion of sexism. It is one of the most insidious forms of social coercion because rape is a constant reminder to all women of their vulnerable condition.

Kate Millett points out that the social meaning of rape, known as eroticism, works to degrade and feminise women. From a radical feminist perspective most heterosexual relations are analogous to rape but concealed by a mystique of romance. Radical feminists, for example Susan Brownmiller, Susan Griffin and Andrea Dworkin, argue that patriarchy legitimises rape by defining rape as 'normal'. Under patriarchy, not only are women defined as sexual objects but men are thought to have 'drives' towards heterosexual intercourse. Because patriarchal culture defines women as being sexually passive and receptive, it is thought reasonable to interpret a woman's uninterested behaviour as *expressive* of sexual interest. See Brownmiller (1975). Brownmiller describes rape as a cultural and social phenomenon which is institutionalised in law and custom. Susan Griffin argues that, as the symbolic expression of a white male hierarchy, rape is the quintessential act of our civilisation (Griffin 1982a). Dworkin adds that rape is both a sexual act and an act of aggression. It is a crime against the person, a crime against property and a political crime.

Adrienne Rich suggests that rape is one of the main means of reinforcing compulsory heterosexuality. Consciousness raising groups reveal that women's experience of rape is not an isolated individual event but a symptom of a society-wide structure of power and powerlessness.

Currently, feminist theory takes the view that rape is a political act of terror against an oppressed group. However, Black feminists draw attention to the need to distinguish power differentials between Black and white women. Racism depends, Angela Davis argues, on a white male belief in Black women's inferiority, enabling her to be sexually abused, and it depends *equally* on the myth of the Black *male* rapist. See Davis (1981). Angela Davis, Adrienne Rich and other feminist critics are working to situate rape historically in order to fully question and demolish its apparent legitimisation. See Rich (1980).

Reasoning

The first thorough feminist account of women's reasoning is Mary Wollstonecraft's *A Vindication of the Rights of Women* (1789). Wollstonecraft made a forceful argument that women had the potential to be fully reasoning and rational creatures and consequently were as capable as men of complete moral responsibility. From this liberal perspective the ideals of reason apply equally to both men and women. But Susan Griffin argues that men have defined reason so as to exclude and oppress women. See Griffin (1982b).

According to radical feminism, patriarchal thinking imposes polarities on reason by conceptually separating aspects that in fact should be inseparable. Although intellectually it is difficult to state women's difference without adopting the polarities that male reason has invented, for example that women are intuitive, many feminists now believe that it is dangerous to ignore difference. This is because Western ideals of reasoning exclude what is simultaneously defined as irrational and female, for example intuition, and that these ideals led to, and legitimate, domination.

Feminist philosophy does argue that there are distinctive 'female' forms of reasoning and that 'neutral' standards of rationality are male biased. One argument coming from psychology claims that differences in women's and men's moral development lead to differences in reasoning. See Gilligan (1982). The other argument is derived from philosophy and claims that given the social context of reasoning, for example in sexual divisions, women do develop a distinctive form of reasoning. See Lorde (1984a) and Griffin (1978). Many French feminists describe how 'reason' is socially and psychologically constituted as 'male' and they suggest we create a distinctive mode of female reasoning. See Kittay and Meyers (1987).

Reich, Wilhelm

A Marxist psychoanalyst whose theories of sexual politics in *The Sexual Revolution* (1945) provoked many New Left and subsequent feminist arguments about sexuality in the 1960s. Reich was the first Marxist to incorporate a theory of sexual repression into a critique of the material conditions of life under capitalism. His argument that sexual repression is revealed in character formation, a kind of social conditioning in physiological form, presaged many feminist accounts of identity formation. Susan Brownmiller attributes her concept of rape to Reich's definition of the masculine ideology of rape. While unhappy about simplistic uses of Reich's theories, for example by Norman Mailer, Kate Millett claims that Reich made the crucial link between social and psychological ills and the negative attitude our culture holds towards sexuality. See Millett (1970).

Juliet Mitchell finds Reich's significance to lie in his view of women's independent sexuality; in his belief that any inferiority in women is due to social attitudes; and in his interest in the pre-Oedipal sexual relationship with the mother. She stresses, however, that Reich's insistence on the superiority of a vaginal orgasm and his biologism limits his theories and his uses for feminism. See Mitchell (1974).

Relativism

The belief that there is no absolute criterion of true or false. Feminist critics address the problems raised by the issue of relativism for feminist theory. In important ways feminist relativism transformed the sociology of knowledge. Fox Keller argues, however, that by rejecting objectivity as being a masculine ideal, relativism exacerbates the very problem it wishes to solve because it nullifies the radical potential of feminist criticism for our understanding of science. See Keller (1978). Rather than total relativism we need to legitimate those elements of scientific culture that are devalued because they are defined as female.

Religion

Generally a system of beliefs. Feminist theorists argue that most of the *organised* religious belief systems which dominate the historical and modern world are profoundly sexist. There are two major feminist theories about religion – the liberal, reformist critique of existing practice and the utopian creation of a new counter culture practice.

Elizabeth Cady Stanton's *The Woman's Bible* (1895–8) made the first major feminist contribution to changes in religion. Stanton believed that the language and interpretation of passages dealing with women in the Bible were a major source of women's inferior status. This was because nineteenth-century women turned so often to the Bible for comfort and inspiration. See Stanton (1895–8).

Contemporary feminist theory documents the facts of male bias and traces its roots. Mary Daly in *The Church and the Second Sex* (1968) and *Gyn/Ecology* (1978) describes how the spell of patriarchy is Christianity which dismembered the original Goddess religion by incorporating some of its elements into a new mythology stripped of any female power. For example the Trinity, the Cross and Virgin birth of Jesus were elements taken from Goddess religions. The central message of Christianity, Daly claims, is sadomasochism legitimised in torture. In Eastern religions, she claims, the practice of Suttee, is a form of sadomasochism. These would be replaced in a future metaphysical feminism by women's warrior comradeship. See Daly (1973, 1978). Susan Griffin also agrees that a fundamental theme of the Western Christian tradition is its hatred of the flesh, which is based on an idea that woman's body calls man back to his animal nature. See Griffin (1981).

Another area in feminist studies aims to discover an alternative history and tradition that could support the personhood of women. This area draws its sources from anthropology and historical scholarship of matriarchal societies and the ancient religions of the Mother Goddess. Adrienne Rich describes a gynocentric far past when, during the period of Great Goddess worship, women were held in respect and awe as sources of primal power. See Rich (1976).

Feminist scholars have been particularly interested in how early religions came to be abandoned or overthrown in favour of patriarchal ones. Peggy Sanday hypothesises that societies which see nature as beneficent worship female deities. See Sanday (1981). Currently, feminist theologians like Rosemary Reuther argue that there are similar patterns of change in human interrelationships and relations with nature in the religious beliefs of contemporary society. These scholars claim that religions must change in order to restore a natural and social balance for future survival. See Reuther (1974). For example they describe how self-blessing rituals derived from oral traditions. The Native American poet Starhawk has created images of nature and the female principle in order to transform cultural traditions. See Christ and Plaskow (1979). Feminist theory is now celebrating the sacrality of women by recovering the religion of the Goddess.

Representation

Feminism, alongside semiology and Marxism, has made a complex appraisal of representation, or the construction of images. The term 'representation' or 'signification' includes *processes* by which meanings are produced. Feminists argue that representation continually creates, endorses, or alters ideas of gender identity. Feminist analysis of advertisements, film, photography, art and craft has produced many strategies for feminist practice. For example feminist critics of pornography use the concept of representation to move from content analysis to understanding the functions of pornography in society and how it is represented in terms of class, race and gender. See Kappeler (1986).

In art, feminism has had to negotiate a new meaning of representation. This is because the ideology of art includes ideas of self-expression which are masculine. See Parker and Pollock (1981). Some feminists look at ideological representations of femininity in terms of the articulation of capitalist production and consumption. See Women's Studies Group (1978). Other feminists focus on the construction of subjectivity and look at the role of language using insights gained from semiotics and Lacanian psychoanalysis. See Coward (1982). Laura Mulvey argues that representation is constructed on the absence or *lack* of female subjectivity because woman is the silent object of a male gaze. See Mulvey (1975).

Feminist film criticism has developed crucial accounts which describe how women are constructed in media representations. Ann Kaplan describes how cinema mechanisms dominate women through the controlling power of the gaze, by the fetishisation of women and often through the destruction of women in plot and narrative. See Kaplan (1983). Feminist film-makers work to demystify representation. For example feminist films foreground the cinematic apparatus as a signifying practice, refuse to construct a fixed spectator, and mix documentary and fiction. In order to suggest how the feminine might be represented outside of patriarchal discourse lesbian film-makers, such as Jan Oxenberg and

Maya Derek, create female images that depart radically from the representations of dominant cinema. Currently, feminism argues that there is no separation between 'real' relationships and representations since representations are part of real experience in the way social discourses are constructed. For example Griselda Pollock claims that we cannot make a separation between reality and signifying practices, for in order to make any intervention in theory or practice we require a soundly-based historical analysis of ideology and codes of representation in their historical specificity. See Pollock (1987).

Black feminism argues that we need a theory that takes into account the economic history of Black women's (mis)representation and ensuing stereotypes, for example the 'mammie' figure of Hollywood cinema. Attempts to represent Black women as cinematic subjects, for example in *The Color Purple*, distort Black ideology by re-asserting patriarchal power. See Miller (1987).

In order to develop a feminist cultural practice and theory that works towards productive social change it is necessary to understand that representation is a political issue and to analyse women's subordination within pariarchal forms of representation.

Reproduction
Juliet Mitchell calls reproduction one of the four main structures of women's oppression. There are two meanings of reproduction in feminist theory: the processes of intergenerational reproduction and the reproduction of daily life in the maintenance and socialisation activities of the home; and, the socially-mediated processes of biological reproduction and sexuality.

Marxists believe that women's work of biological and social reproduction in the home supports an economic and political order dominated by men, while at the same time it prevents women from participating directly in that order. This gives feminist theory one point of departure for an analysis of the subordination of women and sexual divisions. See Barrett and McIntosh (1982).

Marxist theory, however, assumes that the structures of sexuality and capitalist organisation are in unified articulation. Feminist anthropologists point out that sexual oppression precedes capitalism. For example de Beauvoir's claims that the 'mammalian' responsibility of women condemns them to an unfree existence. Sherry Ortner argues that the devaluation of women stems from women's association with reproduction and hence nature, while men participate in the project of culture. See Ortner (1974).

Radical feminists argue that in the wider context of sexual politics male supremacy is grounded in men's attempt to secure control over biological reproduction. Defining women solely as reproductive beings, radicals argue, misshapes women's self-image, sexual preference and expression and women's relations with other women, children and men. For example Shulamith Firestone claims that the prime site of this oppression is the nuclear family and that a feminist revolution needs to seize the means of reproduction. See Firestone (1970).

Two ideas underlie a feminist view of reproductive freedom. First is the idea of bodily self determination and second is the notion that reproductive consciousness is continuous and integrative, constantly affirming women's unity with nature, and cyclical time. See O'Brien (1983).

All radical feminists agree that women's subordination is connected with the sphere of reproduction and that women should aim to transform sexual and procreative practices more than political or economic ones. A number of feminist theorists, however, claim that a connection between women's reproductive activities and our social and political situation is historical not biological. For example Rosalind Petchesky argues that if reproductive freedom for women is justified solely by reference to the fact of female biology it will reinforce the view that all reproductive activity is the special, biologically-destined province of women. See Petchesky (1980).

Feminist theory describes how the social relations of reproduction are now radically altered, for example in the way that reproductive technology has separated copulation and reproduction, which Mary O'Brien calls 'a world-historical event' (O'Brien 1983). Adrienne Rich, more than other theorists, describes the liberating possibilities women have in our reproductive capacities. In reproductive freedom women will, Rich claims, have more highly developed tactile and mental states and a multi-pleasured physicality. See Rich (1976).

Reproductive rights

These include the right to become a mother and to contraception and abortion. Reproductive rights is a category often omitted in traditional, masculine politics. Feminist theory subverts this tradition by comparing public legality with private experience in its argument for reproductive freedom.

The perception that control over the termination of pregnancy is central to the future of women and woman's place informs feminist struggles about abortion. Linda Gordon argues that control of reproduction *is* essentially a political struggle about women's right to self-determination. See Gordon (1976). Adrienne Rich suggests that reproductive rights lie at the core of feminism, both in the sense of freedom *from* reproductive obligations and in a recuperation of motherhood. See Rich (1976). With reproductive rights women would be the creators of a new relationship with the universe.

Research
The aim of feminist research is to create theories grounded in the actual experiences and language of women by investigating women's lives and experience in their own terms. See Du Bois (1983). In addition, feminist research courts subjective involvement in its bid to gain that new theoretical understanding.

Integrating personal praxis and research is not unique to feminism, but feminist theory adds the point that both the content *and* the process of feminist research must involve fresh thinking about gender. For example research must make explicit the everyday knowledge of the researcher as well as that of the researched. See Stanley and Wise (1983). Second, the *process* of personal research must be included as much as any other data. Feminist research must adopt, Shulamit Reinharz claims, a nonhierarchical, nonauthoritarian, nonmanipulative relation to the 'subject' (Reinharz 1983).

Maria Mies has set out specific criteria for feminist research: it must be consciously partial, must be research from below, create change by involvement in women's liberation, be consciousness raising, use women's histories, and be part of collective discussion with women. See Mies (1983).

Reserve army theory
A term coined by Irene Bruegal to describe how women function as a reserve army of labour in capitalist patriarchy. She argues that, although women's employment has grown in the service sector, women are more easily disposed of than men in manufacturing in any economic crisis. Women's work is *regarded* as marginal, or in reserve, because of ideologies such as the 'male bread winner' and 'woman's place is in the home'. See Bruegal (1979).

Re-vision
A term used by Adrienne Rich which became the powerful slogan of contemporary feminist writing. A feminist re-vision makes a historical, cultural and psychic examination of women's cultural past, and creates a women's history. Rich's concept is close to Michel Foucault's notion of 'archaeology' — the exposure of moral values encoded in language. Rich took the term from Robert Duncan's *The Artist's View* (1953). But where Duncan uses 're-vision' merely to describe his *own* past, Rich's re-vision is a method for all women to share. See Rich (1979a) and Humm (1986).

Revolution

Has different meanings in feminist theory. Kate Millett suggested that the first revolution would need to be the abolition of the social construction of gender differences in consciousness. Revolution is associated with radical in radical feminism because uprooting sexism would create a new form of change going beyond existing political transformation. Eliminating women's oppression would create a new form of revolutionary change. See Morgan (1970).

Shulamith Firestone defines revolution as the seizing of control of the means of reproduction by women, which would lead to the dissolution of the biological family. Radicalesbians argue that revolution depends on the practice of women relating to women. The new identity, of woman-identified woman, would create a consciousness with revolutionary force. See Radicalesbians (1973).

Carolyn Heilbrun and feminist psychoanalysts claim that androgyny could be a revolutionary state since it would be based on a new concept of human nature. See Heilbrun (1973) and Bem (1976).

Revolution can also mean a physiological state. Adrienne Rich argues that if institutions of repression were abolished (like the institution of motherhood) then women's new mental and tactile capacities would gain us a new revolutionary relationship to the universe. See Rich (1976). French feminists argue that revolutionary potential derives from the subject position we take up. If we allow pleasure and *jouissance* to disrupt the symbolic order then specific practices of writing, by their very existence, testify to the possibilities of revolution. See Kristeva (1980).

Rich, Adrienne

American poet and critic who, in *Of Woman Born* (1976), *On Lies, Secrets and Silence* (1979) and 'Compulsory heterosexuality and lesbian existence' (1980), creates a feminist theory which she calls her 'Re-vision' or rewriting of patriarchal culture. The term refers to a new feminist perspective which could link women's culture to the realities of our past and contemporary history. Rich uses the technique in her own work to mix research and personal experience. Making a major contribution to feminism with her accounts of education, sexual politics, reproduction and ethnic identity, Rich argues that the English language and the intellectual tradition have been used as weapons of colonialisation and describes how a woman's university and female-identified education could provide an alternative to this tradition.

Rich recuperated the concept of motherhood for contemporary feminism by distinguishing between a patriarchal institutional-isation of motherhood and the joy and experience of motherhood.

Similarly Rich redefined the concept of 'lesbian' and greatly expanded the boundaries of lesbian history and experience by distinguishing the historical existence of lesbian from lesbian continuum, or women-identified experience. Rich's theories of ethnicity and Jewish identity in her more recent work depend on an exciting mixture of psychoanalysis and historical paradigm. In all her writings, and in her gynocentric view of world history, Rich creates a new tradition of feminist scholarship.

Romance

Early feminist theory generally denigrated romance as being a false construction of love. Mary Wollstonecraft criticised romance fiction because it encouraged the patriarchal socialisation of women. Second wave feminism began by arguing that romance is a cultural tool of male power which conceals a false eroticism. Shulamith Firestone claims that romance identifies women as 'love objects', and hence contributes to our devaluation. See Firestone (1970). Germaine Greer accounted for the falsity of romance in social-class terms and argued that romance had replaced coercion in heterosexual marriage. See Greer (1970). On the other hand, Juliet Mitchell argues that psychoanalytically, Eros and the death drive are intertwined in romantic love which represents the triumph of death over life. See Mitchell (1984).

Feminist sociologists draw attention to how older women are wholly categorised by exclusion from romance in media representation. See Itzin (1986). A discourse of romantic love so dominates culture that romance even provides definitions for lesbianism. Celia Kitzinger argues that liberal apologists fallaciously draw on this rhetoric to claim the isomorphism of heterosexuality and homosexuality. See Kitzinger (1986).

Currently, feminist theorists in popular culture analyse romance fiction to define its psychological appeal to women, for example by giving 'safe' expression to female fears about heterosexuality or entrapment. Feminists claim that there is no one kind of woman reader because although the text is a fixed structure, its meaning is constituted by historically situated subjects. These readings draw on psychoanalysis to counter gender stereotyping. See Radford (1986).

For example Janice Radway argues that the act of reading romance is very pleasurable, while of course leaving women's domestic role within patriarchal culture intact. See Radway (1984). Other critics investigating the way teenage girls read romances, argue that codes of romance represent autonomy and peer collectivity to girls. See Thompson (1984).

All feminist theory agrees that negatively or positively the rhetoric of romantic love still provides the only legitimating context for sexual activity in Western culture.

Rosaldo, Michelle

American anthropologist who co-edited *Women, Culture and Society* (1974) and made a major contribution to feminist theories of anthropology. Rosaldo argued that the subordination of women is due to a universal association of women with domestic activities. Later she expressed dissatisfaction with the universalistic theorisation of gender difference, and argued that the 'search for origins' had been taken over too uncritically by contemporary feminism. See Rosaldo (1980).

Rossi, Alice

American sociologist who in *Essays on Sex Equality* (1970) and *The Feminist Papers* (1973) provided a historical background for the contemporary women's movement and placed women in social science history. Rossi claimed that there is some 'biosocial' basis for women's nurturing role and that sex roles are equally biosocially determined. This view created some controversy in feminist theory.

Rowbotham, Sheila

British historian and activist who in *Women, Resistance and Revolution* (1972), *Hidden from History* (1973a), *Woman's Consciousness, Man's World* (1973b) and *Beyond the Fragments* (1979) created a systematic feminist theory about women's exclusion from culture and history. Rowbotham examined language and the symbolic order in terms of the needs of women's consciousness and politics. She reappraised the relation of the women's movement to the Left in Britain and argued for the creation of new feminist theory which would link psychology and materialism.

Rubin, Gayle

American anthropologist who in 'The traffic in women' (1975) coined the influential term 'sex-gender system' to define how women in different societies experience similar processes of gender identity formation. Using the theories of Lévi-Strauss and Freud, Rubin argues that feminism must revolutionise current systems of kinship to eliminate the symbolic exchange of women in the social contract.

Sadomasochism

The use of interpersonal psychic and physical violence as a source of sexual pleasure which feminism customarily defines as part of patriarchy. For radical feminists, lesbian sadomasochism is a matter of intense political debate which focuses on whether sadomasochism can be accepted as a legitimate part of womenculture. Some theorists argue that sadomasochism is coercive and typically patriarchal. For example Mary Daly claims that the central message of Christianity is sadomasochism. See Daly (1973). Susan Griffin argues that sadomasochistic images in pornography are evidence of the desecration of the female and that sadomasochism is essentially a male phenomenon. See Griffin (1981).

Other theorists argue that sadomasochism is concerned with fantasy not reality. See Califia (1981). The discussion illustrates how central sexuality is to a radical feminist concept of human nature and gender politics. Underlying this discussion is a theoretical difference about woman's 'true' nature and the correct direction for feminist politics.

Sapphic sexuality

A term for the expression of sexuality in women's writing, a term used particularly by French critics. Critics point to the shift in writing from limited, restrained descriptions of relationships between women, for example the sentimentality of Colette's lesbianism, to the limitless revolutionary expression of passion between women seen in Monique Wittig's creation of autonomous and mobile lesbian women. See Moi (1985).

Scholarship

Feminist theory's greatest contribution to feminist activism lies in creating a new tradition of feminist scholarship.

The stages of feminist scholarship are defined as: first, the development of 'compensatory' scholarship which adds women's history and work to existing disciplines; second, the radical reconstruction of disciplines and third, the reconstruction of philosophical and scientific reality from a feminist perspective. See Boxer (1982).

The need for feminist scholarship is made clear in Mary Daly's account of male scholarship which describes its bias and legitimisation of the oppression of women. See Daly (1978). Feminist scholarship is unique in its essential duality: that is, feminist scholarship is rooted simultaneously in the disciplinary structures of contemporary intellectual enquiry *and* in a political movement.

Science

The branches of science which most often describe and interpret women's nature are biology and psychology. Feminists argue that observation and analysis in both fields are marked by bias and distortion, for example biology uses primate study to deduce inappropriate behavioural patterns for humans, and psychology argues that sex hormones purportedly create differences between male and female behaviour. Ruth Wallsgrove argues that these common characteristics of science − detachment, rationality and the desire for control − are a reaction against the caring and emotional characteristics traditionally defined as feminine. See Wallsgrove (1980).

Feminist theories of science have two tasks: to point out ways in which scientific methods and theories are sexist and to devise new approaches. Feminist historians of science point to the 'masculinisation' of science in the sixteenth and seventeenth centuries. For example the Baconian experimental method encouraged the inquisition of nature by scientists and drew its inspiration from earlier witch trials. Carolyn Merchant argues that the rise of modern science and technology is based on the rise of the male scientist as priest. See Merchant (1983). Liberal critiques of science point to unfair employment practices and the exclusion of women from science. Radical critiques point to bias in science's choice and definition of problems, for example in its devaluation of women's health issues.

Feminist philosophers argue that science is the epitomy of gender dichotomies. Its dualisms of subject/object, culture/nature, thought/feeling, active/passive are all symbolic of and descriptive of the central male/female dualism and the oppositional relations of dominance and dominated. Susan Griffin notes that the pervasive metaphor in Western science is control over nature. See Griffin (1978).

Evelyn Fox Keller argues that science is usually gendered as masculine and antithetical to Eros. The scientist, who is traditionally male, has had to reject the feminine in order to establish his masculine identity, entailing a rejection of nonbinary thinking and an endorsement of either/or objectivity – a hallmark of the Newtonian world view. She argues that this definition of scientific knowledge grew out of a cultural tradition in which nature is seen as female and the knower of nature was male. This masculine style attracts male scientists and only with the dissolution of this mystical connection, Keller claims, can science truly advance. See Keller (1978).

Elizabeth Fee says that at this historical moment what we are developing is not a feminist science but a feminist critique of existing science. She argues that feminist alternatives to the prevailing masculine ideology of science are a cottage industry, but Donna Haraway suggests that a socialist feminist science is in the process of construction. See Haraway (1979).

Feminist science involves women making a collective approach to the knowledge of nature and ourselves, and a commitment to the survival of both.

Second wave
A term coined by Marsha Weinman Lear to refer to the formation of women's liberation groups in America, Britain and Germany in the late 1960s. The term 'second wave' implies that 'first wave' feminism ended in the 1920s. See Lear (1968).

Disillusionment with the politics of Civil Rights, the anti-war movement and Students for a Democratic Society, led American women to form their own consciousness-raising groups. This activity is encapsulated in the slogan 'the personal is political'. Sara Evans claims that, in its trajectory from civil rights to women's liberation, the second wave recapitulated the history of first wave feminism in the sense that a struggle for racial equality was midwife to both feminisms. See Evans (1979).

The main change in second wave feminist theory since 1970 has been the move from minimising differences between men and women to celebrating a woman-centred perspective. Second wave feminism currently is committed to radically extending egalitarianism based on a sophisticated understanding of the oppressiveness of imposed gender divisions. Second wave feminism is a radical transformation project and aims to create a feminised world. See Maroney (1982).

Segregation
Usually the separation of groups by race in restricted areas or facilities. Feminist economic theory uses two definitions of segre-

gation. Catharine Hakim argues that women are occupationally divided into horizontal and vertical segregation. Horizontal occupational segregation exists when men and women are working in two different sectors of a job or industry and vertical occupational segregation exists because men tend to work in higher grade occupations and women in lower grades. This leads to a double discrimination against women workers. See Hakim (1979).

Self

The concept generally has two different uses in feminist theory. It can mean the beliefs that a woman has about herself and her individual potential (as in self-fulfilment) and it can mean the perception of oneself as a member of a community of women (as in self-help women's therapy). Mary Daly describes two other meanings – a woman's true self and her false self. Under patriarchy women have a false self because they are alienated from authentic experience. When this false self is destroyed, a real self will emerge in a spiritual rebirth. See Daly (1978). Daly uses the concept dialectically, arguing that emotional self-sufficiency is best obtained in a cooperative or contractual model of female relationships.

Self-consciousness

The term is used to describe the critical method of feminism. According to Catharine MacKinnon the practice of self-consciousness – of reading, speaking and listening to oneself and other women is the best way to resist institutional recuperation. Self-consciousness is a form of knowledge which involves the political apprehension of self in society. See MacKinnon (1982).

Semiology

A term, originating with the French linguist Saussure, which describes how all sign systems (literature, the media, social codes and ideologies) function like languages.

Feminists use semiology to demystify the myths and codes of pornography, the media and the beauty industry in order to reveal the mechanisms of a misogynistic patriarchal culture. Semiology is particularly helpful to feminist theories of representation since it shows how techniques and social conventions manufacture meaning. Feminists focus on stereotyping and the construction of subjectivity in representation. For example Ros Coward analyses media representation in terms of narrative structure and semiological oppositions of masculine and feminine. See Coward (1985).

In film theory, E. Ann Kaplan uses semiology to describe how women in Hollywood films are marginalised. Semiology is particularly useful to film theory because it demolishes the idea of a privileged aesthetic discourse and it stresses the crucial role played by artistic form as a medium of expression. See Kaplan (1983). Other critics point to the problems inherent in a semiology of the cinema because semiology takes the text as an object and ignores institutional practice or a historical moment. See Kuhn (1985).

Semiology is used in feminist art practice, particularly by artists who create written art texts, for example Mary Kelly. By arguing that an image of woman is not one already given but constructed in and through the art work itself, feminists have evolved a complex theory of representation. See Pollock (1987).

In French theory, *la sémiotique* is the science of signs. Julia Kristeva coins the term *le sémiotique* to refer to the actual organisation, or disposition, within the body of instinctual drives (hence the semiotic disposition) as they affect language and its practice in dialectical conflict with the '*symbolique*' or symbolic. See Kristeva (1980).

Separatism

The belief that women will only develop their own strengths if separated from male dominated institutions. Feminism has always required a degree of separatism. In the 1960s the women's liberation movement separated from the male New Left so that women could discuss women's experience and reinterpret that experience in the light of an explicit recognition of male domination.

There are two main uses of the term 'separatism' in feminist theory which can be summed up in the difference between the socialist feminist concept of alternative institutions and the radical feminist concept of a womanculture. Radical feminism intends that alternative institutions will enable women to withdraw as far as possible from the dominant culture. Socialist feminists, by contrast, argue that alternative institutions will only partially satisfy existing needs and that women and men must experiment with new forms of working together. See Rowbotham (1979). In this sense separatism does not mean segregation but an organisational or political separation from men.

Separatism is proposed as the ultimate goal of the feminist movement by radical feminists like Ti-Grace Atkinson. In this sense separatism means both a social arrangement and a political stance. Radical feminism advocates separate organisations for women and men and that women maintain a separate culture – by dealing as much as possible only with women, by living with women and living by 'feminine' values. See Daly (1978) and Rich (1979b). Charlotte Bunch has argued that only with alternative women's institutions can we weaken male power over our lives. See Bunch (1981).

American women of colour point to the limitations of a separatist politics. They argue that separatism is not a viable political position because it denies the facts of class and race. See Combahee River Collective (1981). In their view autonomy must stand in the place of separatism.

What all feminist theory agrees, is that separatism is a powerful political force if used as part of a conscious strategy of liberation. Women must separate from male dominated or defined institutions which operate to maintain male privilege rather than equal rights.

Sex
Feminist theory defines sex only as the biology of a person – whether he or she is anatomically male or female. A central task in contemporary feminist theory from Kate Millett onwards is to distinguish conceptually between sex and gender so that expectations of sex roles can be altered if they are not perceived to be biological. Ann Oakley argues that sex differences may be 'natural' but gender differences have their source in culture, not nature. See Oakley (1972).

Sex difference
With the re-emergence of feminism in the 1960s, feminist psychology developed theories about sexual inequality and difference. The term refers to a body of research which covers a broad spectrum, beginning with differences between the sexes in attitudes and abilities and research finding the origins of these in terms of sex role socialisation. For example Matina Horner argues that women are conditioned to a different view of success, 'a fear of success'; and Carol Gilligan argues that women are not as motivated as men by individualistic morals. See Horner (1972) and Gilligan (1982).

There are two basic approaches to sex difference within feminism. There are those theorists who argue against the use of masculine/feminine scales because such scales scientifically reinforce 'man-made' sex role stereotypes about what is appropriate 'feminine' or 'masculine' behaviour. See Eichler (1980). Eichler argues that studies basing causal factors on sex differences will be too simplistic unless they explore other mediating variables. Inevitably most studies conclude that there are inherent differences between the sexes. She suggests that men and women have different psychologies because they have different expectations due to social experience and social conditioning.

Other feminists celebrate sex difference. Ellen Moers argues that there are clear sex differences in literature, for example in vocabulary and syntax (women's more frequent use of ellipsis), in associations (women are closer to natural objects) or in specific genres (women write and read gothic or romance novels). See Moers (1977). Elaine Showalter calls this 'gynocentric' research, which is the construction of a female literary tradition on the basis of sex difference. See Showalter (1979).

French feminist theory also celebrates difference. Julia Kristeva argues that there are sex differences in the relationship of subjects to the symbolic contract, a difference in the relationship to power, to language and to meaning. See Kristeva (1982). The French feminist text most in praise of sexual difference is *Parole de femme* (1974) by Annie Leclerc.

Sex–gender system

A term coined by Gayle Rubin, the American anthropologist, in 1975 to describe the universal system of sexual and reproductive relations. Rubin thinks that the theory of the exchange of women accurately describes the oppression of women because the act of exchange so profoundly limits women's lives. Using insights from Freud, Lacan, Marx and Lévi-Strauss, Rubin argues that all societies organise the biological differences between men and women into specific social arrangements. This common sex-gender system is characterised by an asymmetrical exchange in which men always exchange women and not ever the other way around. Further, this sexual division of labour ensures that the interests of men, not women, are met in the act of exchange. According to Rubin the particular *mode* of production alters the *details* of the exchange, but the sex-gender system can be both conceptually and, at particular historical moments, empirically isolated from the mode of production. See Rubin (1975).

Rubin's theory stimulated feminist scholars across the disciplines of philosophy, history, literature, economics and politics as well as anthropology.

Sexism

A social relationship is which males denigrate females. Contemporary feminism argues that sexist social beliefs and practices not only limit the activities of women, but are an impertinent way of making distinctions between the sexes, because they are not founded on evidence. A substantial body of feminist research has documented sexism in the media, for example the use of sex-role stereotyping where women are always mothers and domestic workers. See Williamson (1978). Studies of the vocabulary of sexism by feminist linguists show how both the sexualisation of language *and* the use of euphemisms, for example 'cleaning lady', are degrading to women. See Lakoff (1975).

Feminist psychoanalysis argues that sexism stems from the formation of gender identity as well as from contemporary culture. Nancy Chodorow and Dorothy Dinnerstein claim that women's responsibility for infant care creates male fears of women and hence later sexism. See Chodorow (1978), Dinnerstein (1976). Feminist sociologists agree that sexism is deeply rooted. Jessie Bernard, for example, suggests that it is unconscious and taken for granted. See Bernard (1968).

Hence the deconstruction of sexist myths is an important aim of, and becomes the agenda for, women's studies. The subjective experience of sexist discrimination has been a starting point and guiding principle for these courses. See Mies (1983). Sexism, as Bell Hooks claims, is of primary importance not because it is the *basis* of all other oppression but because it is the practice of domination that *all* people experience. See Hooks (1981).

Sex roles

In conventional sociology 'sex role' is a social role allocated to men and to women on the basis of biological sex. Feminist theory argues that gender-associated behaviour is linked *arbitrarily* by society to each biological sex. An attack on such sex-role stereotyping was the first agenda of contemporary feminism. Proving Simone de Beauvoir's thought that 'one is not born, but becomes a woman' feminists found sex roles to be a learned quality, an assigned status and part of an ideology which attributes women's roles to nature. For example Kate Millett argues that sex-role stereotyping ensures the social control of women, because from childhood women are trained to accept a system which divides society into male and female spheres and gives public power to males. Millett used the language and concepts of social psychology, in particular Robert Stoller's ideas of core gender identity, to argue that women are given expressive traits and men instrumental traits. Sex roles are a form of oppression because they keep women from social activity. See Millett (1970).

Alice Rossi, Jessie Bernard and Betty Friedan use social psychological analysis and argue that the contemporary oppression of women is the result of the inculcation of socially defined sex roles. Feminism thus revolutionised traditional sociology by showing how gender-associated behaviour was created by social propaganda. For example Elizabeth Janeway claims that women are really only defined by domestic roles in popular media. See Janeway (1971).

Much contemporary feminist research proves that observed *psychological* differences between the sexes are not innate but the result of sex-role conditioning, and uses many theoretical approaches from behaviourism to object relations theory. Phyllis Chesler, in *Women and Madness* (1972) argues that expectations of feminine roles are expectations for abnormal or nonfunctioning human beings, and therefore the stereotype of femininity is a prescription for failure and madness. Other psychoanalysts found role theory to be inadequate because it relies on intentionality whereas sex roles are part of a family creation of appropriate personality structures. See Chodorow (1978). Sandra Bem and others claim that sex-role stereotyping could be eliminated by the introduction of androgyny. Among some radical feminists a commitment to abolishing sex roles is taken to imply a commitment to androgyny.

Radical feminism claims that the only solution to the issue would be to refuse the ascription of any characteristic, behaviour or role to women. See Kreps (1973). Sex-role terminology was gradually abandoned by feminist theory with its general shift away from psychologically based accounts. However, it remains true that more work has been done on sex-role stereotyping, for example on sexist imagery in the media, than on woman's *self* concept of her sex role. Sex-role research presupposes the abstract individualistic belief that human beings exist as actors prior to their entry into society. Feminists now point to the debilitating influence of sex-role terminology which does not consider how women actually perceive and experience such roles. See Condor (1986).

Sexual division

Feminist theory cuts across the divisions created by production and reproduction, the public and the domestic to argue that social relations in the family and social production structure experience in every sector. However, there are differences among feminists about which aspects of sexual division to attack.

Marxist feminists argue that the main division of labour is within the family. Here women (through domestic labour) reproduce not only the future generation of labour power but also current members of the employed labour force. This division within the family parallels a sexual division of labour in employment where women habitually occupy the 'secondary' sector of the labour market. See Barrett and McIntosh (1982).

Radical feminism opposes any solidification of the gender system and gives attention to more problematic implications of the division of labour. For example Temma Kaplan argues that sexual division is not necessarily a negative feature if we understand why women might want to *uphold* a sex division of labour. Sexual divisions, Kaplan claims, can give women a sense of who they are in society and culture. The acceptance of sex division as a means of survival can lead women to political arguments about social issues. See Kaplan (1982).

Sexual harassment

The unwanted sexual advances of men to women. Feminist theory describes this in terms of power relations, and argues that sexual harassment symbolises the way men objectify women. See MacKinnon (1979).

Contemporary feminism introduced the term sexual harassment because the term makes it easier to conceptualise sexual harassment as an experience, and it also can aid opposition and resistance. The term has a double function. It implies a realignment in relations as much as a reorganised perception of what sort of things are intrusive or coercive. For example feminist sociologists draw analogies between police harassment, work harassment and husband harassment, arguing that these are similar kinds of experience. See Stanley and Wise (1983).

Sexual identity

A sense of one's own sexuality.

Feminist theory argues that this identity is culturally rather than biologically determined, for example that it represents only the public presentation of sexual aims and objectives as integrated into the personality. See Coward (1982).

Ann Ferguson gives a clear account of the various meanings of the term. She argues that our identities are predicated upon two conditions. First, a person cannot be said to have a sexual identity that is not self-conscious, for example the taking on of a lesbian identity. Second, that one must live in a culture where that concept has relevance, for example a person cannot have a Black identity unless the concept of blackness exists in a person's cultural environment. See Ferguson *et al* (1982).

Sexuality

The social process which creates, organises, expresses and directs desire. Where Freud had characterised female sexuality as inherently passive, masochistic and narcissistic, feminist theory from the 1960s began a thoroughgoing critique of prevailing ideas of sexuality which ignore the realities of women's experience. For example Anne Koedt, in 'The myth of the vaginal orgasm', argued that women's sexuality was not dependent on vaginal penetration but would be diverse and diffuse. See Koedt (1973).

Sexuality is described as one of the four structures of women's oppression by Juliet Mitchell in 'Women: the longest revolution' (1966). Feminist theory argues that men's control over reproduction and the sexuality of women's bodies is a major activity of patriarchy. In this sense feminism believes that forms of sexuality are not innate but reflect political and cultural institutions that affect the condition of individual life and consciousness. See Firestone (1970).

Feminist psychoanalysts, for example Dorothy Dinnerstein, argue that there is a double standard in sexuality, in that men are thought to have a polygamous nature and women are thought to have a monogamous preference.

Feminist educationists argue that the double division of sexuality in ideology and practice is represented in schools as a struggle for female identity. For example the regulation of girls' sexuality and their production as carers conflicts with their positioning as children. The sexuality of girls is converted into maternal nurturance. See Walkerdine (1986).

According to radical feminism, women's oppression comes from male control of fertility and women's sexuality. Radical feminism argues that male domination in *all* its manifestations is grounded ultimately on men's control over procreative capacities. See Rich (1980).

There is a continuing debate in feminist theory about the *nature* of female sexuality. Some feminists claim that female sexuality is only really represented in lesbian relationships while others argue that this romanticisation of a 'pure' form divorces sexuality from issues of power. Defenders of lesbian sadomasochism argue that all sexual expression needs to be explored in order to combat the commoditisation of sexuality and broaden concepts of sexuality. See Califia (1981). But as yet there is no *new* form of feminist sexuality which can construct a female subject in a process of social change.

Sexual objectification

The fetishisation of women's sexuality. The women's movement, in its campaigns against beauty contests and against pornography, made visible a contemporary feminist critique of sexual objectification. In film theory, Laura Mulvey argues that the whole cinematic apparatus is dependent on the concept of a male gaze or the objectification of women. See Mulvey (1975).

Other feminist theory has added to media analysis the explicit recognition that all social process expresses an inequality in social power. Sexual objectification is a primary process in the subjection of women, since objectification makes sexuality a material reality not simply a psychological, attitudinal or ideological one. See MacKinnon (1982). MacKinnon argues that Marxist attempts to deal with sexual objectification, unlike feminism, cannot deal with the duality of sexual objectification with both an aesthetic and a content of subordination.

Sexual orientation

The term usually means that an individual is naturally inclined towards a particular sexual identity. Even within traditional sociology or psychology there is disagreement about the concept. For example some argue, following Freud, that orientations are set up in early childhood, while others argue that orientations may be more flexible and relate to the life cycle. Radical feminists argue that the term connotes that one is *free* to choose a particular sexual identity. Radicalesbians felt that this choice would enable lesbian women to escape from second-class definitions of 'woman'. See Radicalesbians (1973). In *On Lies, Secrets and Silence* Adrienne Rich suggests that lesbian/feminist transcends the category of 'sexual preference' to become a politics of asking women's questions. See Rich (1979).

Sexual relations

Those activities where sensual aims and objectives are integrated into relations, (usually public) with other people.

Second wave feminism began its critique of sexual relationships in consciousness-raising groups. The groups explored women's past and present experiences and created an awareness of the political dimensions of sexual relations and feminism's powerful potential for change. See Shulman (1986). Kate Millett claimed that the medium of sexual relationships, conventionally described as love, was a relationship of domination and subordination and it was in this sense that sexual relations embodied a political dimension. See Millett (1970).

Sexual politics

The political character of sexuality which is based on the unequal power of sexual relations. A major premiss of feminist theory is that sexual politics supports patriarchy in its politicisation of the personal life.

The term comes from Kate Millett's *Sexual Politics* where she used it to articulate a broad theoretical base for the ideas of the women's movement. Millett widened the concept of politics to refer to power structuring in general and shows that this concept defines the essence of male/female arrangements. Using historical and literary models she argues that sexual politics, grounded in misogyny, results in women's oppression both institutionally and at a personal level. Millett itemises the realms within which patriarchy operates, such as biology, education and rape and shows that one of the key features of sexual politics is its invisibility. See Millett (1970).

Feminist theory has developed several forms of analysis in order to examine the relationships between structures of sexuality and capitalist organisations. For example socialist feminism rejects the idea that sexuality is a biologically-determined domain and it insists that the meaning of sexuality is determined within social relations. See Barrett and McIntosh (1982). Radical feminism argues that the humiliation and abuse of women, for example in clitoridectomy, could not be accounted for by cultural politics but only by a throughgoing sexual politics. See Daly (1978).

Sexual revolution
The term generally means the relaxation of social taboos about the sexual behaviour of men and women which occurred in the 1960s. Feminist theory argues that the earlier sexual revolution of the late nineteenth century was a positive advance for women since it enabled women to take their own genital sexual needs seriously, which is a necessary component of self-identity. However, the sexual objectification of women now adds to our material objectification. See Ferguson et al. (1982).

Feminists of the 1970s claim that the 'sexual revolution' of the 1960s is a male fantasy. See Rowbotham (1979). They argue that changes in sexual activity might be due to women's vulnerability rather than self-discovery. See Gordon (1976). Feminist social scientists also criticise the myth of a sexual revolution and stress the persistence of traditional sex values. See Petchesky (1986).

But since women's sense of sexuality is a product of a sexual culture we need to use the concept of 'revolution' to describe changes in sexuality. Kate Millett uses the term to describe the large-scale changes which are required in contemporary sexual relations. Millett argues that the idea of a sexual revolution is within human consciousness even more pre-eminently than it is within human relations.

Ellen Willis gives the most throughgoing definition of a sexual revolution. She argues that a sexual liberation must involve not only the abolition of restrictions but the positive presence of social and psychological conditions that can foster satisfying sexual relations. Sexual freedom, she claims, will only exist within a coherent feminist politics when individuals are not oppressed by a socially-constructed sexuality based on biologically-determined definitions of sexuality. See Willis (1982).

Sherfey, Mary Jane
American psychiatrist whose account of clitoral orgasms and the inductor theory in 'A theory on female sexuality' (1976) and *The Nature and Evolution of Female Sexuality* (1972) laid the groundwork for second wave feminism. Sherfey argued that women's sexual capacity for multiple orgasms is radically different from, and superior to that of men. Her discovery of the inductor theory in medical literature (that the mammalian male is derived from the female) had significant implications for psychiatry and socially-constituted sex roles since it directly contradicts Freudian theory that the clitoris is a vestigial organ. See Sherfey (1972, 1976).

Showalter, Elaine
American literary theorist who in *A Literature of Their Own: British Women Novelists from Brontë to Lessing* (1977) made a major contribution to literary history by rediscovering neglected women writers and situating them in the terrain of female literature. In 'Towards a feminist poetics' (1979) Showalter evolved a theory of feminist aesthetics called 'gynocritics' which distinguishes between women as reader and woman as writer. See Showalter (1977, 1979).

Signs: Journal of Women, Culture and Society
A groundbreaking American journal dedicated to the publication of new feminist scholarship and theory about women, begun in 1975 by Catharine Stimpson.

Significance
A term used by the French writer Julia Kristeva to refer to linguistic operations that are both fluid and archaic and hence feminine. She uses it to describe the work performed in language which enables a text to signify what communicative speech does not say, and which represents a disruption of the patriarchal order. See Kristeva (1980).

Silence
In feminist theory the silence of women stands both for our repression in patriarchy and also for our techniques of passive resistance. Feminist critics try to enable women to 'find a voice' to articulate difference in the articulation of forbidden discourse. See Moi (1985).

Silence also means 'absence' in the theories that take women to be in the situation of absence in relation to language, that is forced to use a discourse that is inadequate to express reality fully. For example Tillie Olsen in *Silences* argues that silence is a central condition of women's culture. Women's voices have gone unheard, masked by male power realities incorporated into language. See Olsen (1978).

In sociology, particular forms of feminist research have helped women break silence. For example the *Hite Report* enabled women's own accounts of sexuality to be heard. In philosophy, Dorothy Smith argues that women's silence stems from social repression, from strong social disapproval of the exercise by women of intellectual leadership and from organisational process. In situations of social interaction women act as a silent or agreeing audience. See D. Smith (1978).

Black feminists describe how the transformation of silence into language and action can be an act of self-revelation. The breaking of silence is the bridging of differences. See Lorde (1984). Adrienne Rich adds that this breaking will be the naming and founding of a women's culture. See Rich (1979a).

Silence can also mean resistance. Gayatri Spivak argues that in literature when women characters *choose* silence, for example Mrs Ramsay in *To the Lighthouse*, this represents a privileged moment allowing the inanimate world to reflect women's reality. See Spivak (1987).

Single mothers

One-parent families represent one in eight of British families and most are headed by women. Sociologists describe the constraints on women's lives caused by single parenthood, which include low incomes and poor housing. See Beechey (1986). Some feminist theorists argue that, potentially, the choice of single motherhood might be a form of liberation for women. Julia Kristeva argues that single mothers represent a refusal of the paternal function as well as a fervent divinisation of maternal power, all of which, she claims, cannot help but trouble an entire legal and moral order although single mothers cannot be an alternative to it. See Kristeva (1982).

Lesbian theorists argue that single motherhood does represent such an alternative. Many women who choose to have children 'outside' society make a significant step in forming a new identity. Single mothers who are lesbians are making an explicit political statement of a lesbian identity and creating a real alternative to the nuclear family. See Hanscombe and Forster (1982).

Sisterhood

Sometimes called sorority, sisterhood includes the idea and

experience of female bonding, and the self-affirmation and identity discovered in a woman-centred vision and definition of womanhood. Because sisterhood is based on a clear awareness that all women, irrespective of class, race, or nation have a common problem – patriarchy, the term is an important part of contemporary feminism.

Radical feminism argues that sisterhood is not at all symmetrical with brotherhood or male comradeship. Sisterhood has at its core the affirmation of freedom and is radically self-affirming. See Daly (1978). Daly claims that in this respect sisterhood is totally different from male comradeship or brotherhood, in which individuals seem to lose their identity. Daly calls sisterhood a gynaesthetic convergence of personal histories.

There are other definitions of sisterhood, for example Catherine Beecher's idea of separate spheres. Sisterhood is also implied in the maternalists' affirmation and celebration of the unique qualities of female experience (see Rich, 1976) as well as in Mary Daly's vision of women-centred separatism.

Bell Hooks and other Black feminists prefer the term 'solidarity' to sisterhood because sisterhood implies the erasing of difference. They argue that political solidarity must be the main feminist agenda. See Hooks (1981).

Smith, Barbara

Black American lesbian writer who in *Toward a Black Feminist Criticism* (1977) made a pioneering contribution to the development of Black feminist theory. Smith attacked the misrepresentation and construction of Black women in texts by white *and* by Black men. Smith argued that literary theory must become politicised. In 'Across the Kitchen Table' (1981) and 'Between a rock and a hard place' (1984) Smith addressed the challenge for women having to combine the identities of Black women, lesbian or artist. Her books create an agenda of Black, sexual and coalition politics from a solidly pro-woman perspective.

Social change

Within equal-rights feminism this term refers to a narrow agenda which promotes the recruitment of women, over a period of time, into areas of power from which they had been previously excluded. For example by increasing political representation or women's representation in the professions.

Radical feminism claims that a truly feminist theory of social change is possible only *within* radical feminism. For example Ti-Grace Atkinson argues that lesbians are the only group who can think radically about the possibility of social change without reference to existing gender arrangements. See Atkinson (1974).

Social consciousness

Feminism, as a set of beliefs and practices, is a form of social consciousness, but it also connotes a theory of social consciousness specific to it. The most important element in this theory is belief in the experiential quality of women's daily lives. Feminism attacks attempts to objectify this quality. See Stanley and Wise (1983). Feminists argue that there are differences between the social consciousness of men and of women, for example in our different perceptions of the world. Women prefer to share social consciousness in women-related groups. See Condor (1986).

Social control

The indirect or direct coercion of women. Feminist theorists use the term in different disciplinary ways in order to examine its linguistic, institutional, economic and psychological forms. Kate Millett argued that social control works by means of engineering the consent of women themselves through sex-role stereotyping and the institution of heterosexuality. Susan Brownmiller and Susan Griffin point to rape as the major agency in the social control of women. Adrienne Rich makes an institutional analysis of social control. She describes women's exclusion from education; and the coercion of women within the institutions of motherhood and heterosexuality. Rich defines 'social control' as social and psychological 'compulsion'. See Rich (1976, 1980). Nancy Henley describes how women are socially controlled in mixed groups and excluded from social space and language. See Henley (1977). Marxist and socialist feminists account for the social and economic controls wielded by the family in maintaining commodity production. See Rowbotham (1973b). The principal theme of all feminist theory is that aspects of social control in patriarchy are diffuse and very complex, involving every social, economic and cultural institution and practice.

Socialisation

The inculcation of gendered values into children from birth. Juliet Mitchell in *Women: The Longest Revolution* (1966) gave the first thorough contemporary account of socialisation. She argues that socialisation is one of four main social structures which need to be transformed in tandem before women can be liberated. The others are production, reproduction and sexuality. See Mitchell (1966).

Socialist feminism

One of the main theories of Western feminism, socialist feminism believes that women are second-class citizens in patriarchal capitalism which depends for its survival on the exploitation of working people, and on the special exploitation of women. Socialist feminism argues that we need to transform not only the ownership of the means of production, but also social experience because the *roots* of women's oppression lie in the total economic system of capitalism. See Reed (1970).

Unlike radical feminism, socialist feminists refuse to treat economic oppression as secondary; unlike Marxist feminists they refuse to treat sexist oppression as secondary.

Socialist feminism argues that men have a specific material interest in the domination of women and that men construct a variety of institutional arrangements to perpetuate this domination. Socialist feminism goes beyond the conventional definition of 'economy' to consider activity that does not involve the exchange of money, for example by including the procreative and sexual work done by women in the home. In analysing all forms of productive activity, socialist feminism joins the analytic tool of gender to that of class. For example Sheila Rowbotham and Juliet Mitchell argue that women who are confined primarily to the lowest paying and least secure jobs can gain real economic independence only in a fully transformed economy. See Rowbotham (1973b), Mitchell (1984). A socialist feminist theory of historical materialism, together with psychoanalysis, helps us evaluate concepts like 'internalised oppression'. Juliet Mitchell links the two in her theory of character formation to explain why women seem to collude with their own subordination and neglect apparent opportunities for individual or collective resistance. See Mitchell (1974).

Socialist feminism has a theory of epistemology which takes the view that all knowledge represents the interests and values of specific social groups, by describing historical variations in practices and in the categories by which values are understood. See Eisenstein (1979). One difficulty with all these aspects of socialist feminism however is that they rely on a concept of the sexual division of labour to explore the relations between women's subordination, specific economic systems and specific ways of organising sexuality.

Socialist feminism is now engaged in a more adequate explanation of women's subordination in order to show how types of production, not ordinarily considered economic, can be understood in economic terms. The ideal is that 'women' and 'men' might disappear as socially constituted categories.

Socialist feminism is attacked by radical feminism because it obscures and occludes an understanding of how central the institution of heterosexuality is to women's oppression. See Ferguson *et al.* (1982).

Writers trying to place these larger feminist issues, such as reproductive self-determination, into the context of an overall political struggle for a feminist socialism are Lydia Sargent (1981), Linda Gordon (1976) and Rosalind Petchesky (1986). In addition, socialist feminists are describing new libertarian grass roots women's groups which could be new models of socialism. See Rowbotham (1979).

Social mythology
A concept created by Elizabeth Janeway in *Man's World, Woman's Place* (1971) to describe the normative set of beliefs and practices which shape social life according to patriarchal values, as in 'woman's place is in the home'. Janeway argues that social mythology springs from a discrepancy of power between the sexes.

Sociobiology
The science of the biological basis of social behaviour present in behaviour traits and genetic evidence. Feminists criticise the science for its biological determinism. Feminist theory argues that sociobiology constructs 'universal' human behaviours which are curiously similar to social organisations in the white Western industrial capitalist world, and that sociobiology is ignorant of the complexity of human social life and cultures. For example sociobiology's concept of dominance hierarchies is an ethnocentric description of human traits, and sociobiology uses arbitrary categorisations of behaviour. See Howell (1979).

Sociology
The science of, and study of, society. Feminist social scientists argue that the science traditionally concentrates attention on the world as men see it. Classical and modern sociology fail to account for women because both decry experiential evidence, which is the way that women shape and articulate our social reality. See Gould (1980). Sociology focuses on public, official, visible and dramatic role players. This focus produces a distorted view of social reality because unofficial, supportive and invisible spheres of social life and organisation may be as important. See Millman and Kanter (1975).

For example sociology has often failed to consider the influence of gender on social behaviour. Gaye Tuckman reveals that studies of recruitment into artistic careers fail to look at gender as an important variable in career choice. See Tuckman (1975).

Neither is social science value free. Black sociologist Joyce Ladner argues that her view is radically different from anything a white male might bring to research. See Ladner (1971). Elizabeth Janeway argues that social scientists often substitute 'prescription' for description and explain how women ought to be rather than how we are. For example Janeway gives the term 'social mythology' to sociology's claim that women are 'naturally' inclined to domesticity. See Janeway (1971). Arlie Hochschild points out that sociology has never developed a theory of feeling and the emotions. See Hochschild (1983).

The two major methods of social science investigation – statistical surveys and participant observation – are also problematic, some feminist social scientists argue, and should be replaced by experiential analysis which takes into account the experiences of both researcher and researched. See Rubin (1976) and Reinharz (1979).

Since the problem seems endemic to sociology, feminists argue that we need careful conceptual work in order to develop a new sociology of knowledge embracing all aspects of women's experiences. See D. Smith (1978). Liz Stanley and Sue Wise advocate 'fag sociology' or 'sociology without balls' which uses the method of ethnomethodology to concentrate on the everyday personal concerns of women rather than on social structure. They argue that feminist social science must begin with the recognition that the personal, 'lived' experience underlies all behaviour and action. See Stanley and Wise (1983).

Sparking

A term for women's language coined by Mary Daly in *Gyn/Ecology* (1978). Sparking is like *écriture féminine*, in which sparking women can speak with tongues of fire igniting the divine spark in women.

Spender, Dale

Australian critic and scholar who in *Man Made Language* (1980) created a feminist theory of language. Spender argues that the meanings our words bear both constitute, and are constituted by our culture, which is misogynist. For example the use of man to include male *and* female is not innocent but a linguistic message that men are more valuable. In *Men's Studies Modified* (1981) and *Invisible Women* (1982a) Spender analysed education showing how in curriculae, institutions and practices men constructed the world and omitted women's reality. Since, Spender claims, women have not been allowed to construct their own meanings, the task for women is to construct an alternative female reality to which Spender herself contributes, for example in her extensive feminist history: *Women of Ideas* (1982b).

Spinning
A metaphor coined by Mary Daly in *Gyn/Ecology* (1978) to describe the destructive/constructive creation of women's knowledge. Spinning knowledge is not fixed, Daly claims, but continues in a state of change, forming threads between hitherto unlinked sections of reality.

Spinster
Generally used to describe an unmarried woman. Because unmarried implies a negative state, feminist anthropologists now point to the positive roles played by spinster women in Native American culture and others. See Weigle (1982). Mary Daly uses the term to refer to a woman who is self-defined and who is contributing to the 'spinning' of women's culture. See Daly (1978).

Spiritual feminism
Sometimes called myth feminism, this is a growing area of feminist theory. The ecology of myth described by critics such as Carol Christ, Mary Daly and Charlene Spretnak involves the construction of cultural archetypes of power useful to women and psychological tools which can enable women to articulate desire through symbols and rituals.

The revival of a spirituality based on Native cultures and on an enlarged history of myth-making and Wicca or witchcraft, grew out of radical feminism in the 1970s.

Spiritual feminism has been attacked by Hester Eisenstein and others for lacking a sociopolitics. See Eisenstein (1984). However, the movement has created a feminist theory of knowledge based on women's mystical experience of connectedness with nonhuman nature and other women. See Christ and Plaskow (1979), Daly (1978), Spretnak (1982).

Spooking
A term coined by Mary Daly in *Gyn/Ecology* (1978) to refer to the recalling and remembering of witches' power which casts spells on those who terrorise women.

Stanton, Elizabeth Cady
American campaigner for women's rights who, with Susan B. Anthony, founded the National Suffrage Association (1869). In *The Woman's Bible* (1895-8) Stanton used natural rights theory to repudiate the validity of biblical ethics and the Judaeo-Christian tradition. She argued that the Godhead was androgynous and that androgyny was the central rule of the Cosmos. Stanton also argued

for the historical existence of matriarchy and created an important new vein in feminist theory: the idea that women, particularly mothers, have special experiences and capabilities that lead them to express a life-affirming, pacifist, creative world-view. See Stanton (1895-8).

State

Generally means an organisation which rules over an area or groups by virtue of a monopoly of the legitimate use of force. Liberal feminism takes for granted that the State is a legitimate authority for enforcing justice and that it can enforce women's rights, for example in a policy of equal employment. In this sense the State is neutral, an arbiter of conflicting social interests whose task is to protect individual rights.

Elizabeth Wilson argues that this concentration on the welfare aspects of the State does not help feminists understand in historical terms how the State defines women and regulates sexuality. See Wilson (1977). Already, liberal feminists think that some areas of State intervention are unjustified, for example the State's responses to prostitution and pornography. Zillah Eisenstein argues that the practice of contemporary liberal feminists will force them to develop a feminist theory of the State which recognises that the State is not neutral but is a condensation of forces, one of the strongest forces being male dominance. Any sex–class analysis of women's oppression is incompatible with the individualist presuppositions of liberal theory. See Eisenstein (1981).

Feminist sociology has made a fruitful analysis of patriarchal ideology as it is expressed through State activities. Ann Oakley argues that the State involvement in processes of biological reproduction has transferred control from women to men just as in other processes of social reproduction. See Oakley (1972).

Marxist feminists believe that the State exists to construct women's dependence on men. The State has power in its statutory provisions on social security and income tax, in regulation of sexual behaviour in marriage, and in control over ideological and cultural representations of sexuality. Irene Bruegal argues that the State has taken over the productive and reproductive functions of the family in order to preserve the capitalist relations of production. See Bruegal (1979).

The most unified assault on the State by the women's movement has been in campaigns about abortion rights.

Stereotypes

Preconceived ideas about individuals, groups or objects. The most extensive feminist account of stereotyping is by Inge Broverman and her colleagues, whose work has even been cited in the American Congress. They conclude that stereotypic thinking about sex-role related personality traits is pervasive. Desirable traits are more likely to be assigned to men with the valued traits for men forming a competence cluster, while women's traits form a warmth-expressive cluster. These stereotypes are found in school settings, children's literature, language styles and occupations. See Broverman *et al.* (1972).

Strachey, Ray
English writer who in *The Cause* (1928), her history of the Women's Movement, and in *Our Freedom and Its Results* (1936) analysed legal, sexual, social and economic changes in women's condition. Strachey's writings encouraged feminist theory. See Strachey (1928, 1936).

Strength
Radical feminism argues that strength is valued both by feminists and by the male culture but that society makes differing judgements for both about what constitutes strength. Joyce Treblicot points out that 'strong' women in patriarchy are assumed to be unattached and unattractive. A feminist account of strong women describes them as noisy and even loud, and argues that strength represents flexibility not rigidity. See Trebilcot (1979).

Subordination
Feminists agree that the subordination of women is a central feature of all structures of interpersonal domination, but feminists choose different locations and causes of subordination.

In approximate chronological order, contemporary feminist theory begins with Simone de Beauvoir's argument that because men view women as fundamentally different from themselves then women are reduced to the status of a second sex and hence subordinate. See de Beauvoir (1953). Kate Millett's theory of subordination argues that women are a dependent sex class under patriarchal domination. See Millett (1970). Shulamith Firestone located women's subordination in the limitations of reproduction and childbirth. See Firestone (1970). Other radical feminists, for example Susan Brownmiller, Andrea Dworkin, Anne Koedt and Susan Griffin in general take the view that a male control of sexuality and a male domination of nature (specifically in rape and pornography) leads to woman's subordination. The sociologist Elizabeth Janeway argues that 'social mythology', or cultural subordination, has a sexual core as its specific ideology. Feminist anthropologists argue that the separation of public and domestic worlds and women's relegation to the domestic (or to nature) ensures subordination. See Rosaldo and Lamphere (1974) and Ortner (1974).

Feminist psychoanalysis argues that women's subordination comes from the construction of sex-role stereotyping based on the practice of women's mothering. See Chodorow (1978) and Dinnerstein (1976).

Since each individual feminist critic locates women's subordination in a different social, cultural or psychic zone each account would be too lengthy to cite, but the rubrics of anthropology, psychology, sociology, philosophy and radical feminism can function as a general indicator.

The project of feminist theory is to end women's subordination. Jean Baker Miller offers the most intriguing possibility of how this might be done by arguing that women's subordination has enabled us to develop specific skills – of cooperation and vulnerability – which could be a psychic starting point for the creation of a new society. See Miller (1976).

Subject
The term subject is unpopular in feminist theory because, in a grammatical sense, it has a dominant/domineering connotation. For example positivism defines the 'subject' as a researcher standing back from the 'objects' of study, or people. The conventional view of the subject is one on whom research operations are performed rendering her passive, in essence an object.

Renate Duelli Klein argues that we should look for a more egalitarian term and that we could borrow the term 'member' from ethnomethodology. See Duelli Klein (1983). Feminist social scientists propose instead the term 'participatory models' which engage 'subjects' in the making of the research project. See Reinharz (1983). The reconceptualisation of the subject role has become a major aim of feminist researchers.

Suffrage
A term used to describe women's campaigns for the vote in America and in Britain from the mid-nineteenth century. Support for suffrage came from several different theoretical positions. Some argued for enfranchisement on the basis of individual rights; others on the basis of the special contribution women might make in the public sphere.

The theory of suffragism is that suffragettes could no longer look to other reform movements to benefit women, but had to look to women themselves not only to articulate the problem but to provide the solution to women's oppression. Winning enfranchisement represented a radical ideological break because it challenged notions of dependency and male authority, and proved that women's social duties outside their households were as great as those of men. See Du Bois (1978).

One example of that radical break in the prevailing social order is that suffrage connected women from all classes.

Symbolic

In French feminist theory symbolic means the language system of patriarchy. Using techniques drawn from linguistics and psychoanalysis writers such as Hélène Cixous and Luce Irigaray argue that the symbolic represents not only a form of language but a way of thinking and ordering the world to the benefit of men. Opposed to the symbolic is the feminine semiotic or the representation of mother/child relations. Julia Kristeva argues that *le symbolique* is a domain of position and judgement. Generally speaking, the symbolic comes into being later than the semiotic – at the time of the 'mirror' stage; and it involves the establishment of a sign system. Synchronically speaking, the symbolic is always present, even in the semiotic which cannot exist without constantly challenging the symbolic. See Kristeva (1980).

Symbolic interactionism

A concern with everday life and face-to-face relationships. In social science research, symbolic interactionism takes social action to be the result of interaction rather than arguing that people's actions are the result of instinct or socialisation.

The method is valuable to those feminists developing a psychology for women, particularly because the method helps us understand that motherhood is a social process rather than a feminine one. See Nicolson (1986). Feminist philosophers use symbolic interactionism to find out about the place of authorities in legitimising certain definitions of morality. Symbolic interactionism, for example in work with women and abortion, allows feminists to question the models of moral explanation assumed by traditional philosophy. See Kittay and Meyers (1987).

Liz Stanley and Sue Wise argue that the method is very much in sympathy with feminism's insistence on the importance of the personal because it is a means of sensitising us to a fuller view of reality. However, they argue that we should be cautious because many versions of symbolic interactionism retain a positivist adherence to science and objectivity. See Stanley and Wise (1983).

Taylor, Harriet

English nineteenth-century writer whose views about women's emancipation were incorporated by her husband John Mill into his *The Subjection of Women* (1869).

In 'The enfranchisement of women' (1851) and her essays on marriage, Taylor argued for complete civil and political equality for women which would include the opening to women of public offices and occupations. Taylor also proposed the abolition of laws relating to marriage. See Mill and Mill (1970).

Teaching

Feminist theory both analyses the existing institutions of teaching and envisages feminist alternatives to them. Feminists research into the interrelated areas of sex differences, teaching practice and children's achievement. Feminist theory describes how feminist teaching is a 'space' which is outside existing traditions of education. See Westkott (1983).

Feminists evaluate how teaching contributes to maintaining sexual divisions in schools and ask to what extent being a teacher involves being an agent of a patriarchal system, whether consciously or unconsciously. For example any separation of the sexes in the school curriculum conditions gender stereotypes. See Byrne (1978).

Feminist theories of teaching claim that the sexual division of labour in education creates in children a sexist perception of the social order because children see men teachers having greater control than women teachers in education administration. Teachers themselves frequently make distinctions between girls and boys, encouraging gender conformity, and these distinctions reinforce gender differences. See Spender (1982a). Other critics attack the whole ideology of 'progressive' pedagogic practice and argue that because it is based on the concept of the teacher as mother it is inherently sexist. See Walkerdine (1986).

One alternative is to create a specifically feminist pedagogy. Here the feminist teacher acts as facilitator in a nonhierarchical classroom.

Feminist teaching validates and integrates the personal; it is committed to changing students' attitudes towards women (most particularly women's images of themselves and their potential). It recognises that no education is value free; and it aims to integrate cognitive and affective learning in action oriented programmes. See Culley and Portuges (1985).

Virginia Woolf's *Three Guineas* is an early feminist theory of teaching. Woolf argued that in a women's college teachers would be drawn from good livers as well as good thinkers and there would be no barriers of wealth or competition. Musicians, painters and writers would teach, she argued, because they could make their teaching be a form of collective learning. See Woolf (1938).

Technology
This is generally characterised as a neutral force where technological innovation occurs within a neutral context and has beneficial effects. In *The Second Sex* (1953) Simone de Beauvoir argued that technology would make a qualitative difference to women's lives because it could ease physical exertion. Shulamith Firestone argued that control over the technology of reproduction would enable women to break out of their social roles because a women-controlled reproductive technology could free women from the tyranny of biology. See Firestone (1970). However, Dorothy Dinnerstein points out that *existing* male-controlled technology will destroy the world if current gender arrangements are perpetuated. See Dinnerstein (1976).

Feminist anthropologists agree that technological 'freedom' cannot ensure feminism because all societies, technologically advanced or otherwise, seem to control fertility. See Rosaldo and Lamphere (1974). They claim that the idea – that women could be revolutionised by advanced features of technology – ignores the social aspects of reproduction and the political question of who controls technology, how control is organised socially and institutionally, and for what ends. See Petchesky (1986).

Juliet Mitchell has shown that, historically, technology is mediated by an economic and social environment of structural unemployment and women's vulnerability to that environment. See Mitchell (1984). Feminist theory argues that technology is embedded within patriarchal social relations. For example new office technology simply adds to work relations already based on male domination and female subordination.

Feminists writing about the Third World question the assumption that all members of a unit, for example the family, share equally the benefits and burdens of technological change. Feminist geographers are now examining the links between technology, female participation in agricultural production and women's social status in a global analysis. See Momsen and Townsend (1987).

Textiles

Feminist art historians argue that textiles are a form of women's art which demands more attention. Feminist historians are not simply validating women's traditional work in textiles but are analysing and criticising the hierarchy of art forms that exclude textiles from the art tradition. For example feminist historians refuse to privilege painting and sculpture. Feminist artists, like Judy Chicago, also mix textiles with sculpture and the fine arts. See Chicago (1979).

Feminists making textiles are linking art with the political practices of the women's movement. For example the peace movement generated a revival of banner-making which incorporated traditional textile arts and political protest in a counter imagery of collage and web.

For some Third World women the making of textiles is their only accessible means of political survival and resistance, for example the Soweto patchworks. See Parker and Pollock (1981).

Theatre

Feminists aim to improve the position of women as theatre workers, to change the representation of women in plays, and to consolidate an experimental and combative alternative theatre movement which can challenge the repressive aspects of the sexual division of labour.

Feminist critics point out that alternative theatre flourishes at times of changing social attitudes to women because the role of women in the theatre is contingent on how images of sexuality are represented. See Wandor (1981). However, theatre is a difficult area for women to work in because women's public status is policed ideologically. Feminist theatre theory argues for alternative approaches to theatre which include collective work, the use of cyclical ritual patterns rather than the linear mode of classical theatre, and the use of autobiography and associative styles. See Reinhardt (1981).

In Britain contemporary feminist theatre developed from street theatre and the visual arts. It can be defined as a theatre of argument which explores the experience of women in a triple process of reclamation, reversal and subversion. For example feminists write about the breaking of sexual taboos like breast cancer (Louise Page's *Tissue*) and the importance of female friendship, and make a reassessment of history (Caryl Churchill's *Light Shining in Buckinghamshire*).

Theory

Broadly, the content of this Dictionary. More particularly feminist theory aims to create a deeper understanding of women's situation.

Feminist theory begins with women's experience of oppression and argues that women's subordination extends from private circumstances to political conditions.

All feminist writers since the Second World War, from Simone de Beauvoir onwards, are theorists as well as writing in various disciplines. Certain themes dominate their work: the use of 'patriarchy' as an organising concept to theorise the subordination of women; the concept that public/private divisions structure women's lives; the importance of utopian ideas; and theories of subjectivity and the ideological.

However, feminist praxis, which is both theory and action, has different priorities in feminist politics. For example radical feminism is concerned to redescribe reality as it appears only to women, and socialist feminists are typically concerned to give a systematic explanation of that reality generally. See Kittay and Meyers (1987). Feminist art historians argue that theories of cultural production can create feminist meanings from the interaction of cultural phenomena and women's work. See Barry and Flitterman (1987).

Nonaligned feminists are often suspicious of theory because they define theory as a dimension of male repression and part of the violence inherent in rationality. For example some feminist writers argue that the *language* of theory can be an instrument of domination. See Rowbotham (1973b). However, Jean Elshtain and others argue that it does not follow that *all* language, including the language of theory, must spring from, or serve only, the dominators. See Elshtain (1982a).

Feminists agree that feminist theory must be distinguished from other theory, for example Marxism, because feminism focuses on sexuality or gender rather than on material conditions as the base for ideological construction. See MacKinnon (1982). In addition feminist theory and methodology relate closely to each other, which prevents feminist theory from becoming static. See Duelli Klein (1983). Feminist theory is simultaneously political and scientific because feminist theorists use a complex network of conceptual, normative, empirical and methodological approaches. See O'Brien (1982). In sum, feminist theory unites immediate and long-range goals in a dynamic unity of thought and the experiential.

Therapy

Feminist therapy is based on the theory and philosophy of consciousness raising. Feminist therapists have an equal relationship with their clients because feminist therapists examine their own values about women and the female experience at the same time as the client. See Eichenbaum and Orbach (1982).

Feminist therapy is distinct from other nonsexist therapy because feminist therapists analyse the forms of social, economic and political oppression that affect women as a group as well as individually. This analysis informs the therapist's understanding of how women function in our society and of how change may occur. Feminist therapists use *Gestalt*, encounter and humanist therapies to revise and reformulate psychoanalytic theory according to feminist insights.

See Psychotherapy.

Third World

Most Western accounts of the Third World homogenise it in the context of nationalism and ethnicity, and make a pedagogic appropriation of Third World texts. See Spivak (1987).

The 1975 United Nations Decade for Women stimulated research into the role of women in the Third World which until then had been seen in male terms. Feminist anthropologists show how women's practices in the Third World have their own rationale, for example women's choice of seclusion. See Anker (1982).

There is a substantial female contribution to the paid labour force of the Third World. Yet, while processes of development increase the burdens of Third World women, women's contribution is devalued because concepts of development are predominantly economic. See Wellesley Editorial Committee (1977).

Feminist theorists argue that the revival of domestic production in the first and second worlds, which is a feature of recession, is close to the Third World lack of investment in welfare. See Momsen and Townsend (1987).

Time

Feminist geographers are researching the various constraints on women's time. They argue that innovation merely serves to increase the workload of women. Time-use analysis reveals how women's access to leisure varies in relation to childcare. For all women domestic activity is more time-consuming than any other activity, and time is an increasingly scarce resource for women in the developing world who have a triple burden of a working day, housework and childcare and food preparation. See Momsen and Townsend (1987). Dale Spender describes how time constraints reduce women's opportunity to write and pre-empt women's participation from the public sphere. See Spender (1980).

In her theory of time Julia Kristeva describes two temporal divisions: the time of linear history or cursive time, and monumental time. Because female subjectivity, she claims, retains repetition *and* eternity, biological rhythm *and* cosmic time, these two types of temporality (cyclical and monumental) are linked to female subjectivity. See Kristeva (1982).

In general, feminist theory argues that women's diffusive, intersubjective relationships are in opposition to the commodification of time necessary for capitalist patriarchy.

Tokenism
Mary Daly argues that women professionals who work within the establishment are token women who simply mask male power. She claims that reforms won by the women's movement are merely examples of tokenism because reforms create the illusion, but not the reality, of women's liberation. See Daly (1978).

Trade unions
Feminist economists criticise existing theory, for example dual labour market theory, for not including an analysis of trade unions into conceptual frameworks. They claim that since trade unions try to restrict women to particular sectors of the labour force and increase sexual divisions, they play a crucial role in the sexual division of labour especially in restrictive practices. See Barrett (1980).

Specifically, trade unions reproduce and reinforce the vulnerable position of women workers. Hence, Heidi Hartmann argues, trade unions are expressly patriarchal. See Hartmann (1976).

Veronica Beechey adds that this is because, historically, trade unions were founded on structures of occupational segregation. Trade unions counter feminist arguments against protective legislation with a defence of the 'family wage'. See Beechey (1986).

In general, feminist theory attacks the trade union agenda because it is restricted to the workplace and ignores the interconnected sexual divisions within the family.

Transcendental feminism
Margaret Fuller, in *Woman in the Nineteenth Century* (1848), defines this as woman's uniqueness (which she called femality). Transcendental feminism, to Fuller, is an electric and magnetic element in women who have a force of intuitive and perceptive power. Fuller believed in the power of inspiration and that women must be free in order to achieve their potential. See Fuller (1845).

Transcendental signified

A theory of literary criticism which takes the author to be the source, origin and meaning of the text. Luce Irigaray argues that the Phallus and Logo are the transcendental signifiers of Western culture. See Moi (1985).

Truth, Sojourner

Black American feminist who, as an ex-slave, spoke at the Akron Women's Rights Convention (1851) and the 'Mob' Convention (1853) about abolition, nonviolence and women's rights. In her remarks to the convention she argued for equal economic rights for women and made links between the double oppression experienced by Black women and her own need to 'sojourn' to the ballot box before her death. See Sojourner Truth (1851).

Contemporary feminists argue that Sojourner Truth's experience is an example of how the alleged benefits of an ideology of femininity did not apply to the Black female and how white women are ignorant of the divergent needs of Black women. See Davis (1981) and Joseph and Lewis (1981).

Unconscious
A psychoanalytic concept. Freud defined the unconscious as that which is repressed from consciousness and argued that access to the unconscious is indirect through dreams, jokes, slippages and free association. For example Freud claims that an unconscious repudiation of femininity is expressed in the setting up of fetish objects.

Feminist theory argues that the unconscious is structured differently under different forms of social relations. Using Lacan's argument that the 'I' is a construction that the unconscious shows to disappear, feminist theory claims therefore that sexual identity is also uncertain. Kate Millett and Shulamith Firestone described the role of the unconscious in terms of power relations and sexual divisions; Juliet Mitchell argues that the content of the unconscious can change. This will occur, she claims, when the potentialities of capitalism − both economic and ideological − are released by its overthrow, new structures will gradually come to be represented in the unconscious. See Mitchell (1974).

Luce Irigaray suggests that the unconscious is desire attempting to speak itself. See Irigaray (1977a). She calls for a new sort of psychoanalytic writing, one in which the analyst's mastery is undercut by a recognition that the analyst too has an unconscious. Virginia Woolf described the unconscious as being a continual pressure on conscious thought and Julia Kristeva argues that this force of the unconscious can disrupt language because of women's strong links with the pre-oedipal mother figure. See Kristeva (1974a).

Utopianism
Utopian thinking has always been a source of political inspiration for feminists. See Taylor (1983). For example the matriarche in nineteenth century feminism which Charlotte Perkins Gilman describes in her utopia *Herland* (1915) is an expression of utopian ideals. Marge Piercy's *Woman on the Edge of Time* (1976) projects a viable communitarian, nonsexist and productive utopia.

Feminist science fiction creates utopian visions of a female world where women are models for humanity. French feminist theorists suggest that utopias are a crucial form of sociological imagination. For example Hélène Cixous describes feminine/female writing and the *jouissance* of the female body as a utopian vision of female creativity. See Moi (1985).

Hester Eisenstein suggests that feminist theory is utopian in itself in the way it creates a space within patriarchy and opens up new horizons. For example Adrienne Rich describes a gynocentric consciousness which produces a women-centred culture. See Eisenstein (1984).

Universalism
The view that all women, whatever their race, religion, class or sexual preference, have something fundamentally in common. Universalism relies on biological or psychological universals. Michelle Rosaldo argues that women are universally associated with the domestic, and men with the public domain and that this underlies the universal subordination of women. See Rosaldo and Lamphere (1974). Nancy Chodorow argues that there is a universally different socialisation of male and female children. See Chodorow (1978).

Universalism is sometimes called metaphysical feminism and radical feminists, for example Adrienne Rich, suggest that a lesbian continuum is available universally to all women. Barbara Ehrenreich suggests that universalism neglects the fact that differences in the position of women in different societies are quite significant from a feminist perspective. See Ehrenreich (1976).

Universalism has come most under attack from Black and lesbian feminists who are reinstating concepts of difference. Audre Lorde sums this up by arguing that universalism will align feminist theory with a form of neo-colonialism. See Lorde (1984b).

Vegetarianism

The renunciation of meat-eating parallels a renunciation of aggression. In the nineteenth century many feminists, for example Margaret Fuller and Matilda Gage, argued that vegetarianism would be part of a desired feminisation of culture and, more specifically, that it was part of the matriarchate period when all life was regarded as holy. In Charlotte Perkins Gilman's novel *Herland* (1915) women have an ecological concern for all forms of life in a harmonic and peaceful vegetarianism. See Donovan (1985).

This vision is at the heart of pacificist feminism as it developed in the twentieth century. Carol Adams argues that carnivorism is linked to sexism, and that vegetarianism must be part of feminist culture. Vegetarianism, she claims, stands for a commitment to pacifism and an ecologically holistic environment. See Adams (1975).

Victimisation

The denigration of women by men as part of segregation and subordination. Feminist theorists agree that the victimisation of women socially, politically, economically and culturally results from a society-wide structure where women are controlled by men. Descriptions of women's victimisation occur throughout feminist criticism and are too numerous to cite, but in general feminists either describe victimisation causally or structurally. For example Phyllis Chesler in *Women and Madness* (1972) argues that victimisation is caused by sex-role stereotyping, while Mary Daly in *Gyn/Ecology* (1978) argues that patriarchy victimises women into a structure of robotitude. Black feminists, for example Audre Lorde, argue that Black women are too often seen only as victims rather than as sources of wisdom. See Lorde (1984b).

Violence

Feminists writing about violence towards women dispel several popular myths, namely that victims of violence 'ask for' or provoke violence or that battered wives 'seek out' a battering partner. Whether violence takes the form of rape, battering, incest, sexual harassment, or pornography, feminist theory proves that violence against women is pervasive and that it is the product of a patriarchal culture in which men control both social institutions and women's bodies. When women understand that their individual experience of male violence has an objective social basis and social origin, they are making feminist theory.

Kate Millett points out that patriarchy depends on institutionalised violence which is inherent in legal systems, illegal abortions and rape. See Millett (1970). Violence is the main mechanism by which unequal power relations are maintained in body politics. Feminist theory followed Millett by discovering, and struggling against other manifestations of male violence such as wife beating and pornography. The origins and political significance of male violence against women are interpreted differently in feminist writings. For example Jessica Benjamin argues that male violence stems from the violence of rationality. This exists in all institutions which control and objectify the other out of existence. See Benjamin (1980). In contrast, Andrea Dworkin attributes violence to a male obsession with pornography and argues that pornography is the chief engine of violence rooted in history. See Dworkin (1981).

Feminist sociologists argue that violence is the form of power differential in marriage. They show that the existence and scale of wife battering and male domestic violence makes the issue of domestic violence a major example of the contradictory forces (the State, money, law and the sexual division of labour) which shape women's lives. Feminist historians reveal that the issue of battered women often becomes an area of social concern during periods of active feminism, but that violence is a common and institutionalised part of marriage in European culture. See Binney (1981).

Feminists writing about the Third World describe how violence is used against women who breach social rules. They argue that male violence is used to contain women within the roles and behaviours allotted to them and argue that violence is specifically used to control women's sexuality and reproductive roles, for example in ritual and symbolic representations of sexual relations. See Brown *et al.* (1981).

Violence against women is both a means of women's subordination and part of institutional and ideological domination.

Vocabulary

Sexist vocabulary is a component of language that has recently begun to be systematically studied by linguists. Investigators point to the sexualisation of terms which refer to women, for example 'mistress', and the prevalence of negative connotations for women. See McConnell-Ginet (1980).

Redefining vocabulary is a central concern of many feminists. Adrienne Rich argues that the breaking of taboos of vocabulary occurs when women name themselves. New terms coined by feminists, such as 'sexism' and 'male chauvenism', show the parallels between different inequalities. See Kramarae and Treichler (1985).

Voice

Feminist literary theorists argue that the representation of the voice in literature by women writers is a textual strategy used by writers to deconstruct images of women inherited from male literature. See Gilbert and Gubar (1979). In this sense the female authorial voice is an essence of feminism.

Hélène Cixous argues that femininity in writing can be defined as a privileging of the voice. Cixous, together with Julia Kristeva and Luce Irigaray, has developed a language where the speaking voice can evoke the mother and the mother's body as part of an eternally present linguistic space. See Moi (1985).

Wages for housework
A campaign which began in the early 1970s in Italy (where relatively few mothers were employed in wage labour) and which spread across Europe to Britain and Canada. The movement argued that wages for housework would recognise the value of work that all women perform. Mariarosa Dalla Costa and Selma James made this issue of women's domestic labour part of feminist theory in their text *The Power of Women and the Subversion of the Community* (1975).

The provision of wages for housework is incompatible in the long run with the goals of feminism because it reinforces the sexual division of labour. However, supporters of the theory argue that such wages can contribute to a redefinition of concepts of 'work' and 'domesticity'.

Wallace, Michele
Black American feminist who, in *Black Macho and the Myth of the Superwoman* (1979), examined ideas about Black masculinity and Black femininity. Wallace contrasted the 'patriarchal macho' (as exemplified by the family man) with the narcissistic machoman of the Black Power Movement. Wallace called on Black women to dispel the myth of the strong, invulnerable superwoman created by the media because she felt that the myth prevented any assessment of the real status of Black women.

War
The definition of war is problematic in feminist theory because women's roles in war are determined by perceptions of gender held by the societies to which women belong. For example where war is defined as a male activity the female warrior, whether an Amazon woman or a woman guerrilla, is seen as inherently unsettling to the social order. In modern Western culture explanations of gender differences in war are based on suppositions of biological drives which serve to support sexual divisions. See Macdonald (1987).

Equal rights theory argues that women should be equal military partners with men but feminist theory points out that political decisions to put women into war are usually made by men. See Goldman (1982).

Virginia Woolf argued that, for social and historical reasons, women should oppose war. She invented a society — The Outsiders — whose pacifist programme would require the dismantling of the whole patriarchal sex/gender system. Woolf argued that war came from men's identification of fighting with masculinity. See Woolf (1938).

Opposition to war is a major part of second wave feminism. For example Susan Brownmiller argues that rape is both a social and a military phenomenon. Cynthia Enloe investigates the structural and ideological interconnections between patriarchy and militarism and argues that these are bound in a symbiotic relationship. See Enloe (1983).

However, currently, feminism has conflicting views about women and war. For example feminist theory is based on a materialist, pacifist feminism, while at the same time it supports women's revolutionary violence in the Sandinista movement in Nicaragua.

Weaving

Feminist artists, for example Judy Chicago, are integrating weaving along with literature into fine art products to give a fuller expression to the history and experiences of women figures they wish to represent. Similarly, feminist art theory uses a critical framework, free of sexist hierarchies, to accommodate both fine and traditional arts. For example Norma Broude and Mary Garrard argue that the whole concept of fine art is a very recent one and that crafts like weaving and potmaking are the world's principal forms of artmaking. See Broude and Garrard (1982).

Feminist theory also attacks the way traditional criticism translates the 'craft' of weaving into principles of abstraction, for example in the current 'recuperation' of Navajo blankets. See Parker and Pollock (1981).

Weisstein, Naomi

American psychologist who was one of the first feminist theorists to describe the damaging effects of Freudian therapy on women. In '"Kinde, kuche, kirche" as scientific law: psychology constructs the female' she questioned the construction of the concept of femininity in psychology and argued that the practices of psychology agreed with conventional and sexist social expectations. See Weisstein (1970).

Welfare

The key issues in feminist theories of women's welfare are: the implications of women's position in the family and the relationship between paid and unpaid work. Most conventional analyses of the Welfare State in Britain and America work from an inadequate theoretical base because they ignore the State's concern with maintaining gender hierarchy. In contrast, feminist analysis emphasises that the Welfare State is not just a set of services but a set of ideas about society, particularly in the way the State organises family life. See Petchesky (1986).

A major contemporary feminist account of welfare is in Elizabeth Wilson's *Women and the Welfare State* (1977). She argues that the Welfare State embodies a set of assumptions about women expressed in its ideology and manifested in its practices. One main assumption is that a woman's role is principally that of housewife and mother. Wilson shows how psychology combines with sociology and government reports to reinforce this ideology. 'Welfarism' masks women's unpaid housework and turns women into an industrial reserve army of labour.

Some feminists dismiss welfare as simply a family ideology; others take a more defensive position, arguing that the Welfare State acts as a crucial safety net. A third feminist approach is to call for radical reforms which could make sex equality a welfare priority. These arguments all focus on the way women's position in the family structures our position in welfare *and* in work. See Lewis (1986).

For example Hilary Land and Mary McIntosh show how State social security systems subordinate women, in the interests of men, within marriage. They argue that the State supports a specific form of household where the family depends on a male wage and female domestic servicing. See McIntosh (1978). In America Zillah Eisenstein has extended this feminist critique of the Welfare State into an analysis of contemporary neo-conservative politics. See Eisenstein (1982).

West, Rebecca (Cicily Fairfield Andrews)

British feminist and critic who in her work for women's suffrage, her journalism in *The Freewoman* and her fiction described male power and defined new concepts which would help women to be independent. West aimed to reform the Victorian status of women and she wrote frequently about the exploitation of women and feminist politics. She contributed a new psychosocial criticism to feminist theory and a new understanding of the gendered context of issues like authority and difference. See West (1982) and Humm (1986).

White

White women have a different history, culture and experience from Black women but ignorance of Black experience is a primary form of racism in the women's movement, as in any other. See Joseph and Lewis (1981).

White Western feminists dominate theory but the *meaning* of whiteness can be experienced only in Black writing. White feminism has created a woman's tradition and history but often only by silencing and making absent the Black woman. Feminist historians describe the specific differences in Black and white women's history, economic and social situation. For example white women are more likely to marry, have access to education, have fewer children and earn more. See Lerner (1972).

Feminist literary theorists describe how the Victorian iconography of female whiteness is related to a Victorian ideal of feminine purity and that one way for women to escape that constraint was through a further deployment of a complex symbolism of whiteness. See Gilbert and Gubar (1979). Anthropologists show how this cultural dualism projects physicality and sexuality onto the Black woman making the white woman 'virginal'. See Reuther (1974).

Adrienne Rich has made a major feminist critique of white-centred theory which she argues has not dealt adequately with the texts of Black feminism. Whiteness has a circumscribing nature because white women marginalise others in confusing white and Western with the general 'woman'. Rich argues that white women can only disengage from their system of objectification by *not* identifying with whites and acknowledge that dynamic between their identity as white feminists and commitment to anti-racism. See Rich (1986).

Wilson, Elizabeth

British critic and writer who in *Women and the Welfare State* (1977) and *Only Halfway to Paradise: Women in Post-war Britain 1945–1968* (1980) analysed patriarchal ideology and institutions in the State, the family and the media. Wilson reveals how familial ideology obscures social relations, making women dependent on men, and she examines the various discourses of 'femininity'.

Witch

Most modern writers use the Old English word *Wicca*, meaning 'wisewoman' which is a positive term for maiden, mother and crone. Wicca creates rituals and ceremonies using the symbolism of woman-hood. Matilda Gage was one of the first theorists to describe witches as bearers of an alternative feminine tradition which could give women community powers feared by the churches. See Gage (1873).

Feminist theorists suggest that witches are women goddesses. See Christ and Plaskow (1979). Feminist theory also argues that witchcraft occurs between individuals who have social relationships with each other. For example Mary Daly suggests that the term 'wicca' can stand for the 'sparking of Amazons' and a new women's culture. See Daly (1978). Margot Adler suggests that witches make deep connections between humans and the universe because they claim that nonhuman nature is divine and the human body is holy. See Adler (1979). Since witches' traditional wisdom may be connected to the 'Lost World', Hélène Cixous suggests that witches are model women who operate on the edges of language and culture, together with madwomen and hysterics. See Cixous (1976).

Barbara Starrett suggests that this female sensitivity and value system needs a new set of symbols which she feels could be rooted in reinterpreted myths of past witchcraft. See Starrett (1975). Female spiritual leaders, such as Starhawk, have prophesied the dawning of a new religion: feminist witchcraft. This would be the first modern theistic religion which takes its deity, the Goddess, to be an *internal* set of images and attitudes. See Starhawk (1982).

Wittig, Monique
French writer and lesbian theorist. In *Les Guérillères* (1969) and *Lesbian Peoples: Material for a Dictionary* (1976) Wittig defined Western culture as phallogocentric but differed from other feminism in insisting that the theory and practice of feminism must focus only on women not on men's views of women. Wittig explores what social relationships among women-identified women are, or might be, and locates the lesbian subject outside the male linguistic universe. For example she creates new lesbian metaphors and genres. See Jones (1985).

Wittig argues that culture has a crucial role in the constitution of difference, and calls for a new conception of female sexuality based upon pleasure, not reproduction and the heterosexual enslavement of women. Wittig claims that 'lesbianism' is the mechanism by which this new conception will be realised since 'lesbian', unlike 'woman', is a positive term, signifying a healthy, unoppressed sexual identity. Wittig claims that lesbianism not only destroys categories of material enslavement (for example where women are defined as an oppressed group like 'the proletariat') but it also gives women the semantic power to name and to redefine themselves.

Wollstonecraft, Mary
Known as the first British feminist theorist. Wollstonecraft wrote *Thoughts on the Education of Daughters* (1787) and *A Vindication of the Rights of Woman* (1789) in response to a flood of advice literature

directed at young women. She argued that women are enslaved by a corrupt process of socialisation which stunts their intellect and teaches them to be subordinate to men. Wollstonecraft believed that the principles of the Enlightenment were principles that ought to apply equally to women as well as to men. Her liberal, egalitarian ideas underlie many contemporary political programmes, for example the argument for equal rights and equal opportunities for women.

Wollstonecraft's texts, which are now the classics of feminist theory, are based on three key assumptions. Reason – the capacity of acquiring knowledge, of forming judgements and of choosing general maxims of moral conduct – is the same in women as in men; reason is a necessary condition of woman's virtue; and the emancipation of women demands the dominance of reason over the passions, or of rational feelings over love. Women's excessive interest in themselves as objects and subjects of desire, Wollstonecraft argues, is the effect of the inscription of male desire on female subjects.

Wollstonecraft's argument is analogous to Virginia Woolf's metaphor of woman as looking glass to man. But Wollstonecraft differs from Woolf by believing that the domestic sphere, which represents community and a network of relationships with children and kin, is a paradigm of social order. Wollstonecraft argues that the beginning point of women's civic and political emancipation is education.

Juliet Mitchell suggests that Wollstonecraft moves away from liberalism to radical humanism by linking the liberation of women to egalitarian ideas. See Mitchell (1984).

Woman

The term for the social construction of the female whose identity (of femininity) is imposed and constructed through representation. Contemporary feminists argue that the term depends on its opposition, man, and has no meaning. De Beauvoir first asked the question in *The Second Sex* (1953): does the word 'woman' have any specific content? and answered that one is not born but rather becomes a woman. Catharine MacKinnon argues that the social process of sexuality defines 'woman', and Mary O'Brien suggests that the term is simply a generalised abstraction which is a product of male praxis. See MacKinnon (1982) and O'Brien (1982).

Currently, many French feminists refuse to use the term 'woman'. They argue that attempts to define a feminine subjectivity as a contrast to the phallocentric view of women will founder on masculine/feminine oppositions and cannot move beyond them.

Monique Wittig, in particular, calls for a political deconstruction of the term 'woman' in order to disassociate 'women' our class from 'woman' the myth. Because lesbians are outside the man/woman dyad, Wittig claims that a 'lesbian' is not a woman. Wittig has created a lesbian language which avoids words for woman (*la femme*) by repeating the feminine plural (*elles*) to designate women as a historical class rather than woman as a feminine essence. See Wittig (1981).

Woman-centredness
The term defines that branch in feminist theory which is based on a notion of women's difference and which argues for the creation of a holistic world culture. This theory draws on the writings of lesbian feminism of the early 1970s, for example the Radicalesbians, and the debates about women's psychology.

Woman-centredness argues that female experience ought to be a prime topic of study and a source of values for culture as a whole. The term is usually applied to the work of feminist historians, for example Gerda Lerner and radical feminists, such as Adrienne Rich and Susan Griffin. In psychology, Jean Baker Miller in *Toward a New Psychology of Women* outlined the character attributes a woman-centred world might adopt. Dorothy Dinnerstein claims that woman-centredness is crucial for world survival. See Miller (1976) and Dinnerstein (1976).

Currently, woman-centred analysis focuses on a woman's language (*écriture féminine*) and the idea of a wild zone or female space. The landmark text of woman-centredness is Mary Daly's *Gyn/Ecology* (1978) which embraces female difference and articulates a new vocabulary for a woman's world.

Womanculture
Barbara Burris defines womanculture as a fourth world. See Burris (1971). Hypotheses of womanculture have been developed over the last decade by feminist anthropologists, sociologists and social historians to help theory move away from masculine systems and values, and to describe the primary nature of female cultural experience. The concept of womanculture is a controversial one in women's history but historians agree on its significance in defining female groups. Historians distinguish between roles and behaviour prescribed *for* women (women's sphere) and activities and functions generated *out* of women's lives. See Smith-Rosenberg (1975). Gerda Lerner, in particular, argues against defining womanculture as a *sub*culture since women are in the majority.

Feminist anthropologists provide a terminology for womanculture, for example Shirley Ardener calls womanculture a 'muted group' which is a useful term for feminist literary theory since it agrees with a literary notion of absence. See Ardener (1981). In literary criticism the term is used by critics to define the specificity and difference of women's writing. The representation of womanculture in literature includes images of women's bodies, language and psyche and the social contexts in which these occur. The concept enables theorists to acknowledge important differences between women in terms of class, race and sexual preference while accepting that womanculture forms a collective experience. See Showalter (1982). However, Adrienne Rich suggests that although there is concrete evidence of womanculture, for example in prehistory, existing images might keep us immobilised. See Rich (1986).

Ann Ferguson and Nancy Folbre argue that a womanculture can ideologically and materially support women outside of patriarchy. See Ferguson and Folbre (1981). The term currently stands for a separatist dream of a woman-centred culture like Charlotte Perkins Gilman's *Herland* (1915), where symbols associated with the feminine are part of a matriarchal cultural utopia. See Covina and Galena (1976).

In French feminist theory womanculture stands for a wild zone, the 'alter ego' of official society, in which real or fantasised possibilities for *jouissance* could occur. See Kristeva (1982). In this sense womanculture is positioned against the socio-symbolic contract and means a harmonious women's world without prohibitions which is free and fulfilling.

Black feminism uses the concept womanculture to describe a counter culture of art and craft which retains connections with maternal images. See A. Walker (1983). Lesbian culture has been defined as womanculture in the writings of Adrienne Rich and lesbian novels which map out feminist utopias. Cultural separatists define womanculture as pacifist and ecologically holistic and Cherríe Moraga and Gloria Anzaldúa have given womanculture the title *El mundo zurdo* or the left-handed world. See Moraga and Anzaldúa (1981).

Woman-identified woman

A term for women who relate emotionally and/or sexually to other women rather than to men. The phrase came from the title of an influential essay by the Radicalesbians who referred exclusively to lesbians although the term, technically, can apply to feminist heterosexual women.

Feminist theory depends on woman-identified women. Nine-teenth-century cultural feminists, for example Margaret Fuller and

Charlotte Perkins Gilman, participated in woman-identified networks, and the practices of contemporary woman-identified women
are regarded as sources of revolutionary change. See Darty and Potter
(1984).

Radical feminism uses the term in different ways. In *Gyn/Ecology*
Mary Daly calls woman-identified environments 'Hagocentric'
psychic spaces. Adrienne Rich extends the meaning of woman-
identified woman in her important essay 'Compulsory heterosexuality
and lesbian existence'. Rich wrote the essay to enable women to
know the depth and breadth of women identification and women
bonding which, she argues, is often rendered invisible by compulsory heterosexuality. Rich claims that all women need to explore
lesbian culture. See Rich (1980). The notion of woman-identified
woman is important to creative writers and women's writing has for
some time depicted women bonding and women's communities. See
Auerbach (1978).

Womanism

The term now implies Black feminism although in the nineteenth
century it referred to those who supported women's rights. A
feminist who believes in womanism is a womanist. Alice Walker
provides a full account of womanism in *In Search of our Mothers'
Gardens* (1983). She argues that womanism is not separatism, and
that it derives from the expressions Black mothers use with female
children as in 'you acting womanish', that is, like a woman or
courageously and seriously. Walker outlines four features of
womanism: Black feminism; woman who love other women sexually
or nonsexually and appreciate and prefer women's culture, emotions
and strength; women who love music, dance and themselves; and
'womanist is to feminist as purple is to lavender' (Walker 1983,
p. xi).

Womanspirit

A feminist spiritual philosophy which weaves together strands of
women's history and mythology. Womanspirit is based on a belief
in the Great Goddess and it advocates study of astrology, dreams,
the I Ching, Tarot and Yoga.

Like its symbol, the circle, womanspirit is embracing and
unending and spiritual feminists are anxious to overcome mind/
body, subject/object dualities. In *Gyn/Ecology* (1978) Mary Daly
suggests that womanspirit will redefine political relationships and
create gynocentric environments. In *The Spiral Dance*, Starhawk
elides womanspirit with Wicca because both stand for a feminist

ecological religion, based on natural rhythms, which connects our bodies with the cosmic body. See Starhawk (1979).

Women: The Longest Revolution
Written by Juliet Mitchell, this is a pioneering account of British feminist theory which appeared in *New Left Review* (1966). Mitchell argued that the family must be analysed in terms of four component structures and functions: production, reproduction, sexuality and socialisation. It should not be analysed simply, as in existing Marxist theory, in terms of a capitalist division of labour.

Women's liberation
The name of the contemporary women's movement which was adopted by feminists in the 1960s in a conscious effort to avoid earlier connotations of 'the woman question'. Gayle Yates character- ises women's liberation as one of three periods, or ideological divisions, in the women's movement – the others being 'feminist' and 'androgynous'. See Yates (1975).

Women's liberation is the major version of feminism in contemporary Western society and its name both reflects the political context from which it emerged (the American New Left) and also provides a clue to the way in which it differs from earlier forms of feminism. Earlier feminists used the language of 'rights' and 'equality' but in the late 1960s 'oppression' and 'liberation' were the key words of feminist activism. But, Sheila Rowbotham argues, women's liberation has a long tradition – from democratic religious groups to the American New Left. See Rowbotham (1983).

Women's liberation came from women's pooled experience in consciousness raising groups and expanded into a more specialised theoretical study of the social relations of capitalist patriarchy. The contemporary women's movement, then, argues that the shaping of consciousness is a central dynamic of women's oppression and therefore that sexual politics is a central area of struggle. See Deckard (1975). Its basic premiss is that women are oppressed legally, economically and culturally and that changes in law, social policy and attitudes are needed to redress the unequal status of women. Women's liberation has several aims: equal pay; equal educational and job opportunities; free contraception and abortion on demand; free 24-hour childcare; legal and financial independence for women; an end to discrimination against lesbians and the right to self-defined sexuality; and an end to rape and violence against women.

Currently there is debate about the extent to which feminist theory can be congruent with the purposes of the women's liberation movement. Some feminists see a fundamental contradiction between the social scientific methods of theory and the principles of the movement. See Mies (1983). Other feminists argue that theory only has purpose if it *is* compatible with women's liberation politics. See Stanley and Wise (1983).

Certainly women's liberation is a unique political movement. This is because it redefines the nature of politics. For example since the sex-role system underlies all social institutions and social relationships, questions and issues never before considered political have been made political by women's liberation. Second, liberation women define themselves as a group which can include all women irrespective of race, nationality, socio-economic background and religion or sexual preferences.

Some feminists argue that women's liberation is pitched at a level of generality because the concept depends on identity between women and the idea that women share the same experiences. See Delmar (1986). There is a paradox now between the generality of a categorical appeal to all women and an emphasis on difference and ethnicity. For example Mary Daly rejects the women's movement because it is reformist and it masks male power; while Betty Friedan argues in reverse, that radical feminism's sexual politics alienate and divert women's liberation. See Daly (1978) and Friedan (1981).

However, women's liberation coheres around the struggle against sexism (or false consciousness) and for women's control over our own bodies. Women's battle for collective self-definition validates attributes and categories culturally coded as 'feminine'. Hence women's liberation has an intimate connection with women's studies since the principles of the movement are part of the content and method of teaching women's studies. See Rutenberg (1983).

The main success of women's liberation has been to make the debate over gender difference a thoroughgoing critique of prevailing mores and this has led to an irreversible process of change. Women's liberation is the most far reaching of contemporary social ideas because women's liberation does not address its demands to some external agency, for example the State, but addresses itself to people in their most intimate human relations, the relationship between women and men, and between women and women.

Women's studies
Although difficult to define in a simple way, women's studies is the study of power and gender relationships and it uses educational techniques of cooperation and consciousness raising to enable women to learn together as women. See Hughes and Kennedy (1985).

Adrienne Rich suggests that there are two kinds of women's studies: those in the academic community and those grounded in the feminist community which have a more diverse style and language. However, both share, she argues, a strong relatedness to politics and both make a dialogic exploration of subjectivity. See Rich (1986). Women's studies relates to political and social movements outside the walls of the university, and criticises traditional disciplines for ignoring women's history and experience by questioning the supposed objectivity of academic knowledge and deconstructing its assumptions. Women's studies emerged in the late 1960s from women's experiences in the New Left. The first British course was taught by Juliet Mitchell at the Anti-University in 1968–9. In 1966 Cathy Cade and Peggy Dobbins taught a course on women at New Orleans Free School as did Naomi Weisstein at the University of Chicago and Annette Baxter taught women's history at Barnard College. The first officially established integrated Women's Studies programme was at San Diego State in 1970. Women's studies scholarship was disseminated through new journals such as *Signs, Feminist Studies* and *Woman's Studies International Forum*. Both inside and outside higher education women researched the construction of femininity, the family, in history and society, sexual divisions, work and economic theory. See Boxer (1982).

Women's studies has been defined by the founders of the National Women's Studies Association as an 'educational strategy' for change, with a double purpose: to expose *and* to redress the oppression of women. See *Women's Studies Newsletter* (1977). Women's studies is the intellectual and research arm of the women's movement. Women's studies aims to transform all areas of education including curriculum, research, writing and teaching, and to prepare women to change society. It argues that a systematic consideration of gender is a fundamental condition of any adequate analysis or knowledge of contemporary society. Women's studies has the potential to alter fundamentally the nature of all knowledge by shifting the focus from androcentricity to a frame of reference in which women's differing ideas, experiences, needs and interests are valid in their own right and form the basis of our teaching and learning. See Bowles and Duelli Klein (1983).

A major debate now focuses on whether women's studies should stand alone as an autonomous discipline or whether feminist scholarship should be integrated into, and then change, existing disciplines. Feminists who advocate the former view argue that the disciplines cannot accommodate feminist claims or that the process of change would take too long. See Bowles and Duelli Klein (1983). Integrationist feminists agree that a separate area of women's studies can function as a powerhouse and conscience of all education, keeping feminist ideas, research and teaching actively visible. See Hughes and Kennedy (1985).

Another and equally major debate focuses on method. Theorists argue that women's studies must not be imagined as the *sum* of other disciplines but be a self-conscious proof that both the content *and* form of existing knowledge is related to the unequal distribution of social power between men and women. See Evans (1983). It is the collective mode of women's studies which can validate personal experience within the context of academia. However, the debate between the value of informal networks and the formality of the academy, between integration and separation, between disciplinary autonomy and integration, is subsumed in the current sensitivity within women's studies to combat its own racism and ageism. Adrienne Rich envisions a women's studies which will contest homophobia and racism in a woman's university transformed by feminist principles and where women use power constructively in cooperation, not competition. See Rich (1979b). Currently Black women's studies is giving an essential revolutionary edge to women's studies because it requires that fundamental political and social change take place in a dialectic between knowledge and social action. See Hull *et al.* (1981). However it is defined, women's studies can change the androcentricity of existing knowledge and look at human experience from a woman's point of view to enable women to gain full self-determination.

Woodhull, Victoria

American feminist who, as a candidate of the New Equal Rights Party, was the first woman to run for President of the United States in 1872. Her journal *Woodhull and Chaplin's Weekly* printed the first American edition of the Communist Manifesto and her writings articulate a romantic, anarchist view of women's liberation in which marriage would be abolished and women would be free of social restrictions. See Donovan (1985).

Woolf, Virginia

British writer. Woolf's theories of feminism are in *A Room of One's Own* (1928) and *Three Guineas* (1938) and her ideas resurface in most contemporary feminist theory. For example Adrienne Rich points to Virginia Woolf's writing as the basis of her own anti-imperialist theory. Woolf's novels, for example *Mrs. Dalloway* (1922), *To The Lighthouse* (1927) and *Orlando* (1928) are pioneering works of female modernism whose fictional worlds question patriarchal assumptions about the conformity between gender ascription and social values.

In *A Room of One's Own* Woolf describes women's restricted access to literary production and social visibility. She analyses both the historical production, and distribution, of literature and its social reception.

In *Three Guineas* Woolf argues that women can prevent war which is a product of masculinity. Woolf describes fundamental differences between men and women, between our psychologies, culture and value systems, and claims that only feminism can struggle against patriarchal fascism. The book is structured as a response to three letters: the first from a man asking for contributions to a pacifist society; the second from a woman soliciting funds for rebuilding a women's college; and the third asking for money for a society dedicated to helping women enter the professions. Woolf argues that these causes are interrelated. Women, she argues, are custodians of an anti-fascist feminine value system and fascism is a sexism that depends on the derogation of women. Woolf believes that a women's college and the Outsiders Society can preserve a subversive women's culture, and, more adequately than later feminism, Woolf explores the ways in which patriarchy has historically structured oppression.

Work

Feminist theories about work argue that the social relations of work, its cognitive and affective domains, and its sexual divisions are structured around gender. Feminist theory has developed an epistemology of feminist materialism which provides contemporary politics with its most thorough account of work to date.

Feminist historians point out that women's work spans community and industry. For example feminists analysing women's work in England and France from 1500 to 1700 challenge the traditional view that industrialisation separated the family from work and demonstrate that the family had a role in production. See Tilly and Scott (1978). In *Woman's Estate* (1971), Juliet Mitchell analysed the historical changes in women's work and argued that these changes must be put alongside the history of reproduction. Currently the history of women's exclusion from work by practices of protective legislation is cited by feminist scholars as an instance of the collaboration between capitalism and patriarchy.

Feminist theory argues that women's work must be seen in the context of the family economy. Christine Delphy in *The Main Enemy* suggests that it is the domestic mode of production which benefits men and enables them to control the labour of women. See Delphy (1977). Sheila Rowbotham argues that capitalist patriarchy depends on *both* domestic production in the family *and* commodity production. See Rowbotham (1983).

Adrienne Rich suggests that, commonly, women's domestic labour is not defined as work. See Rich (1976). Contemporary feminism argues that dominant conceptions of work make the home invisible. Tillie Olsen eloquently explores some of these issues in *Silences* (1978).

Radical feminists argue that work constraints will end only with a major revolution in the structure of the economy and society. For example Ann Ferguson and Nancy Folbre suggest that women's participation and exploitation in work has *increased* because of the burden of domestic labour. They argue that the social relations of women's nurturance work account for our oppression but might be our strength in a new revolutionary culture. See Ferguson and Folbre (1981).

Feminist theorists point to the way the sexual division of labour assigns to women different work from that of men. Dorothy Smith argues that women's work is primarily in what she calls 'the bodily mode', because it transforms the immediate and concrete world. Men's work, by contrast, is in what Smith calls the 'abstracted conceptual mode' which is the ruling mode of society. Women's work, in effect, facilitates the domination of men in this conceptual mode. See D. Smith (1979).

Nancy Hartsock claims that women's bodies in pregnancy have epistemological consequences because the directly sensuous nature of women's labour leads women to a more profound unity of mental and manual labour. See Hartsock (1979). The understanding that women's work is caring labour enables feminism to describe 'caring' work as transformative knowledge of the social. A utopian idea of transformed work is the anarchic society of Ursula Le Guin's *The Dispossessed* (1975).

Working class

There has always been a tension between feminism and definitions of class throughout the history of the women's movement. This is because most women have a dual class status. In Britain women are defined by the census in terms of the class status of the men with whom they may cohabit but they may have another class location in terms of education or parentage. For example a divorced woman may have a working-class income but a middle-class education. See Beechey (1986).

Other feminists draw attention to how sociological theory needs to be more complex in its definitions of working-class girls. For example girls' deviancy is frequently defined by their sexuality but not, as it might be, by class. See McRobbie and Nava (1984). Working-class women have a different relation to feminist theory than middle-class women. For example many working-class women find consciousness-raising groups too middle class and that the women's movement excludes working-class issues. See Fisher-Manick (1981).

Feminist theory argues that the working-class woman wage labourer is likely to be more radical than the housewife. This is because women workers see the reality of wage differentials and therefore know that women's rights do not exist in practice. See Eisenstein (1981). Kinship networks provide working-class women with a basis for feminist struggle. However, radical feminism argues that feminist theory must not restrict itself to economic issues at the expense of cultural and sexual liberation.

Wright, Frances

Scottish-American writer. Wright argued, in *A Course of Popular Lectures* (1829), that individual conscience was a more reliable source of truth than any established institution or tradition because all real knowledge derived from emotions. Influenced by Jeremy Bentham's ideas, Wright developed utilitarian arguments for women's equality and described a programme of enlightenment liberal feminism. See Wright (1829).

Young women

Conventional sociology concentrates on white working-class men. Young women are either ignored or young men are taken as the norm against which young women's experiences are judged. There are two consequences of this sexism. First, gender-specific theories are presented as if they applied universally and, second, feminist researchers are forced to battle with unsatisfactory models. See Griffin (1986).

The differential regulation of boys and girls inside and outside the family is one of a range of phenomena which prove that any concept of youth as a unitary category must be inadequate. Unlike boys, young girls are controlled by the family, since girls are expected to take on a larger share of labour and responsibility in the domestic sphere. Young women have a different experience of generational boundaries than boys. The boundary between girlhood and womanhood is far less accentuated. See McRobbie and Nava (1984).

Ideas on what counts as valid feminist theory about young women are not uniform. For example Valerie Amos and Pratibha Parmer argue that most theory about the experience of Black young women is integrationist and denies the autonomy of Black culture, for example by implying that white girls have a 'free choice' in marriage as opposed to the arranged marriages of some Black young women. See Amos and Parmer (1981).

Zetkin, Clara
Wrote about 'the woman question' from within a socialist perspective. Like Friedrich Engels and August Bebel, Zetkin was convinced that the only route to women's emancipation was women's involvement in production and the overthrow of the capitalist system. Clara Zetkin helped initiate International Women's Day (8 March). See Zetkin (1972).

BIBLIOGRAPHY

AAWORD (1980) *Resources for Feminist Research*, vol. 9, no. 1, pp. 8–9.

Abdalla, D. (1982) *Sisters in Affliction: Circumcision and Infibulation of Women in Africa*, Zed Books: London.

Abel, E. (ed.) (1983) *The Voyage In: Fictions of Female Development*, University Press of Maryland: Hanover, NH.

Adams, C. (1975) 'Oedible complex: feminism and vegetarianism', in *The Lesbian Reader*, Covina, G. and L. Galana (eds). Amazon Press: Oakland, CA.

Adams, C. and Laurikietis, R. (1980) *The Gender Trap, A Closer Look at Sex Roles 3: Messages and Images*, Virago: London.

Addams, J. (1965), *The Social Thought of Jane Addams*, Lasch, C. (ed), Bobbs-Merrill: Indianapolis.

Addelson, K.P. (1987) 'Moral passages', in *Women and Moral Theory*, Kittay, E. F. and D. T. Meyers (eds), Rowman & Littlefield: Totowa, NJ.

Adler, M. (1979) *Drawing Down the Moon*, Beacon Press: Boston, Mass.

Allen, P. (1970) *Free Space: A Perspective on the Small Group in Women's Liberation*, Times Change Press: New York.

Althusser, L. (1971) *Lenin and Philosophy and Other Essays*, New Left Books: London.

Amos, V. and Parmar, P. (1981) 'Resistances and responses', in *Feminism for Girls*, McRobbie, A. and T. McCabe (eds), Routledge & Kegan Paul: London.

Amos, V. and Parmar, P. (1984) 'Challenging imperial feminism', *Feminist Review*, 17, pp. 3–21.

Anker, R. (ed.) (1982) *Women's Roles and Population Trends in the Third World*, Croom Helm: London.

Anthony, S.B. and Harper, I. (1902) *History of Woman Suffrage*, Hollenbeck Press: Indianapolis.

Ardener, S. (ed.) (1981) *Women and Space*, Croom Helm: London.

Aries, E. (1976) 'Interaction patterns and themes of male, female, and mixed groups', *Small Group Behavior*, 7, pp. 7–18.

Ariès, P. (1960) *L'enfant et la vie familiale sous l'ancien régime*, Plon: Paris. Translated as *Centuries of Childhood* by Baldick, R. (1973) Penguin: Harmondsworth.

Arms, S. (1975) *Immaculate Deception*, Houghton Mifflin: Boston, Mass.

Atkinson, Ti-Grace (1974) *Amazon Odyssey*, Links Books: New York.

Auerbach, N. (1978) *Communities of Women: An Idea In Fiction*, Harvard University Press: Cambridge, Mass.

Baehr, H. (1981) 'The impact of feminism on media studies: just another commercial break?', in *Men's Studies Modified*, Spender, D. (ed.), Pergamon: Oxford.

Banner, L. (1983) *American Beauty*, Alfred A. Knopf: New York.

Barrett, M. (ed.) (1979) *Ideology and Cultural Production*, Croom Helm: London.

Barrett, M. (1980) *Women's Oppression Today: Problems in Marxist Feminist Analysis*, Verso: London.

Barrett, M. and McIntosh, M. (eds) (1982) *The Anti-Social Family*, Verso: London.

Barry, J. and Flitterman, S. (1987) 'Textual strategies', in *Framing Feminism*, Parker, R. and G. Pollock (eds), Routledge & Kegan Paul: London.

Bart, P. (1971) 'Depression in middle-aged women', in *Women in Sexist Society*, Gornick, V. and B.K. Moran (eds), Basic Books: New York.

Bartky, S. (1978) 'Toward a phenomenology of feminist consciousness', in *Feminism and Philosophy*, Vetterling-Braggin, M. (ed.), Littlefield, Adams: Totowa, NJ.

Bartky, S. (1979) 'On psychological oppression' in *Philosophy and Women*, Bishop, S. and M. Weinzweig (eds), Wadsworth: Belmont, CA.

Bartky, S. (1982) 'Narcissism, femininity and alienation', *Social Theory and Practice*, vol. 8, no. 2, p. 137.

Beard, M.R. (1946) *Women as a Force in History: A Study in Traditions and Realities*, Macmillan: New York.

Beardsley, E. (1977) 'Traits and genderization', in *Feminism and Philosophy*, Vetterling-Braggin, M. (ed.) Littlefield, Adams: Totowa, NJ.

Beauvoir, S. de (1953) *The Second Sex*, Penguin: Harmondsworth.

Beck, E.T. (1984) *Nice Jewish Girls: A Lesbian Anthology*, Crossing Press: Trumansburg, New York.

Beck, L. and Keddie, N. (eds) (1978) *Women in the Muslim World*, Harvard University Press: Cambridge, Mass.

Beddoe, D. (1983) *Discovering Women's History*, Pluto Press: London.

Beechey, V. (ed.) (1985) *Subjectivity and Social Relations*, Open University: Milton Keynes.

Beechey, V. (ed.) (1986) *Women in Britain Today*, Open University: Milton Keynes.

Belenky, M. *et al.* (1986) *Women's Ways of Knowing: the Development of Self, Voice and Mind*, Basic Books: New York.

Bem, S.L. (1974) 'The measurement of psychological androgyny', *Journal of Consulting and Clinical Psychology*, vol. 42, no. 12, pp. 155–62.

Bem, S.L. (1976) 'Probing the promise of androgyny', in *Beyond Sex-Role Stereotypes: Readings Toward a Psychology of Androgyny*, Kaplan, A. and J.P. Bean (eds), Little, Brown: Boston, Mass.

Benjamin, J. (1980) 'The bonds of love: rational violence and erotic domination', *Feminist Studies*, vol. 6, no. 1, pp. 144–74.

Benston, M. (1969) 'The political economy of women', *Monthly Review*, vol. 21, no. 4, pp. 13–27.

Berger, J. (1980) *Ways of Seeing*, Writers and Readers: London.

Bernard, J. (1968) *The Sex Game*, Prentice-Hall: Englewood Cliffs, NJ.

Bernard, J. (1974) *The Future of Motherhood*. Dial Press: New York.

Bernard, J. (1975) *Women, Wives, Mothers: Values and Options*, Aldine: Chicago.

Betterton, R. (ed.) (1987) *Looking On*, Pandora: London.

Bickner, M. (1974) *Women at Work*, University of California Press: Los Angeles.

Binney, V. (1981) 'Domestic violence' in *Women and Society*, The Cambridge Women's Studies Group (ed.), Virago: London.

Bleier, R. (1984) *Science and Gender: A Critique of Biology and its Theories on Women*, Pergamon: New York.

Boserup, E. (1970) *Women's Role in Economic Development*, St. Martin's Press: New York.

Boston Women's Health Collective (1971) *Our Bodies, Ourselves*, Simon & Schuster: New York.

Boulding, E. (1976) *The Underside of History: A View of Women Through Time*, Westview Press: Boulder, Col.

Boulding, E. (1977) *Women in the Twentieth-Century World*, Halstead Press: New York.

Bowlby, J. (1965) *Child Care and the Growth of Love*, 2nd edn, Penguin: Harmondsworth.

Bowles, G. and Duelli Klein, R. (eds) (1983) *Theories of Women's Studies*, Routledge & Kegan Paul: London.

Boxer, M.J. (1982) 'For and about women: the theory and practice of women's studies in the United States', in *Feminist Theory*, Keohane, N.O. *et al.*, Harvester Press: Brighton.

Branca, P. (1975) *Silent Sisterhood: Middle-Class Women in the Victorian Home*, Croom Helm: London.

Bridenthal, R. (ed.) (1984) *When Biology Became Destiny: Women in Weimar and Nazi Germany*, Monthly Review Press: New York.

Broude, N. and Garrard, M.D. (eds) (1982) *Feminism and Art History: Questioning the Litany*, Harper & Row: New York.

Broverman, I. *et al.* (1972) 'Sex role stereotypes: a current appraisal', *Journal of Social Issues*, 28, pp. 59–78.

Brown, G.W. and Harris, T. (1978) *The Social Origins of Depression*, Tavistock: London.

Brown, P. and Jordanova, L.J. (1981) 'Oppressive dichotomies: the nature/culture debate', in *Women in Society*, Cambridge Women's Studies Group, (ed.), Virago: London.

Brown, P. *et al.* (1981) 'A daughter: a thing to be given away', in *Women in Society*, Cambridge Women's Studies Group (ed.), Virago: London.

Brown, R.M. (1976) *A Plain Brown Rapper*, Diana Press: Oakland CA.

Brownmiller, S. (1975) *Against Our Will: Men, Women and Rape*, Simon & Schuster: New York.

Brownmiller, S. (1984) *Femininity*, Simon & Schuster: New York.

Bruegal, I. (1979) 'Women as a reserve army of labour', *Feminist Review*, 3, pp. 12–23.

Brundsdon, C. (ed.) (1986) *Films for Women*, British Film Institute: London.

Bulkin, E. (1980) 'Heterosexism and women's studies', *Radical Teacher*, 17, pp. 25–31.

Bulkin, E. *et al.* (1984) *Yours in Struggle*, Long Haul Press: New York.

Bullough, V. *et al.* (1977) *A Bibliography of Prostitution*, Garland: New York.

Bunch, C. (1975) *Lesbianism and the Women's Movement*, Diana Press: Oakland, CA.

Bunch, C. (1976) 'Beyond either/or: feminist options', *Quest*, vol. 3, no. 1, Summer, pp. 2–18.

Bunch, C. *et al.* (ed.) (1976) 'Leadership', *Quest*, vol. 2, no. 4, Spring, pp. 2–13.

Bunch, C. (ed.) (1981) *Building Feminist Theory: Essays from Quest*, Longman: New York.

Bunch, C. and Myron, N. (eds) (1974) *Class and Feminism*, Diana Press: Baltimore, MD.

Bunch, C. and Pollack, S. (eds) (1983) *Learning Our Way: Essays in Feminist Education*, The Crossing Press: New York.

Burris, B. (1971) 'The fourth world manifesto', in *Radical Feminism*, Koedt, A. *et al.* (eds), Quadrangle: New York.

Burton, C. (1985) *Subordination: Feminism and Social Theory*, George Allen & Unwin: Sydney.

Butler, R. (1975) *Why Survive: Being Old in America*, Harper & Row: New York.

Byrne, E. (1978) *Women and Education*, Tavistock: London.

Califia, P. (1981) 'Feminism and sadomasochism', *Heresies*, 12.

Capra, F. and Spretnak, C. (1984) *Green Politics*, Dutton: New York.

Castellanos, R. (1973) *Mujer que Sabe Latín . . .* , Secretaría de Educación Publica: Mexico City.

Castellanos, R. (1975) *El Eterno Femenino*, Farsa, Fondo do Cultura Económica: Mexico City.

Chapkis, W. and Enloe, C. (1983) *Of Common Cloth: Women in the Global Textile Industry*, Transnational Institute: Amsterdam.

Chernin, K. (1981) *The Obsession: Reflections on the Tyranny of Slenderness*, Harper & Row: New York.

Chesler, P. (1972) *Women and Madness*, Doubleday: New York.

Chicago, J. (1979) *The Dinner Party: A Symbol of Our Heritage*, Anchor Press/Doubleday: Garden City, NY.

Chicago, J. (1985) *The Birth Project*, Doubleday: New York.

Chodorow, N. (1978) *The Reproduction of Mothering: Psychoanalysis and the Sociology of Gender*, University of California: Berkeley, CA.

Christ, C. and Plaskow, J. (eds) (1979) *Womanspirit Rising*, Harper & Row: San Francisco.

Christian, B. (1985) *Black Feminist Criticism: Perspectives on Black Women Writers*, Pergamon: Oxford.

Churchill, C. (1978) *Light Shining in Buckinghamshire*, Pluto Press: London.

Cixous, H. (1976) 'The laugh of the medusa', *Signs*, Summer, pp. 875–93.

Cixous, H. (1981) 'Castration or decapitation', *Signs*, Fall, pp. 41–55.

Cixous, H. and Clement, C. (1975) *La jeune née*, Union Générale d'Editions: Paris.

Clavir, J. (1979) 'Choosing either/or: a critique of metaphysical feminism', *Feminist Studies*, vol. 5, Summer, no. 2, pp. 404–5.

Combahee River Collective (1981) 'A black feminist statement', in *This Bridge Called My Back: Writings by Radical Women of Color*, Moraga, C. and G. Anzaldúa (eds), Persephone Press: Watertown, Mass. pp. 210–18.

Condor, S. (1986) 'Sex role beliefs' in *Feminist Social Psychology*, Wilkinson, S. (eds), Open University Press: Milton Keynes.

Cott, N.F. (1977) *The Bonds of Womanhood: 'Woman's Sphere' in New England 1780–1835*, Yale University Press: New Haven, CT.

Cott, N.F. (1987) *The Grounding of Modern Feminism*, Yale University Press: Yale, Conn.

Cott, N.F. and Pleck, E.H. (eds) (1979) *A Heritage of Her Own: Towards a New Social History of American Women*, Simon & Schuster: New York.

Covina, G. and Galena, L. (eds) (1976) *The Lesbian Reader*, Amazon Press: Oakland, CA.

Coward, R. (1978) 'Rethinking Marxism', *M/F*, 2, pp. 85–96.

Coward, R. (1980) '"This novel changes lives": are women's novels feminist novels?', *Feminist Review* 5, pp. 53–64.

Coward, R. (1982) 'Sexual politics and psychoanalysis', in *Feminism, Culture and Politics*, Brunt, R. (ed.), Lawrence & Wishart: London.

Coward, R. (1983) *Patriarchal Precedents: Sexuality and Social Relations*, Routledge & Kegan Paul: London.

Coward, R. (1984) 'Introduction', in *Desire: The Politics of Sexuality*, Snitow, A. *et al.* (eds), Virago: London.

Coward, R. (1985) 'The royals', in *Subjectivity and Social Relations*, Beechey, V. and J. Donald (eds), Open University: Milton Keynes.

Coward, R. and Ellis, J. (1977) *Language and Materialism: Developments in Semiology and the Theory of the Subject*, Routledge & Kegan Paul: London.

Cox, S. (1976) *Female Psychology: The Emerging Self*, Science Research Associates: Chicago.

Coyner, S. (1983) 'Women's studies as an academic discipline: why and how to do it', in *Theories of Women's Studies*, Bowles, G. and R. Duelli Klein (eds), Routledge & Kegan Paul: London.

Culley, M. and Portuges, C. (eds) (1985) *Gendered Subjects*, Routledge & Kegan Paul: London.

Culpepper, E. (1975) 'Female history/myth making', *The Second Wave*, vol. 4, no. 1, pp. 14–17.

Dahlerup, D. (1986) *The New Women's Movement*, Sage: New York.

Dalla Costa, M. and James, S. (1975) *The Power of Women and the Subversion of the Community*, Falling Wall Press: Bristol.

Daly, M. (1968) *The Church and the Second Sex*, Harper & Row: New York.

Daly, M. (1973) *Beyond God the Father: Toward a Philosophy of Women's Liberation*, Beacon Press: Boston, Mass.

Daly, M. (1978) *Gyn/Ecology: The Metaethics of Radical Feminism*, Beacon Press: Boston, Mass.

Daly, M. (1984) *Pure Lust: Elemental Feminist Philosophy*, Beacon Press: Boston, Mass.

Daly, M. (1987) *Webster's First New Intergalactic Wickedary of the English Language*, Beacon Press: Boston, Mass.

Darling, M.J. (1987) 'The disinherited as source: rural black women's memories', in *Women and Memory: Special Issue, Michigan Quarterly Review*, vol. XXVI, no. 1, Winter, pp. 48–64.

Darty, T. and Potter, S. (1984) *Woman-Identified Women*, Mayfield: Palo Alto, CA.

Davidson, C.N. (ed.) (1980) *The Lost Tradition: Mothers and Daughters in Literature*, Frederick Ungar: New York.

Davis, A. (1971) *If They Come in the Morning: Voices of Resistance*, Third Press: New York.

Davis, A. (1981) *Women, Race and Class*, Random House: New York.

Davis, E.G. (1971) *The First Sex*, G.P. Putnam: New York.

Davis, M. *et al.* (eds) (1987) *The Year Left 2*, Verso: London.

Deckard, B. (1975) *The Women's Movement: Political, Socio-Economic and Psychological Issues*, Harper & Row: New York.

Deem, R. (ed.) (1978) *Women and Schooling*, Routledge & Kegan Paul: London.

Delmar, R. (1986) 'What is feminism?', in *What is Feminism?*, Mitchell, J. and A. Oakley (eds), Basil Blackwell: Oxford.

Delphy, C. (1977) *The Main Enemy: A Materialist Analysis of Women's Oppression*, Women's Research and Resources Centre: London.

Delphy, C. (1980) 'For a materialist feminism', in *New French Feminisms*, Marks, E. and I. de Courtivron (eds), Harvester Press: Brighton; University of Massachusetts Press: Amherst.

Delphy, C. (1984) *Close to Home: A Materialist Analysis of Women's Oppression*, University of Massachusetts Press: Amherst.

Derrida, J. (1967) *Grammatologie*, Editions de Minuit: Paris.

Diamond, A. and Edwards, L. (eds) (1977) *The Authority of Experience*, University of Massachusetts Press: Amherst.

Diner, H. (1932) *Mothers and Amazons: The First Feminine History of Culture*, reprinted 1973 by Anchor Press: Garden City, NY.

Dinnerstein, D. (1976) *The Mermaid and the Minotaur: Sexual Arrangements and Human Malaise*, Harper & Row: New York.

Divine, D. (1989) 'Unveiling the mysteries of Islam: the art of studying Muslim women', in the *Endless Waterfall: Studies on Women and Social Change*, Addelson, K.P. and M. Ackelsberg (eds), forthcoming.

Dobash, R.J. and Dobash, R.P. (1980) *Violence Against Wives: A Case Against the Patriarchy*, Free Press: New York.

Donovan, J. (1985) *Feminist Theory*, Frederick Ungar: New York.

Douglas, M. (1966) *Purity and Danger*, Routledge & Kegan Paul: London.

Doyal, L. and Elston, M.A. (1986) 'Women, health and medicine', in *Women in Britain Today*, Beechey, V. and E. Whitelegg (eds), Open University: Milton Keynes.

Du Bois, B. (1983) 'Passionate scholarship: notes on values, knowing and method in feminist social science', in *Theories of Women's Studies*, Bowles, G. and R. Duelli Klein (eds), Routledge & Kegan Paul: London.

DuBois, E. (1978) *Feminism and Suffrage*, Cornell University Press: Ithaca, NY.

DuBois, E. (ed.) (1985) *Feminist Scholarship: Kindling in the Groves of Academe*, University of Illinois Press: Urbana.

DuBois, E.C. and Gordon, L. (1984) 'Seeking ecstasy on the battlefield: danger and pleasure in nineteenth-century feminist sexual thought' in *Pleasure and Danger*, Vance, C.S. (ed.), Routledge & Kegan Paul: London.

Duchen, C. (1987) *French Connections*, Hutchinson: London.

Duchen, C. (ed.) (1986) *Feminism in France: From May 1968 to Mitterrand*, Routledge & Kegan Paul: London.

Duelli Klein, R. (1983) 'How to do what we want to do: thoughts about feminist methodology', in *Theories of Women's Studies*, Bowles, G. and R. Duelli Klein (eds), Routledge & Kegan Paul: London.

Duncan, R. (1953) *The Artist's View*, in *The New American Poetry* (1960), Allen, D. (ed.), Grove Press: New York.

DuPlessis, R.B. (1985) 'For the Etruscans', in *Feminist Criticism*, Showalter, E. (ed.), Random House: New York.

Dworkin, A. (1974) *Woman Hating*, E.P. Dutton: New York.

Dworkin, A. (1981) *Pornography: Men Possessing Women*, G.P. Putnam: New York.

Dworkin, A. (1983) *Right-Wing Women: The Politics of Domesticated Females*, Putnam: New York.

Dworkin, A. (1987) *Intercourse*, Free Press: New York.

Eastman, C. (1978) 'On women and revolution', in *Crystal Eastman on Women and Revolution*, Cook, B.W. (ed.), Pergamon Press: Oxford.

Echols, A. (1984) 'The new feminism of Yin and Yang', in *Desire: The Politics of Sexuality*, Snitow, A. (ed.), Virago: London.

Ecker, G. (1985) *Feminist Aesthetics*, The Women's Press: London.

Ehrenreich, B. (1976) 'What is socialist feminism?', *WIN*, vol. 7, June, no. 3.

Ehrenreich, B. and English, D. (1979) *For Her Own Good: 150 Years of the Experts' Advice to Women*, Anchor Press: Garden City, NY.

Ehrlich, C. (1979) 'Socialism, anarchism and feminism', in *Reinventing Anarchy*, Ehrlich, H.J. *et al.* (ed.), Routledge & Kegan Paul. London.

Eichenbaum, L. and Orbach, S. (1982) *Outside In, Inside Out*, Penguin: Harmondsworth.

Eichler, M. (1980) *The Double Standard: A Feminist Critique of Feminist Social Science*, Croom Helm: London.

Eisenstein, H. (1984) *Contemporary Feminist Thought*, George Allen & Unwin: London.

Eisenstein, H. and Sacks, S.R. (1975) 'Women in search of autonomy: an action design', *Social Change*, vol. 5, no. 2, pp. 4–6.

Eisenstein, S. (1983) *Bread and Roses: Working Women's Consciousness in the United States, 1890 to World War I*, Routledge & Kegan Paul: London.

Eisenstein, Z.R. (ed.) (1979) *Capitalist Patriarchy and the Case for Socialist Feminism*, Monthly Review Press: New York.

Eisenstein, Z.R. (ed.) (1981) *The Radical Future of Liberal Feminism*, Longman: New York.

Eisenstein, Z.R. (1982) 'The sexual politics of the new right', in *Feminist Theory*, Keohane, N.O. *et al.* (eds), Harvester Press: Brighton.

Eisenstein, Z.R. (1984) *Feminism and Sexual Equality: Crisis in Liberal America*, Monthly Review Press: New York.

Elliott, J. and Walden, P. (1984) 'The struggle for peaceful conflict resolution: feminist teaching and learning', *Women's Studies Quarterly*, vol. XII, Summer, no. 2.

Ellmann, M. (1968) *Thinking About Women*, Harcourt Brace Jovanovich: New York.

Elshtain, J.B. (1979) 'Methodological confusion and conceptual confusion: a critique of mainstream political science', in *The Prism of Sex: Essays in the Sociology of Knowledge*, Sherman, J.A. and E.T. Beck (eds), University of Wisconsin Press: Madison.

Elshtain, J.B. (1981) *Public Man, Private Woman: Women in Social and Political Thought*, Martin Robertson: Oxford.

Elshtain, J.B. (1982a) 'Feminist discourse and its discontents: language, power and meaning', in *Feminist Theory*, Keohane, N.O. *et al.* (eds), Harvester Press: Brighton.

Elshtain, J.B. (1982b) *The Family in Political Thought*, Harvester Press: Brighton.

Elston, M.A. (1981) 'Medicine as "old husbands' tales": the impact of feminism', in *Men's Studies Modified*, Spender, D. (ed.), Pergamon: Oxford.

Emecheta, B. (1979) *The Joys of Motherhood*, Heinemann: London.

Enloe, C. (1983) *Does Khaki Become You? The Militarization of Women's Lives*, South End Press: Boston, Mass.

Erlemann, C. (1985) 'What's feminist architecture?', in *Feminist Aesthetics*, Ecker, G. (ed.), The Women's Press: London.

Ettore, E.M. (1978) 'Women, urban social movements, and the lesbian ghetto', *International Journal of Urban and Regional Research* vol. 2, no. 3, pp. 499–520.

Evans, J. (ed.) (1986) *Feminism and Political Theory*, Sage: London.

Evans, M. (1983) 'In praise of theory: the case for women's studies', in *Theories of Women's Studies*, Bowles, G. and R. Duelli Klein (eds), Routledge & Kegan Paul: London.

Evans, S. (1979) *Personal Politics*, Vintage Books: New York.

Faderman, L. (1981) *Surpassing the Love of Men: Romantic Friendship and Love Between Women from the Renaissance to the Present*, William Morrow: New York.

Fee, E. (1973) 'The sexual politics of Victorian social anthropology', *Feminist Studies*, 1.

Ferber, M.A. and Teiman, M.L. (1981) 'The impact of feminism on economics', in *Men's Studies Modified*, Spender, D. (ed.), Pergamon: Oxford.

Ferguson, A. (1979) 'Women as a new revolutionary class in America', in *Between Labor and Capital*, Walker, P. (ed.), South End Press: Boston, Mass.

Ferguson, A. (1983) 'On conceiving motherhood and sexuality: a feminist materialist approach', in *Mothering: Essays on Feminist Theory*, Trebilcot, J. (ed.), Rowman & Allanheld: Totowa, NJ.

Ferguson, A. *et al.* (1982) 'On "compulsory heterosexuality"', in *Feminist Theory*, Keohane, N.O. *et al.* (eds), Harvester Press: Brighton.

Ferguson, A. and Folbre, N. (1981) 'The unhappy marriage of patriarchy and capitalism', in *Women and Revolution*, Sargent, P. (ed.), South End Press: Boston, Mass.

Ferguson, M. (1986) 'Feminist polemic: British women's writings in English from the late Renaissance to the French Revolution', *Women's Studies International Forum*, vol. 19, no. 5–6 pp. 451–64.

Fetterley, J. (1978) *The Resisting Reader: A Feminist Approach to American Fiction*, Indiana University Press: Bloomington.

Finch, S. *et al.* (1986) 'Socialist-feminists and Greenham', *Feminist Review*, 23, Summer, pp. 93–101.

Firestone, S. (1968) *Notes from the First Year*, Radical Feminism: New York.

Firestone, S. (1970) *The Dialectic of Sex: The Case for Feminist Revolution*, William Morrow: New York.

Fisher, B. (1981) 'What is feminist pedagogy?' *Radical Teacher*, 18, pp. 20–24.

Fisher-Manick, B. (1981) 'Race and class: beyond personal politics', in *Building Feminist Theory*, the *Quest* staff (ed.), Longman: New York.

Flax, J. (1980) 'Mother-daughter relationships: psychodynamics, politics and philosophy', in *The Future of Difference*, Eisenstein, H. and A. Jardine (eds), G.K. Hall: Boston, Mass.

Flax, J. (1983) 'Political philosophy and the patriarchal unconscious: a psychoanalytic perspective on epistemology and metaphysics', in *Discovering Reality*, Harding, S. and M. Hintikka, (eds), D. Reidel: Boston, Mass.

Foreman, A. (1977) *Femininity as Alienation: Women and the Family in Marxism and Philosophy*, Pluto Press: London.

Foucault, M. (1969) *L'Archéologie du Savoir*, Gallimard: Paris.

Foucault, M. (1979) *The History of Sexuality*, Allen Lane: London.

Frazier, N. and Sadker, M. (1973) *Sexism in School and Society*, Harper & Row: New York.

Freedman, E.B. (ed.) (1985) *The Lesbian Issue: Essays from Signs*, University of Chicago Press: Chicago.

Freeman, J. (1970) *The Bitch Manifesto*, KNOW: Pittsburgh.

Freeman, J. (1973) 'Women on the move: roots of revolt', in *Academic Women on the Move*, Rossi, A. and A. Calderwood (eds), Russell Sage: New York.

Freeman, J. (1975) *The Politics of Women's Liberation*, David McKay: New York.

Freeman, J. (1976) 'The women's liberation movement: its origins, structures, impact and ideas', in *Women's Studies: The Social Realities*, Watson, B.B. (ed.), Harper & Row: New York.

Freire, P. (1970) *Pedagogy of the Oppressed*, Seabury Press: New York.

French, M. (1975) *Beyond Power: Women, Men and Morals*, Jonathan Cape: London.

Freud, S. (1905) *Three Essays on the Theory of Sexuality* in *On Sexuality* (1977) Penguin: Harmondsworth.

Friedan, B. (1963) *The Feminine Mystique*, W.W. Norton: New York.

Friedan, B. (1981) *The Second Stage*, Summit Books: New York.

Frye, M. (1980) 'On second thought . . .', *Radical Teacher*, 17, November, pp. 37–8.

Frye, M. (1983) *The Politics of Reality: Essays in Feminist Theory*, Crossing Press: Trumansburg, NY.

Fuller, M. (1845) *Women in the Nineteenth Century*, reprinted 1971 by W.W. Norton: New York.

Furner, M. (1975) *Advocacy and Objectivity*, University of Illinois Press, Urbana.

Gage, M.J. (1873) *Woman, Church and State*, Charles Kerr: Chicago; reprinted 1980 by Persephone Press: Watertown, Mass.

Gallop, J. (1982) *Feminism and Psychoanalysis: The Daughter's Seduction*, Macmillan: London.

Gavison, R. (1980) 'Privacy and the limits of law', *Yale Law Journal*, vol. 89, no. 3, pp. 421–71.

Gearhart, S. (1978) 'The spiritual dimension: death and resurrection of a hallelujah dyke', in *Our Right to Love*, Vida, G. (ed.), Prentice-Hall: Englewood Cliffs, NJ.

Geiger, S.N.G. (1986) 'Women's life histories: method and content', *Signs*, vol. II, Winter, no. 2, pp. 334–51.

Gelfand, E.D. and Hules, V.T. (1985) *French Feminist Criticism: Women, Language and Literature: An Annotated Bibliography*, Garland: New York.

Gilbert, S. and Gubar, S. (1979) *The Madwoman in the Attic: The Woman Writer and the Nineteenth Century Literary Imagination*, Yale University Press: New Haven, CT.

Gilligan, C. (1982) *In a Different Voice: Essays on Psychological Theory and Women's Development*, Harvard University Press: Cambridge, Mass.

Gilman, C.P. (1898) *Women and Economics*, Small Maynard: Boston, Mass.

Gilman, C.P. (1903) *The Home, its Work and Influence*, Heinemann: London.

Gilman, C.P. (1911) *The Man-Made World or Our Androcentric Culture*, T. Fisher Unwin: London.

Gilman, C.P. (1915) *Herland*, reprinted 1979 by Pantheon: New York.

Githens, M. and Prestage, J. (1975) *A Portrait of Marginality: The Political Behaviour of American Women*, David McKay: New York.

Goldenberg, N. (1979) *Changing of the Gods: Feminism and the End of Traditional Religions*, Beacon Press: Boston, Mass.

Goldman, E. (1970) *The Traffic in Women and Other Essays on Feminism*, Times Change: New York.

Goldman, N. (ed.) (1982) *Female Soldiers*, Greenwood Press: Westport, Conn.

Gordon, L. (1976) *Woman's Body. Woman's Right: A Social History of Birth Control in America*, Grossman: New York.

Gould, C.C. (ed.) (1976) *Women and Philosophy: Toward a Theory of Liberation*, G.P. Putnam: New York.

Gould, C.C. (ed.) (1982) *Beyond Domination: New Perspectives on Women and Philosophy*, Rowman & Allanheld: Totowa, NJ.

Gould, M. (1980) 'The new sociology', *Signs*, 5, pp. 459–67.

Greer, G. (1970) *The Female Eunuch*, McGibbon & Kee: London.

Greer, G. (1984) *Sex and Destiny: The Politics of Human Fertility*, Secker & Warburg: London.

Gregory, C.E. (1980) 'Black activists', *Heresies*, 3:1 issue 9, pp. 14–17.

Griffin, C. (1986) 'From school to the job market', in *Feminist Social Psychology*, Wilkinson, S. (ed.), Open University: Milton Keynes.

Griffin, S. (1978) *Woman and Nature: The Roaring Inside Her*, Harper & Row: New York.

Griffin, S. (1979) *Rape: The Power of Consciousness*, Harper & Row: New York.

Griffin, S. (1981) *Pornography and Silence: Culture's Revenge Against Nature*, Harper & Row: New York.

Griffin, S. (1982a) *Made from this Earth*, The Women's Press: London.

Griffin, S. (1982b) 'The way of all ideology', in *Feminist Theory*, Keohane, N.O. *et al.* (eds), Harvester Press: Brighton.

Grimké, S. (1838) *Letters on the Equality of the Sexes and the Condition of Women*, Isaac Knapp: Boston, Mass.

Grimshaw, J. (1986) *Feminist Philosophers: Women's Perspectives on Philosophical Traditions*, Harvester Press: Brighton.

Guillaumin, C. (1981) 'The practice of power and belief in nature, part 1', *Feminist Issues*, vol. 1, no. 2, pp. 3–28.

Guillaumin, C. (1982) 'The question of difference', *Feminist Issues*, vol. 2, no. 1, pp. 33–52.

Guillaumin, C. (1983a) 'The practice of power and belief in nature, part 2', *Feminist Issues*, vol. 1, no. 3, pp. 87–109.

Guillaumin, C. (1983b) 'The masculine: denotations/connotations, *Feminist Issues*, vol. 5, no. 1, pp. 65–73.

Haber, B. (1979) 'Is personal life still a political issue?', *Feminist Studies*, vol. 5, Fall, no. 3, pp. 417–30.

Haber, B. (1982) *The Women's Annual 1981: the Year in Review*, G.K. Hall & Co: Boston, Mass.

Haber, B. (1983) *The Women's Annual 1982–1983*, G.K. Hall: Boston, Mass.

Haber, B. (1983) *The Women's Annual 1982–1983*, G.K. Hall: Boston, Mass.

Hacker, H.M. (1951) 'Women as a minority group', *Social Forces*, 30, pp. 60–9.

Hakim, C. (1979) *Occupational Segregation*, Department of Employment: London.

Hall, J.A. (1984) *Non Verbal Sex Differences*, Johns Hopkins University Press: Baltimore, Mass.

Hall, N. (1980) *The Moon and the Virgin: Reflections on the Archetypal Feminine*, Harper & Row: New York.

Hanisch, C. (1971) 'The personal is political', in *The Radical Therapist*, Agel, J. (ed.), Ballantine Books: New York.

Hanscombe, G.E. and Forster, J. (1982) *Rocking the Cradle – Lesbian Mothers/A Challenge to Family Living*, Sheba: London.

Harding, S. (1978–9) 'Is the equality of opportunity principle democratic?', *The Philosophical Forum*, vol. 10, Winter/Summer, no. 2/4.

Harding, S. and Hintikka, M.B. (eds) (1983) *Discovering Reality: Feminist Perspectives on Epistemology, Metaphysics, Methodology and Philosophy of Science*, D. Reidel: Boston, Mass.

Haraway, D. (1979) 'The biological enterprise: sex, mind and profit from human engineering to sociobiology', *Radical History Review*, 20, Spring/Summer.

Harris, O. (1984) 'Households as natural units', in *Of Marriage and the Market*, Young, K. *et al.* (eds), Routledge & Kegan Paul: London.

Hartmann, H. (1976) 'Capitalism, patriarchy and job segregation by sex', in *Women and the Workplace: The Implications of Occupational Segregation*, Blaxall, M. and B. Reagan (eds), University of Chicago Press: Chicago.

Hartmann, H. (1981) 'The unhappy marriage of marxism and feminism', in *Women and Revolution*, Sargent, P. (ed.), South End Press: Boston, Mass.

Hartsock, N. (1975) 'Fundamental feminism: process and perspective', *Quest*, vol. 2, Fall, no. 2.

Hartsock, N. (1979) 'Feminist theory and the development of revolutionary strategy', in *Capitalist Patriarchy and the Case for Socialist Feminism*, Eisenstein, Z. (ed.), Monthly Review Press: New York.

Hartsock, N. (1981) *Money, Sex and Power: An Essay on Domination and Community*, Longman: New York.

Haug, F. (1987) *Female Sexualization*, Verso: London.

Hayden, D. (1976) *Seven American Utopias: the Architecture of Communitarian Socialism, 1790–1975*, MIT Press: Cambridge, Mass.

Hayden, D. (1980a) *A 'Grand Domestic Revolution': Feminism, Socialism and the American Home, 1870–1930*, MIT Press: Cambridge, Mass.

Hayden, D. (1980b) 'What would a non-sexist city be like?', *Signs*, vol. 5, Spring, no. 3, pp. 170–187.

Heilbrun, C. (1973) *Toward a Recognition of Androgyny*, Alfred A. Knopf: New York.

Held, V. (1987) 'Feminism and moral theory', in *Women and Moral Theory*,

Kittay, E.F. and D.T. Meyers (eds), Rowman & Littlefield: Totowa, NJ.

Henley, N.M. (1977) *Body Politics*, Prentice Hall: Englewood Cliffs, NJ.

Heschel, S. (ed.) (1983) *On Being a Jewish Feminist: A Reader*, Schocken Books: New York.

Hochschild, A. (1983) *The Managed Heart*, University of California Press: Los Angeles.

Hole, J. and Levine, E. (eds) (1971) *The Rebirth of Feminism*, Quadrangle: New York.

Holland, P. *et al.* (1986) *Photography/Politics: Two*, Comedia: London.

Hooks, B. (1981) *Ain't I a Woman: Black Women and Feminism*, South End Press: Boston, Mass.

Hooks, B. (1984) *Feminist Theory: From Margin to Center*, South End Press: Boston, Mass.

Hooks, B. (1987) 'Feminism: a movement to end sexist oppression', in *Feminism and Equality*, Phillips, A. (ed.), Basil Blackwell: Oxford.

Horner, M.S. (1972) 'Toward an understanding of achievement-related conflicts in women', *Journal of Social Issues*, 28, pp. 157–75.

Horney, K. (1967) *Feminine Psychology*, W.W. Norton: New York.

Howe, F. (1978) 'Breaking the disciplines', in *The Structure of Knowledge: A Feminist Perspective*, Proceedings of the Fourth Annual GLLA Women's Studies Conference: Wellesley.

Howe, F. (ed.) (1975) *Women and the Power to Change*, McGraw Hill: New York.

Howell, N. (1979) 'Sociobiological hypotheses explored', *Science*, 206, pp. 1294–5.

Hubbard, R. (1983) 'Have only men evolved?', in *Discovering Reality*, Harding, S. and M.B. Hintikka (eds), Reidel: Boston, Mass.

Hughes, M. and Kennedy, M. (1985) *New Futures*, Routledge & Kegan Paul: London.

Hull, G. *et al.* (1981) *Black Women's Studies*, Feminist Press: Old Westbury, NY.

Humm, M. (1986) *Feminist Criticism: Women as Contemporary Critics*, Harvester Press: Brighton.

Humm, M. (1987) *An Annotated Bibliography of Feminist Criticism*, Harvester Press: Brighton.

Humm, M. (1988) 'Is the gaze feminist? Pornography, film and feminism', in *Perspectives on Pornography*, Day, G. and C. Bloom (eds), Macmillan: London.

Humphries, J. (1982) 'The working-class family: a Marxist perspective', in *The Family in Political Thought*, Elshtain, J.B. (ed.), Harvester Press: Brighton.

Hunter College Women's Studies Collective (1983) *Women's Realities, Women's Choices*, Oxford University Press: New York.

Interrante, J. and Lasser, C. (1979) 'Victims of the very songs they sing: a critique of recent work on patriarchal culture and the social construction of gender', *Radical History Review*, 20, Spring/Summer.

Irigaray, L. (1974a) *Speculum de l'autre femme*, Editions de Minuit: Paris.

Irigaray, L. (1974b) 'La "Mécanique" des fluides', *L'Arc*, 58, pp. 49–55.

Irigaray, L. (1977a) 'La Misère de la psychanalyse', *Critique*, 30, 365, October, pp. 879–903.

Irigaray, L. (1977b) *Ce sexe qui n'en est pas un*, Editions de Minuit: Paris.

Itzin, C. (1986) 'Media images of women: the social construction of ageism and sexism', in *Feminist Social Psychology: Developing Theory and Practice*, Wilkinson, S. (ed.), Open University: Milton Keynes.

Jacobus, M. (1987) 'Freud's mnemonic: women, screen memories, and feminist nostalgia', in *Women and Memory: Special Issue, Michigan Quarterly Review*, vol. XXVI, no. 1, pp. 117–40.

Jaggar, M.A. (1983) *Feminist Politics and Human Nature*, Harvester Press: Brighton.

Jaggar, M.A. and Rothenberg, S.P. (1978) *Feminist Frameworks: Alternative Theoretical Accounts of the Relations Between Women and Men*, McGraw Hill: New York.

Janeway, E. (1971) *Man's World, Woman's Place: A Study in Social Mythology*, Dell: New York.

Janeway, E. (1981) *The Powers of the Weak*, Morrow Quill: New York.

Jardine, A.A. (1985) *Gynesis: Configurations of Women and Modernity*, Cornell University Press: Ithaca, NY.

Jayaratne, T.E. (1983) 'The value of quantitative methodology for feminist research', in *Theories of Women's Studies*, Bowles, G. and R. Duelli Klein (eds), Routledge & Kegan Paul; London.

Jayawardena, K. (1982) *Feminism and Nationalism in the Third World in Nineteenth and Early Twentieth Centuries*, Institute of Social Studies: The Hague.

Jehlen, M. (1982) 'Archimedes and the paradox of feminist criticism', in *Feminist Theory*, Keohane, N.O. *et al.* (eds), Harvester Press: Brighton.

Jenkins, L. and Kramer, C. (1978) 'Small group processes; learning from women', *Women's Studies International Quarterly*, vol. 1, no. 1, pp. 67–84.

Johnston, J. (1974) *Lesbian Nation: The Feminist Solution*, Simon & Schuster: New York.

Jones, A.R. (1985) 'Writing the body: toward an understanding of *l'écriture féminine*', in *Feminist Criticism*, Showalter, E. (ed.), Pantheon: New York.

Jordanova, L.J. (1981a) 'Mental illness, mental health', in *Women in Society*, Cambridge Women's Studies Group (ed.), Virago: London.

Jordanova, L.J. (1981b) 'The history of the family', in *Women in Society*, Cambridge Women's Studies Group (ed.), Virago: London.

Joseph, G.I. (1983) 'Review of woman, race and class', *Signs*, vol. 9, no. 1, pp. 134–6.

Joseph, G.I. and Lewis, J. (1981) *Common Differences: Conflicts in Black and White Feminist Perspectives*, Anchor Press/Doubleday: Garden City, NY.

Kaplan, A.E. (ed.) (1978) *Women in Film Noir*, British Film Institute: London.

Kaplan, A.E. (1983) *Women and Film*, Methuen: New York.

Kaplan, C. (1986) *Sea Changes*, Verso: London.

Kaplan, T. (1982) 'Female consciousness and collective action', in *Feminist Theory*, Keohane, N.O. *et al.* (eds), Harvester Press: Brighton.

Kappeler, S. (1986) *The Pornography of Representation*, Polity Press: Cambridge.

Katzenstein, M.F. and Laitin, D.D. (1987) 'Politics, feminism and the ethics of caring', in *Women and Moral Theory*, Kittay, E.F. and D.T. Meyers (eds), Rowman & Littlefield: Totowa, NJ.

Keller, E.F. (1978) 'Gender and science', *Psychoanalysis and Contemporary Thought*, VI, pp. 409–33.

Keller, E.F. (1982) 'Feminism and science', in *Feminist Theory*, Keohane, N.O. *et al.* (eds), Harvester Press: Brighton.

Kelly-Gadol, J. (1974) *Women's History*, Sarah Lawrence College: Bronxville, NY.

Kelly-Gadol, J. (1976) 'The Social relations of the sexes: methodological implications of women's history', *Signs*, 1, pp. 809–24.

Kelly-Gadol, J. (1979) 'The doubled vision of feminist theory: a postscript to the "Women and power" Conference', *Feminist Studies*, vol. 5, no. 1, Spring.

Kelly-Gadol, J. (ed.) (1984) *Women, History and Theory*, University of Chicago Press: Chicago.

Kendrigan, M.L. (1984) *Political Equality in a Democratic Society: Women in the United States*, Greenwood Press: Westport, Conn.

Kenner, C. (1985) *No Time For Women*, Pandora: London.

Kimmel, M.S. (1987) *Changing Men*, Sage: London.

Kittay, E.F. and Meyers, D.T. (eds) (1987) *Women and Moral Theory*, Rowman & Littlefield: Totowa, NJ.

Kitzinger, C. (1986) 'Introducing and developing Q as a feminist methodology: a study of accounts of lesbianism', in *Feminist Social Psychology*, Wilkinson, S. (ed.), Open University: Milton Keynes.

Klein, E. (1984) *Gender Politics*, Harvard University Press: Cambridge, Mass.

Koedt, A. (1973) 'The myth of the vaginal orgasm', in *Radical Feminism*, Koedt, A. *et al.* (eds), Quadrangle: New York.

Koedt, A. *et al.* (eds) (1973) *Radical Feminism*, Quadrangle: New York.

Kofman, S. (1987) 'The narcissistic woman: Freud and Girard', in *French Feminist Thought*, Moi, T. (ed.), Basil Blackwell: Oxford.

Kollontai, A. (1977) *Selected Writings*, Holt, A. (ed.), Allison & Busby: London.

Kolodny, A. (1975) *The Lay of the Land: Metaphor as Experience and History in American Life and Letters*, University of North Carolina Press: Chapel Hill.

Komarovsky, M. (1964) *Blue-Collar Marriage*, Random House: New York.

Kornegger, P. (1979) 'Anarchism: the feminist connection', in *Reinventing Anarchy*, Ehrlich, H.J. *et al.* (eds), Routledge & Kegan Paul: London.

Kramarae, C. and Treichler, P.A. (1985) *A Feminist Dictionary*, Pandora: London.

Kreps, B. (1973) 'Radical feminism: 1', in *Radical Feminism*, Koedt, A. *et al.* (eds), Quandrangle: New York.

Kristeva, J. (1974a) *La Révolution du langage poétique*, Tel Quel: Paris.

Kristeva, J. (1974b) *Des Chinoises*, Editions des femmes: Paris.

Kristeva, J. (1980) *Desire in Language: A Semiotic Approach to Literature and Art*, Basil Blackwell: Oxford.

Kristeva, J. (1982) 'Women's time', in *Feminist Theory*, Keohane, N.O. *et al.* (eds), Harvester Press: Brighton.

Kuhn, A. (1985) *The Power of the Image*, Routledge & Kegan Paul: London.

Kuhn, A. and Wolpe, A.M. (1978) *Feminism and Materialism: Women and Modes of Production*, Routledge & Kegan Paul: London.

Kuhn, T. (1962) *The Structure of Scientific Revolutions*, University of Chicago Press: Chicago.

Lacan, J. (1966) *Ecrits*, Editions du Seuil: Paris.

Ladner, J.A. (1971) *Tomorrow's Tomorrow: The Black Woman*, Doubleday: New York.

Lakoff, R. (1975) *Language and Woman's Place*, Harper & Row: New York.

Lancaster, J. (1975) *Primate Behaviour and the Emergence of Human Culture*, Holt Rinehart and Winston: New York.

Land, H. (1981) 'The family wage', *New Statesman*, 18 December, pp. 16–18.

Langland, E. and Gore, W. (1981) *A Feminist Perspective in the Academy: The Difference it Makes*, University of Chicago Press: Chicago.

de Lauretis, T. (ed.) (1986) *Feminist Studies: Critical Studies*, Indiana University Press: Bloomington.

Lear, M.W. (1968) 'The second feminist wave', *New York Times Magazine*, 10 March.

Leclerc, A. (1974) *Parole de Femme*, Grasset: Paris.

Lederer, L. (ed.) (1980) *Take Back the Night: Women on Pornography*, William Morrow: New York.

Le Guin, U. (1969) *The Left Hand of Darkness*, Macdonald: London.

Le Guin, U. (1975) *The Dispossessed*, Avon: New York.

Le Guin, U. (1976) 'Is gender necessary?' in *Aurora: Beyond Equality*, McIntyre, V.N. and S.J. Anderson (eds), Fawcett: Greenwich, Conn.

Lerner, G. (1971) *The Women in American History*, Addison-Wesley: Menloe Park, CA.

Lerner, G. (ed.) (1972) *Black Woman in White America*, Pantheon: New York.

Lerner, G. (1978) *The Majority Finds its Place: Placing Women in History*, Oxford University Press: New York.

Lerner, G. (1986) *The Creation of Patriarchy*, Oxford University Press: Oxford.

Lesage, J. (1981) 'Celine and Julie go boating', *Jump-Cut*, 24–25 March.

Lévi-Strauss, C. (1949) *The Elementary Structures of Kinship*, 1969 edition, Beacon Press: Boston, Mass.

Lewis, J. (1986) 'Feminism and welfare', in *What is Feminism?*, Mitchell, J. and A. Oakley (eds), Basil Blackwell: Oxford.

Lippard, L. (1976) *From the Center*, E.P. Dutton: New York.

Lopata, H. (1971) *Occupation: Housewife*, Oxford University Press: New York.

Lorde, A. (1981) *The Black Unicorn*, W.W. Norton: London.

Lorde, A. (1984a) 'Uses of the erotic', in *Sister Outsider*, Crossing Press: Trumansburg, NY.

Lorde, A. (1984b) 'An open letter to Mary Daly', in *Sister Outsider*, Crossing Press: Trumansburg, NY.

Love, B. and Shanklin, E. (1983) 'The answer is matriarchy', in *Mothering: Essays in Feminist Theory*, Trebilcot, J. (ed.), Rowman & Allanheld: Totowa, NJ.

Lowe, M. and Hubbard, R. (1983) *Woman's Nature: Rationalizations of Inequality*, Pergamon: Oxford.

Luxemburg, R. (1970) *Rosa Luxemburg Speaks*, Waters, M.A. (ed.), Pathfinder Press: London.

Macciochi, M.A. (1979) 'Female sexuality in fascist ideology', *Feminist Review*, 1, pp. 67–82.

Maccoby, E. and Jacklin, C.N. (1974) *The Psychology of Sex Differences*, Stanford University Press: Palo Alto, CA.

McConnell-Ginet, S. (ed.) (1980) *Women and Language in Literature and Society*, Praeger: New York.

Macdonald, S. (ed.) (1987) *Images of Women in Peace and War*, Macmillan: London.

McDonough, R. and Harrison, R. (1978) 'Patriarchy and relations of production', in *Feminism and Materialism*, Kuhn, A. and A. Wolpe (eds), Routledge & Kegan Paul: London.

McIntosh, M. (1978) 'The state and the oppression of women', in *Feminism and Materialism*, Kuhn, A. and A. Wolpe (eds), Routledge & Kegan Paul: London.

MacKinnon, C. (1979) *The Sexual Harassment of Working Women*, Yale University Press: New Haven, Conn.

MacKinnon, C. (1982) 'Feminism, marxism, method and the state: an agenda for theory', in *Feminist Theory*, Keohane, N.O. *et al.* (eds), Harvester Press: Brighton.

MacLeod, S. (1981) *The Art of Starvation*, Virago: London.

McRobbie, A. and Nava, M. (1984) *Gender and Generation*, Macmillan: London.

Mainardi, P. (1970) 'The politics of housework', in *Sisterhood is Powerful*, Morgan, R. (ed.), Vintage: New York.

Maitland, S. (1983) *A Map of the New Country: Women and Christianity*, Routledge & Kegan Paul: London.

Maitland, S. and Garcia, J. (1983) *Walking on the Water*, Virago: London.

Makward, C. (1980) 'To be or not to be . . . a feminist speaker', in *The Future of Difference*, Eisenstein, H. and A. Jardine (eds), G.K. Hall: Boston, Mass.

Malveaux, J. (1987) 'The political economy of black women', in *The Year Left 2*, Davis, M. (ed.), Verso: London.

Marcuse, H. (1955) *Eros and Civilization*, Beacon Press: Boston, Mass.

Marks, E. and Courtivron, I. de (eds) (1981) *New French Feminisms*, Harvester Press: Brighton.

Maroney, H.J. (1982) 'Embracing motherhood', in *Feminist Theory*, Keohane, N.O. *et al.* (eds), Harvester Press: Brighton.

Martineau, H. (1832–4) *Illustrations of Political Economy*, Charles Fox: London.

Martineau, H. (1838) *How to Observe, Morals and Manners*, Charles Knight: London.

Martyna, W. (1980) 'The psychology of the generic masculine', in *Women and Language in Literature and Society*, McConnell-Ginet, S. (ed.), Praeger: New York.

Mathieu, N.C. (1978) 'Man-culture and woman nature?', *Women's Studies International Quarterly*, 1, pp. 55–65.

Mathieu, N.C. (1984) 'Biological paternity, social maternity', *Feminist Issues*, vol. 4, no. 1, pp. 63–71.

Mead, M. (1935) *Sex and Temperament in Three Primitive Societies*, William Morrow: New York.

Mead, M. (1949) *Male and Female: A Study of the Sexes in a Changing World*, Dell: New York; reprinted 1971.

Merchant, C. (1983) *The Death of Nature: Women, Ecology and the Scientific Revolution*, Harper & Row: San Francisco.

Mickelwait, D.R., Riegelman, M.A. and Sweet, C.F. (1976) *Women in Rural Development*, Westview Press: Boulder, Col.

Mies, M. (1983) 'Towards a methodology for feminist research', in *Theories of Women's Studies*, Bowles, G. and R. Duelli Klein (eds), Routledge & Kegan Paul: London.

Mies, M. (1986) *Patriarchy and Accumulation on a World Scale*, Zed: London.

Mill, J.S. (1869) *The Subjection of Women*, reprinted 1974 by Oxford University Press: Oxford.

Mill, J.S. and Mill, H.T. (1970) *Essays on Sex Equality*, Rossi, A.S. (ed.), University of Chicago Press: Chicago.

Miller, C. and Swift, K. (1976) *Words and Women: New Language in New Times*, Anchor Press/Doubleday: Garden City, NY.

Miller, J.A. (1987) 'From Sweetback to Celie', in *The Year Left 2*, Davis, M. (ed.), Verso: London.

Miller, J.B. (1976) *Toward a New Psychology of Women*, Beacon Press: Boston, Mass.

Millett, K. (1970) *Sexual Politics*, Doubleday: New York.

Millman, M. and Kanter, R.M. (eds) (1975) *Another Voice: Feminist Perspectives on Social Life and Social Science*, Anchor Press: Garden City, NY.

Minnich, E. (1982) 'A devastating conceptual error: how can we *not* be feminist scholars?', *Change*, vol. 14, no. 3, pp. 7–9.

Mitchell, J. (1966) 'Women: The Longest Revolution', *New Left Review*, 40.

Mitchell, J. (1971) *Woman's Estate*, Penguin: Harmondsworth.

Mitchell, J. (1974) *Psychoanalysis and Feminism*, Penguin: Harmondsworth.

Mitchell, J. (1984) *Women: The Longest Revolution*, Virago: London.

Mitchell, J. and Oakley, A. (eds) (1976) *The Rights and Wrongs of Women*, Penguin: Harmondsworth.

Modleski, T. (1982) *Loving with a Vengeance*, Archon: Hamden, Conn.

Moers, E. (1977) *Literary Women*, Anchor Press/Doubleday: Garden City, NY.

Moi, T. (1985) *Sexual/Textual Politics*, Methuen: London.

Momsen, J.H. and Townsend, J. (1987) *Geography of Gender in the Third World*, Hutchinson: London.

Montefiore, J. (1987) *Feminism and Poetry*, Pandora: London.

Montrelay, M. (1977) *L'Ombre et le nom*, Minuit: Paris.

Moraga, C. and Anzaldúa, G. (1981) *This Bridge Called My Back: Writings by Radical Women of Color*, Persephone Press: Watertown, Mass.

Moraga, C. (1986) 'From a long line of Vendidas', in *Feminist Studies: Critical Studies*, Lauretis, T. de (ed.), Indiana University Press: Bloomington.

Morahan, S. (1981) *A Woman's Place: Rhetoric and Readings for Composing Yourself and Your Prose*, SUNY Press: Albany, NY.

Morgan, R. (ed.) (1970) *Sisterhood is Powerful*, Vintage: New York.

Morgan, R. (1977) *Going Too Far: The Personal Chronicle of a Feminist*, Random House: New York.

Moschkovich, J. (1981) '— "But I know you, American woman"', in *This Bridge Called My Back*, Moraga, C. and G. Anzaldúa (eds), Persephone Press: Watertown, Mass.

Mulvey, L. (1975) 'Visual pleasure and narrative cinema', *Screen*, vol. 16, no. 3, Autumn, pp. 6–19.

Nash, J. and Fernandez, K. (1983) *Women, Men and the International Division of Labor*, SUNY Press: Albany, NY.

Nash, J. and Safa, H. (1975) *Sex and Class in Latin America*, Praeger: New York.

Nestle, J. (1984) 'Living with *Herstory*', in *Women-Identified Women*, Darty, T. and S. Potter (eds), Mayfield: Palo Alto, CA.

Newton, E. and Walton, S. (1984) 'The misunderstanding: toward a more precise sexual vocabulary', in *Pleasure and Danger*, Vance, C.S. (ed.), Routledge & Kegan Paul: Boston, Mass.

Newton, J. (1981) *Women: Power and Subversion: Social Strategies in British Fiction 1778–1860*, University of Georgia Press: Athens, GA.

Nicolson, P. (1986) 'Developing a feminist approach to depression following childbirth', in *Feminist Social Psychology*, Wilkinson, S. (ed.), Open University: Milton Keynes.

Nochlin, L. (1971) 'Why have there been no great women artists?', in *Women in Sexist Society: Studies on Power and Powerlessness*, Gornick, V. and B. Moran (eds), Basic Books: New York.

Oakley, A. (1972) *Sex, Gender and Society*, Maurice Temple-Smith: London.

Oakley, A. (1982) *Subject Women*, Fontana: London.

Oakley, A. (1984) *Taking It Like a Woman*, Jonathan Cape: London.

O'Brien, M. (1982) 'Feminist theory and dialectical logic', in *Feminist Theory*, Keohane, N.O. *et al.* (eds), Harvester Press: Brighton.

O'Brien, M. (1983) *The Politics of Reproduction*, Routledge & Kegan Paul: London.

O'Donovan, K. (1981) 'Before and after: the impact of feminism on the academic discipline of law', *Men's Studies Modified*, Spender, D. (ed.), Pergamon: Oxford.

O'Leary, V.I. (1977) *Towards Understanding Women*, Brooks/Cole: Belmont, CA.

Olsen, T. (1978) *Silences*, Delacorte Press: New York.

Orbach, S. (1978) *Fat Is a Feminist Issue*, Paddington Press: London.

Ortner, S. (1974) 'Is female to male as nature is to culture?', in *Women, Culture and Society*, Rosaldo, M. and L. Lamphere (eds), Stanford University Press: Stanford, CA.

Ortner, S. and Whitehead, H. (eds) (1981) *Sexual Meanings: The Cultural Construction of Gender and Sexuality*, Cambridge University Press: Cambridge.

Ostriker, A.S. (1986) *Stealing the Language*, Beacon Press: Boston, Mass.

Page, L. (1982) *Tissue* in *Plays by Women vol. 1*, Wandor, M. (ed.), Methuen: London.

Pagels, E. (1979) *The Gnostic Gospels*, Random House: New York.

Parker, K. and Leghorn, L. (1981) *Woman's Work: Sexual Economics and the World of Women*, Routledge & Kegan Paul: Boston, Mass.

Parker, R. (1987) *Framing Feminism*, Routledge & Kegan Paul: London.

Parker, R. and Pollock, G. (1981) *Old Mistresses*, Routledge & Kegan Paul: London.

Parlee, M.B. (1979) 'Psychology and women', *Signs*, vol. 5, no. 1, pp. 121–33.

Parsons, K. (1977) 'Moral revolution', in *The Prism of Sex*, Sherman, J.A. and E.T. Beck (eds), University of Wisconsin Press: Madison.

Passerini, L. (1979) 'Work ideology and consensus under Italian fascism', *History Workshop Journal*, 8, Autumn, pp. 82–108.

Pearce, D. (1978) 'The feminization of poverty: women, work and welfare', *Urban and Social Change Review*, February.

Petchesky, R.P. (1980) 'Reproductive freedom: beyond "A woman's right to choose"', *Signs*, vol. 5, no. 4, pp. 661–85.

Petchesky, R.P. (1986) *Abortion and Woman's Choice*, Verso: London.

Piercy, M. (1976) *Woman on the Edge of Time*, Fawcett: Greenwich, Conn.

Pizan, C. de (1983) *The Book of the City of Ladies*, Pan: London.

Polan, J. (1982) 'Toward a theory of law and patriarchy', in *The Politics of Law: A Progressive Critique*, Kairy, D. (ed.), Pantheon: New York.

Pollock, G. (1987) 'What's wrong with "images of women"?', in *Framing Feminism*, Parker, R. and G. Pollock (eds), Pandora: London.

Pool, J. (1977) *Women in Music History: A Research Guide*, Pool: Ansonia Station, NY.

Pratt, A. (1982) *Archetypal Patterns in Women's Fiction*, Harvester Press: Brighton.

Pritchard, S.M. (1984) *The Women's Annual 4 1983–1984*, G.K. Hall: Boston, Mass.

Radford, J. (ed.) (1986) *The Progress of Romance*, Routledge & Kegan Paul: London.

Radicalesbians (1973) 'The woman-identified woman', in *Radical Feminism*, Koedt, A. (ed.), Quadrangle: New York.

Radway, J. (1984) *Reading the Romance: Women, Patriarchy and Popular Literature*, University of North Carolina Press: Chapel Hill.

Raymond, J. (1975) 'The illusion of androgyny', *Quest*, vol. 11, no. 1, p. 61.

Reddock, R. (1984) *Women, Labour and Struggle in Twentieth-Century Trinidad and Tobago 1898–1960*, Institute of Social Studies: The Hague.

Reed, E. (1970) *Problems of Women's Liberation*, Pathfinder: New York.

Reed, E. (1975) *Women's Evolution: From Matriarchal Clan to Patriarchal Family*, Pathfinder: New York.

Reed, E. (1978) 'Women: caste, class or oppressed sex?', in *Feminist Frameworks*, Jagger, A. and P.R. Struhl (eds), McGraw-Hill: New York.

Reich, W. (1945) *The Sexual Revolution*, reprinted 1951 by Vision Press: London.

Reinhardt, N. (1981) 'New directions for feminist criticism in theatre and the related arts', in *A Feminist Perspective in the Academe*, Langland, E. and W. Gore (eds), University of Chicago Press: Chicago.

Reinharz, S. (1979) *On Becoming a Social Scientist: From Survey Research and Participant Observation to Experiential Analysis*, Jossey-Bass: San Francisco.

Reinharz, S. (1983) 'Experiential analysis: a contribution to feminist research', in *Theories of Women's Studies*, Bowles, G. and R. Duelli Klein (eds), Routledge & Kegan Paul: London.

Reinharz, S. (1986) 'Friends or foes: gerontology and feminist theory', *Women's Studies International Forum*, vol. 9, no. 5/6, pp. 503–14.

Reiter, R.R. (1975) *Toward an Anthropology of Women*, Monthly Review Press: New York.

Reuther, R. (1974) *Religion and Sexism*, Simon & Schuster: New York.

Rich, A. (1976) *Of Woman Born: Motherhood as Experience and Institution*, W.W. Norton: New York.

Rich, A. (1977) 'Forward: conditions for work: the common world of woman', in *Working It Out: Twenty-Three Women Writers, Artists, Scholars Think About Their Lives and Work*, Pantheon: New York.

Rich, A. (1979a) 'When we dead awaken: writing as re-vision', in *On Lies, Secrets and Silence*, W.W. Norton: New York.

Rich, A. (1979b) 'Toward a woman-centered university', in *On Lies, Secrets and Silence*, W.W. Norton: New York.

Rich, A. (1980) 'Compulsory heterosexuality and lesbian existence', *Signs*, vol. 5, no. 4, pp. 631–60.

Rich, A. (1986) *Blood, Bread and Poetry*, W.W. Norton: New York.

Richards, J.R. (1980) *The Sceptical Feminist*, Routledge & Kegan Paul: London.

Rieger, E. (1985) '"Dolce semplica"? On the changing role of women in music', in *Feminist Aesthetics*, Ecker, G. (ed.), The Women's Press: London.

Rigney, B.H. (1978) *Madness and Sexual Politics in the Feminist Novel*, University of Wisconsin Press: Madison.

Rihani, M. (1977) *Development as if Women Mattered: An Annotated Bibliography with a Third World Focus*, Overseas Development Council: Washington, DC.

Riley, D. and Leonard, D. (1986) 'Women in the family', in *Women in Britain Today*, Beechey, V. and E. Whitelegg (eds), Open University: Milton Keynes.

Roberts, H. (ed.) (1981) *Women, Health and Reproduction*, Routledge & Kegan Paul: London.

Robertson, C. and Berger, I. (eds) (1986) *Women and Class in Africa*, Holmes and Meier: New York.

Rosaldo, M. (1980) 'The use and abuse of anthropology: reflections on feminism and cross-cultural understanding', *Signs*, vol. 5, no. 3, pp. 389–417.

Rosaldo, M.Z. and Lamphere, L. (eds) (1974) *Women, Culture and Society*, Stanford University Press: Stanford, CA.

Rose, H. (1986) 'Women's work: women's knowledge', in *What is Feminism?*, Mitchell, J. and A. Oakley (eds), Basil Blackwell: Oxford.

Rossi, A. (1970) *Essays on Sex Equality*, University of Chicago Press: Chicago.

Rossi, A. (1973) *The Feminist Papers*, University of Columbia Press: New York.

Rowbotham, S. (1972) *Women, Resistance and Revolution*, Penguin: Harmondsworth.

Rowbotham, S. (1973a) *Hidden from History*, Pluto Press: London.

Rowbotham, S. (1973b) *Woman's Consciousness, Man's World*, Penguin: Harmondsworth.

Rowbotham, S. (1977) *A New World for Women: Stella Browne, Socialist Feminist*, Pluto Press: London.

Rowbotham, S. (ed.) (1979) *Beyond the Fragments: Feminism and the Making of Socialism*, Merlin: London.

Rowbotham, S. (1983) *Dreams and Dilemmas*, Virago: London.

Rubin, G. (1975) 'The traffic in women: notes on the "political economy" of sex', in *Toward an Anthropology of Women*, Reiter, R.R. (ed.), Monthly Review Press: New York.

Rubin, G. (1984) 'Thinking sex', in *Pleasure and Danger*, Vance, C.S. (ed.), Routledge & Kegan Paul: London.

Rubin, L.B. (ed.) (1976) *Worlds of Pain: Life in the Working-Class Family*, Basic Books: New York.

Ruddick, S. (1980) 'Maternal thinking', *Feminist Studies*, vol. 6, no. 2, pp. 342–67.

Ruddick, S. (1984) 'Preservative love and military destruction', in *Mothering: Essays in Feminist Theory*, Trebilcot, J. (ed.), Rowman & Allanheld: Totowa, NJ.

Russ, J. (1973) 'What can a heroine do? Or why women can't write', in *Images of Women in Fiction: Feminist Perspectives*, Cornillon, S.K. (ed.), Bowling Green University Popular Press: Bowling Green, Ohio.

Rutenberg, T. (1983) 'Learning women's studies', in *Theories of Women's Studies*, Bowles, G. and R. Duelli Klein (eds), Routledge & Kegan Paul: London.

Sabrosky, J. (1979) *From Rationality to Liberation: The Evolution of Feminist Ideology*, Greenwood Press: Westport, Conn.

Sacks, K. (1974) 'Engels revisited: women, the organization of production and private property', in *Women, Culture and Society*, Rosaldo, M. and L. Lamphere (eds), Stanford University Press: Stanford, CA.

Sanchez, R. and Cruz, R.M. (eds) (1978) *Essays on La Mujer*, Chicano Studies Center Publications, University of California Press: Los Angeles.

Sanday, P. (1981) *Female Power and Male Dominance*, Cambridge University Press: Cambridge.

Sarah, E. (ed.), (1983) *Reassessment of 'First Wave' Feminism*, Pergamon Press: Oxford.

Sargent, L. (ed.) (1981) *Women and Revolution: A Discussion of the Unhappy Marriage of Marxism and Feminism*, South End Press: Boston, Mass.

Sayers, J. (1987) 'Melanie Klein, psychoanalysis and feminism', *Feminist Review*, 25, pp. 23–37.

Schechter, S. (1982) *Women and Male Violence: the Visions and Struggles of the Battered Women's Movement*, South End Press: Boston, Mass.

Shange, N. (1987) 'Interview', *Spare Rib*, May, pp. 14–18.

Sharff, J. (1981) 'Free enterprise and the ghetto family', *Psychology Today*, March, pp. 41–8.

Sherfey, M.J. (1972) *The Nature and Evolution of Female Sexuality*, Random House: New York.

Sherfey, M.J. (1976) 'A theory on female sexuality', in *Female Psychology: the Emerging Self*, Cox, S. (ed.), Science Research Associates: Chicago.

Shostak, M. (1981) *Niga: the Life and Words of a Kang (Kong?) Woman*, Cambridge University Press: Cambridge.

Showalter, E. (1971) 'Women in the literary curriculum', *College English*, 32, pp. 853–62.

Showalter, E. (1977) *A Literature of Their Own: British Women Novelists from Brontë to Lessing*, Princeton University Press: Princeton, NJ.

Showalter, E. (1979) 'Towards a feminist poetics', in *Women Writing and Writing About Women*, Jacobus, M. (ed.), Croom Helm: London.

Showalter, E. (1982) 'Feminist criticism in the wilderness', in *Writing and Sexual Difference*, Abel, E. (ed.), Harvester Press: Brighton.

Showalter, E. (ed.) (1986) *The New Feminist Criticism: Essays on Women, Literature and Theory*, Pantheon: New York.

Shulman, A. (1986) 'Sex and power: the sexual bases of radical feminism', *Signs*, vol. 5, no. 4, pp. 590–604.

Slocum, S. (1975) 'Woman the gatherer: male bias in anthropology', in *Toward an Anthropology of Women*, Reiter, R.R. (ed.), Monthly Review Press: New York.

Smart, C. (1977) *Women, Crime and Criminology*, Routledge & Kegan Paul: London.

Smith, B. (1978) 'The structure of knowledge: a feminist perspective', *Great Lakes College Association Women's Studies Conference Proceedings*, pp. 11–16.

Smith, B. (1979) 'Notes for yet another paper on black feminism', *Conditions: Five*, 27, pp. 123–7.

Smith, B. (1980) *Toward a Black Feminist Criticism*, Out and Out Books: Trumansburg, NY.

Smith, B. (1982) 'On separatism', *Sinister Wisdom*, 20, Spring, pp. 100–4.

Smith, B. (1984) 'Between a rock and a hard place', in *Yours In Struggle* Bulkin, E., M.B. Pratt and B. Smith (eds), Long Haul Press: New York.

Smith, B. and Smith, B. (1981) 'Across the kitchen table', in *This Bridge Called My Back*, Moraga, C. and G. Anzaldúa (eds), Kitchen Table Press: New York.

Smith, D. (1974) 'Women's perspective as a radical critique of sociology', *Sociological Inquiry*, vol. 44, no. 1, pp. 7–13.

Smith, D. (1978) 'A peculiar eclipsing', *Women's Studies International Quarterly*, vol. 1, no. 4, pp. 281–5.

Smith, D. (1979) 'A sociology for women', in *The Prism of Sex: Essays in the Sociology of Knowledge*, Beck, E.T. and J. Sherman (eds), University of Wisconsin Press: Madison.

Smith-Rosenberg, C. (1972) 'The hysterical woman: sex roles and conflict in nineteenth-century America', *Social Research*, 39, pp. 652–78.

Smith-Rosenberg, C. (1975) 'The female world of love and ritual: relations between women in nineteenth-century America', *Signs*, vol. 1, no. 1, pp. 1–29.

Smith-Rosenberg, C. (1985) *Disorderly Conduct: Visions of Gender in Victorian America*, Alfred A. Knopf: New York.

Snitow, A. (1980) 'The front line: notes on sex in novels by women, 1969–1979', *Signs*, vol. 5, no. 4, pp. 702–18.

Sojourner, Truth (1851) 'Address' in *The History of Woman Suffrage*, vol. 2 (1891–86), Stanton, C.E., S.B. Anthony and M.J. Gage, Charles Mann: Rochester, New York.

Spence, J. (1987) 'New portraits for old: the use of the camera in therapy', in *Looking On*, Betterton, R. (ed.), Pandora: London.

Spender, D. (1980) *Man Made Language*, Routledge & Kegan Paul: London.

Spender, D. (ed.) (1981) *Men's Studies Modified*, Pergamon: Oxford.

Spender, D. (1982a) *Invisible Women: The Schooling Scandal*, Writers and Readers: London.

Spender, D. (1982b) *Women of Ideas and What Men Have Done to Them: From Aphra Benn to Adrienne Rich*, Routledge & Kegan Paul: London.

Spender, D. (1983) 'Theorising about theorising', in *Theories of Women's Studies*, Bowles, G. and R. Duelli Klein (eds), Routledge & Kegan Paul: London.

Spivak, G. (1987) *In Other Worlds: Essays in Cultural Politics*, Methuen: London.

Spretnak, C. (ed.) (1982) *The Politics of Women's Spirituality: Essays on the Rise of Spiritual Power within the Feminist Movement*, Anchor Press: Garden City, NY.

Stanley, L. and Wise, S. (1983) "'Back into the personal" or our attempt to construct "feminist research"', in *Theories of Women's Studies*, Bowles G. and R. Duelli Klein (eds), Routledge & Kegan Paul: London.

Stanton, E.C. (1895–8) *The Woman's Bible*, Arno Press: New York; reprinted 1974 as *The Original Feminist Attack on the Bible*.

Stanworth, M. (1981) *Gender and Schooling*, Hutchinson: London.

Starhawk (1979) *The Spiral Dance*, Harper & Row: San Francisco.

Starhawk (1982) *Dreaming the Dark*, Beacon Press: Boston, Mass.

Starrett, B. (1975) 'I Dream in female: the metaphors of evolution', in *The Lesbian Reader*, Covina, G. and L. Galena (eds), Amazon Press: Oakland, CA.

Steedman, C. (ed.) (1985) *Language, Gender and Childhood*, Routledge & Kegan Paul: London.

Stimpson, C.R. (ed.) (1981) *Women and the American City*, University of Chicago Press: Chicago.

Stone, M. (1976) *The Paradise Papers: the Suppression of Women's Rites*, Virago: London.

Strachey, R. (1928) *The Cause: A Short History of the Women's Movement in Great Britain*, G. Bell & Sons: London; reprinted 1979 by Virago: London.

Strachey, R. (1936) *Our Freedom and Its Results by Five Women*, Hogarth Press: London.

Strathern, M. (1987) 'An awkward relationship: the case of feminism and anthropology', *Signs*, vol. 12, no. 2, Winter, pp. 276–92.

Taylor, B. (1983) *Eve and the New Jerusalem*, Virago: London.

Thompson, S. (1984) 'Search for tomorrow: on feminism and the reconstruction of teen romance', in *Pleasure and Danger*, Vance, C.S. (ed.), Routledge & Kegan Paul: London.

Thomson, J. (1975) 'The right to privacy', *Philosophy and Public Affairs*, vol. 4, no. 4, pp. 295–314.

Thorne, B. and Henley, N. (eds) (1975) *Language and Sex: Difference and Dominance*, Newbury House: Rowley, Mass.

Thorne, B. and Yalom, M. (1982) *Rethinking the Family: Some Feminist Questions*, Longman: New York.

Tiger, L. (1969) *Men in Groups*, Nelson: London.

Tilly, L. and Scott, J. (1978) *Women, Work and the Family*, Holt Rinehart and Winston: New York.

Todd, J. (1988) *Feminist Literary History: A Defence*, Polity Press: Cambridge.

Trask, H.K. (1986) *Eros and Power: The Promise of Feminist Theory*, University of Pennsylvania Press: Philadelphia, PA.

Trebilcot, J. (1977) 'Two forms of androgynism', in *Feminism and Philosophy*, Vetterling-Braggin, M. (ed.), Rowman & Littlefield: Totowa, NJ.

Trebilcot, J. (1979) 'Conceiving women: notes on the logic of feminism', *Sinister Wisdom*, Fall, pp. 43–50.

Trebilcot, J. (ed.) (1983) *Mothering: Essays in Feminist Theory*, Rowman & Allanheld: Totowa, NJ.

Tuchman, G. (1975) 'Women and the creation of culture', in *Another Voice: Feminist Perspectives on Social Life and Social Science*, Millman, M. and R.M. Kanter (eds), Anchor Press: Garden City, NY.

Tuttle, L. (1986) *Encyclopedia of Feminism*, Longman: Harlow.

Vaughter, R. (1976) 'Psychology', *Signs*, vol. 2, no. 1, pp. 120–46.

Vetterling-Braggin, M. (ed.) (1977) *Feminism and Philosophy*, Rowman & Littlefield: Totowa, NJ.

Vetterling-Braggin, M. (1981) *Sexist Language: A Modern Philosophical Analysis*, Littlefield, Adams: Totowa, NJ.

Vickers, J. (1983) 'Memoirs of an ontological exile: the methodological rebellions of feminist research', in *Feminism in Canada*, Miles, A. and G. Finn (eds), Black Rose Press: Montreal.

Vogel, L. (1984) *Marxism and the Oppression of Women: Towards a Unitary Theory*, Rutgers University Press: New Brunswick, NJ.

Walker, A. (1983) *In Search of Our Mothers' Gardens*, Harcourt Brace Jovanovitch: New York.

Walker, B.G. (1983) *The Woman's Encyclopedia of Myths and Secrets*, Harper & Row: New York.

Walkerdine, V. (1986) 'Post structuralist theory and everyday social practices: the family and the school', in *Feminist Social Psychology*, Wilkinson, S. (ed.), Open University: Milton Keynes.

Walkowitz, J. (1984) 'Male vice and female virtue' in *Desire*, Snitow, A. *et al.* (eds), Virago: London.

Wallace, M. (1979) *Black Macho and the Myth of the Superwoman*, Dial Press: New York.

Wallsgrove, R. (1980) 'The masculine face of science', in *Alice through the Microscope*, Kelly, A. (ed.), Virago: London.

Wandor, M. (1981) *Understudies: Theatre and Sexual Politics*, Methuen: London.

Warner, M. (1981) *Joan of Arc: The Image of Female Heroism*, Weidenfeld and Nicolson: London.

Washbourn, P. (1979) *Seasons of Woman: Song, Poetry, Ritual, Prayer, Myth, Story*, Harper & Row: New York.

Washington, M.H. (1975) *Black-Eyed Susans*, Doubleday: Garden City, NY.

Webster, P. (1984) 'The forbidden: eroticism and taboo' in *Pleasure and Danger*, Vance, C.S. (ed.), Routledge & Kegan Paul: London.

Weigle, M. (1982) *Spiders and Spinsters: Women and Mythology*, University of New Mexico: Albuquerque.

Weisstein, N. (1970) '"Kinder, kuche, kirche" as scientific law:

psychology constructs the female', in *Sisterhood is Powerful*, Morgan, R. (ed.), Random House: New York.

Weitz, M.C. (1985) *Femmes: Recent Writings on French Women*, G.K. Hall: Boston, Mass.

Wekerle, G.R. (1981) 'Women in the urban environment', in *Women and the American City*, Stimpson, C.R. *et al.* (eds), University of Chicago Press: Chicago.

Wellesley Editorial Committee (1977) *Women and National Development: The Complexities of Change*, University of Chicago: Chicago.

Werlhof, F. *et al.* (1983) 'Frauen, die letzte Kolonie', *Rorora Aktuell, Technik: Politik*, 20.

West, R. (1913) 'Mr. Chesterton in hysterics', *The Clarion*, 14 November.

West, R. (1982) *The Young Rebecca*, Marcus, J. (ed.), Macmillan: London.

Westkott, M. (1979) 'Feminist criticism of the social sciences', *Harvard Educational Review*, vol. 49, no. 4, pp. 422–50.

Westkott, M. (1983) 'Women's studies as a strategy for change: between criticism and vision', in *Theories of Women's Studies*, Bowles, G. and R. Duelli Klein (eds), Routledge & Kegan Paul: London.

Whitbeck, C. (1983) 'A different reality: feminist ontology', in *Beyond Domination: New Perspectives on Women and Philosophy*, Gould, C.C. (ed.), Rowman & Allanheld: Totowa, NJ.

Wilkinson, S. (ed.) (1985) *Affirmative Action: Special Issue, Canadian Women's Studies*, vol. 2, no. 4.

Williams, V. (1986) *Women Photographers*, Virago: London.

Williamson, J. *et al.* (eds) (1979) *Women's Action Almanac*, William Morrow: New York.

Williamson, J. (1978) *Decoding Advertisements: Ideology and Meaning in Advertising*, Marion Boyars: London.

Willis, E. (1982) 'Toward a feminist sexual revolution', *Social Text*, vol. VII, Fall, no. 3, pp. 3–21.

Willis, E. (1984) 'Feminism, moralism and pornography', in *Desire: The Politics of Sexuality*, Snitow, A. *et al.* (eds), Virago: London.

Wilson, E. (1977) *Women and the Welfare State*, Tavistock: London.

Wilson, E. (1980) *Only Halfway to Paradise: Women in Post-War Britain 1945–1968*, Tavistock: London.

Wilson, E. (1985) *Adorned in Dreams*, Virago: London.

Wilson, E. and Weir, A. (1986) *Hidden Agendas: Theory, Politics and Experience in the Women's Movement*, Tavistock: London.

Wittig, M. (1969) *Les Guérillères*, Minuit: Paris.

Wittig, M. (1981) 'One is not born a woman', *Feminist Issues*, vol. 1, no. 2, pp. 47–54.

Wittig, M. (1982) 'The category of sex', *Feminist Issues*, vol. 2, no. 2, pp. 63–8.

Wittig, M. and Zeig, S. (1976) *Lesbian Peoples: Material for a Dictionary*, Avon: New York.

Wolff, J. (1981) *The Social Production of Art*, Macmillan: London.

Wollstonecraft, M. (1787) *Thoughts on the Education of Daughters: With*

Reflections on Female Duties, in the more Important Duties of Life, Joseph Johnson: London.

Wollstonecraft, M. (1789) *A Vindication of the Rights of Woman*, reprinted 1967 by W.W. Norton: New York.

Women's Studies Group (1978) *Women Take Issue*, Hutchinson: London.

Women's Studies Newsletter (1977) 'Constitution of the NWSA', vol. 5, no. 1, p. 6.

Woolf, V. (1929) *A Room of One's Own*, Hogarth Press: London.

Woolf, V. (1938) *Three Guineas*, Hogarth Press: London.

Wright, F. (1829) *A Course of Popular Lectures*, Free Enquirer: New York; reprinted 1973 in *The Feminist Papers: From Adams to de Beauvoir*, Rossi, A. (ed.), Bantam: New York.

Yates, G. (1975) *What Women Want: The Ideas of the Movement*, Harvard University Press: Cambridge, Mass.

Yerkovich, S. (1977) 'Gossiping as a way of speaking', *Journal of Communication*, vol. 27, pp. 192–6.

Young, I. (1980) 'Socialist feminism and the limits of dual systems theory', *Socialist Review*, vol. 10, no. 2/3, pp. 158–69.

Young, K. and Harris, O. (1976) 'The subordination of women in cross-cultural perspective', in *Papers on Patriarchy*, Women's Publishing Collective: Lewes.

Zimmerman, B. (1981) 'What has never been: an overview of lesbian feminist criticism', *Feminist Studies*, 7, pp. 451–75.

Zetkin, C. (1972) 'Lenin on the Woman Question' in *The Emancipation of Women: From the Writings of V.I. Lenin*, Lenin, V.I., International: New York.

DATE DUE